THE BODY ECONOMIC

THE
BODY
ECONOMIC

Why Austerity Kills

**Recessions, Budget Battles,
and the Politics of Life and Death**

DAVID STUCKLER
SANJAY BASU

HarperCollins*PublishersLtd*

Published by HarperCollins Publishers Ltd

First published by HarperCollins Publishers Ltd in a hardcover edition: 2013
This HarperCollins Publishers Ltd trade paperback edition: 2014

HarperCollins books may be purchased for educational, business,
or sales promotional use through our Special Markets Department.

HarperCollins Publishers Ltd
2 Bloor Street East, 20th Floor
Toronto, Ontario, Canada
M4W 1A8

www.harpercollins.ca

Library and Archives Canada Cataloguing in Publication
information is available upon request

ISBN 978-1-44342-045-7

Printed and bound in the United States of America
RRD 9 8 7 6 5 4 3 2

Politics is nothing but medicine on a grand scale.
Rudolph Virchow, 1848

CONTENTS

PREFACE

Thank you for participating in this clinical trial. You might not recall signing up for it, but you were enrolled in December 2007, at the start of the Great Recession. This experiment was not governed by the rules of informed consent or medical safety. Your treatment was not administered by doctors or nurses. It was directed by politicians, economists, and ministers of finance.

During this study, you were assigned, along with billions of others around the world, to one of two major experimental treatments: austerity or stimulus. Austerity is medicine intended to reduce symptoms of debts and deficits, and to cure recessions. It cuts government spending on healthcare coverage, assistance to the unemployed, and housing support. At the start of the trial, its potential side-effects were not well understood.

When the austerity experiment began, your prognosis was grim and uncertain. The US housing market bubble burst in 2007, battering economies across the world. Some politicians, such as British Prime Minister David Cameron, decided to pursue austerity to reduce deficits. Elsewhere in Europe, the International Monetary Fund and the European Central Bank pressured governments in Greece, Spain, and Italy to experiment with austerity: cutting billions of dollars from social programs. If you received an experimental dose of austerity, you might have noticed some serious changes to your world.

Meanwhile, other politicians chose to invest in health and social safety net programs. If you were in the stimulus group—that is, if you are currently living in Sweden, Iceland, or Denmark—your community was massively affected by unemployment and the recession, but was largely spared from austerity. Instead, stimulus funds were used to bolster health and social safety nets during the recession. If you lived in a stimulus country, you may not have noticed many changes to your neighborhood, waiting lines at the hospital, food prices, or rates of homelessness.

This experiment was not the first pitting stimulus against austerity. Eighty years ago, one of the largest such tests took place in the United States. As a way out of the Great Depression, President Franklin Delano Roosevelt proposed a raft of programs known as the New Deal, and Congress adopted them. The New Deal created jobs and strengthened the social safety net. But while many state governments in the US adopted the New Deal programs, others refused to implement them. They experienced wildly different outcomes as a result. Public health improved in pro–New Deal states but not in anti–New Deal states. Two decades ago, austerity was also tested in post-Communist Russia, and in East Asia, with strikingly similar results.

These experiments provided critical insights about the central findings in this book: economic choices are not only matters of growth rates and deficits, but matters of life and death.

The Body Economic is about data, and the stories behind those data. Over the past decade, we've been concerned about how our health is affected by economic crises—including this Great Recession. Our interest is not just academic—it is personal.

Both of us have experienced financial vulnerability, and the health consequences that attend it. David dropped out of high school to follow his passion and play in a band. Music didn't earn much money (and in retrospect, the band wasn't that great), so he worked odd jobs waiting tables and doing maintenance work at an apartment complex to make ends meet. But when he was unexpectedly laid off, he couldn't afford to pay rent. He variously lived in a tent, his car, and on friends' sofas. When winter came, he started to get sick. Having suffered asthma since childhood, he caught bronchitis and then pneumonia—while out of work, he had no health insurance, money, or a place to go of his own. Eventually he was able to get back on his feet and go to college with the support of his family. There, he studied health economics and statistics, and learned that his situation was not unique: all across America, people were one paycheck away from becoming homeless and needing help, just as he had done.

From a young age, Sanjay's life was affected by illness as well. His mother was sick for years from a lung infection called coccidiomycosis (the "Valley Fever" of the American Southwest). His father traveled across states to find work and make ends meet. The family moved in and out of hospitals; oxygen machines were delivered every week to the garage. He was good at math, though, and when he enrolled as an undergraduate at MIT, he discovered the mathematics of life and death—how statistics described the reasons behind who lived and who died.

We met in graduate school, studying public health and medicine because we wanted to help others. Since that time, we have studied how social and economic policies affect our health. That's because ultimately these policies make more of an impact on who lives and who dies than any pill, surgery, or insurance plan. Good health doesn't start in hospitals and clinics; it starts in our homes and our neighborhoods, in the food we eat, the air we breathe, and the safety of our streets. Indeed, a top predictor of your life expectancy is your zip code. That's because much of what keeps us healthy has to do with our social environment.[1]

All of the research on health and social policy presented in this book has been subjected to extensive peer review. Leading independent economists, epidemiologists, physicians, and statisticians have checked our data, our methods, and how we present these findings. We draw on the most recent research in the field, as well as many studies of our own. Our work has been published in respected scientific and medical journals, such as *The Lancet, British Medical Journal*, and *PLoS Medicine*, in addition to economics and social science journals.

Academic journals can be obscure, however, and so this book is an attempt to translate that data into plain English. Our goal is to provide people with the information they need to make informed, democratic choices about their economy and their health. We also want to inject hard evidence into the debate about austerity—a debate that has been shaped far more by ideology than facts.

The political debate about the Great Recession has been intense. Free marketeers and proponents of austerity tend to believe in paying off debt, regardless of the human price. Some of their opponents believe in maintaining a strong social safety net, even if that means less economic growth. Their longstanding disagreement about these basic principles has devolved into a cacophony of shrill voices and combative viewpoints. And both sides have grossly failed to see the false dichotomy in this debate.

Making smart policy choices can boost growth without human costs. Often those choices require up-front investment in public health programs. These programs, if administered correctly, can help spur growth in the short run, in addition to their long-term benefits. In other words, our data reveal that we can have good health, and tackle our debts too. But creating this balance requires funding the right government programs.

To identify the best drugs and treatments in medicine, doctors use large, randomized controlled trials. But it is difficult, if not impossible, to enroll entire societies into randomized controlled trials to test out the best social policies. So to understand how policies affect our health, we use rigorous statistical methods to study what are known as "natural experiments." These experiments arise, for example, when policy makers face similar problems such as a large recession, but choose different courses of action. This divergence creates the potential for us, as researchers, to learn how political choices ultimately come to affect our health, for better and for worse.

Can we afford to pay for social protection programs—for healthcare, mental health programs, food stamps, and housing programs—when we face a large national debt? The results of our research demonstrate that stimulus spending on specific public health programs actually helps to reduce debt by sparking new economic growth. Every $1 invested in these programs returns $3 back in economic growth that can be used to pay off debt. By contrast, those countries participating in steep short-term cuts end up with long-term economic declines. When the government cuts its spending during a recession, it drastically reduces demand at a time when demand is already low. People spend less; businesses suffer, ultimately leading to more job losses and creating a vicious spiral of less and less demand and more and more unemployment. Ironically, austerity has the opposite of its intended effect. Far from decreasing debt, austerity increases it as the economy slows. And so debt gets worse in the long run when we don't stimulate economic growth.

The economic consequences of austerity can already be seen in the early results of the US and UK experiments. As shown in Figure P.1, the US and UK both had a major economic collapse after the financial meltdown on Wall Street. Starting in 2009 when President Obama came into office, the US began

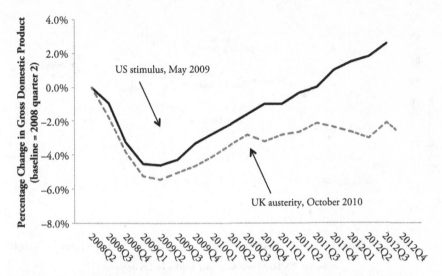

FIGURE P.I   US Economy Is Recovering After Stimulus but UK Still in Recession After Austerity[2]

to pursue a stimulus path. That choice marked a turning point in the US recession—since then, the economy has been recovering, and now its GDP is greater than it was before the crisis began. In contrast, after the Conservatives came to power in 2010, the British government started cutting billions of pounds in government spending. Its economy has been recovering at less than half the rate of the US, has yet to fully recover, and now shows signs of entering a dreaded "triple-dip recession."

This pattern—the benefits of stimulus, the harms of austerity—plays out in nearly a century of data on recessions and the economy, from countries all over the world.

Conventional wisdom holds that recessions are inevitably bad for human health. Thus, we ought to expect a rise in depression, suicide, alcoholism, infectious disease outbreaks, and many other health problems. But this is false. Recessions pose both threats and opportunities for public health, and sometimes can even improve health outcomes. Sweden had a massive economic crash in the early 1990s, larger than it experienced in the Great Recession, but saw no increase in suicides or alcohol-related deaths. Similarly, in

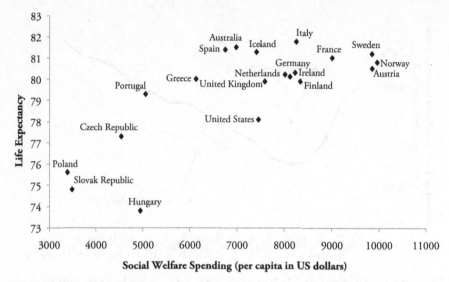

FIGURE P.2. Social Welfare Spending Increases Life Expectancy at Birth, Year 2008[3]

this recession we have seen health improve in Norway, Canada, and even for some people in the US.[4]

What we've learned is that the real danger to public health is not recession per se, but austerity. When social safety nets are slashed, economic shocks like losing a job or a home can turn into a health crisis. As shown in Figure P.2, a strong determinant of our health is the strength of our social safety nets. When governments invest more in social welfare programs—housing support, unemployment programs, old-age pensions, and healthcare—health improves for reasons we'll explain. And this is not merely a correlation, but a cause-and-effect relationship seen across the world.

That's why Iceland—rocked by the worst bank crisis in history—didn't experience rising deaths in the Great Recession. It chose to uphold its social welfare programs, and went even further to bolster them. By contrast, Greece, Europe's guinea pig for austerity, was pressured to undertake draconian cuts— the largest seen in Europe since World War II. Its recession was smaller than Iceland's at first, but now has worsened with austerity. The human costs have become dramatically clear: a 52 percent rise in HIV, a doubling in suicide, rising homicides, and a return of malaria—all as critical health programs were cut.

These dangers of austerity are as consistent as they are profound. In history, and decades of research, the price of austerity has been recorded in death statistics and body counts.

Too much of the conversation surrounding the Great Recession has focused on lost GDP, deficits, and debt reduction. Too little has focused on human health and well-being. In March 1968, Senator Robert Kennedy criticized this fetishization of economic growth:

> Our gross national product now is over eight hundred billion dollars a year, but that gross national product—if we should judge the United States of America by that—that gross national product counts air pollution and cigarette advertising and ambulances to clear our highways of carnage. It counts special locks for our doors and the jails for the people who break them. It counts the destruction of the redwoods and the loss of our natural wonder in chaotic sprawl. It counts napalm, and it counts nuclear warheads, and armored cars for the police to fight the riots in our cities. It counts the television programs which glorify violence in order to sell toys to our children.
>
> Yet the gross national product does not allow for the health of our children, the quality of their education, or the joy of their play. It does not include the beauty of our poetry or the strength of our marriages, the intelligence of our public debate or the integrity of our public officials. It measures neither our wit nor our courage; neither our wisdom nor our learning; neither our compassion nor our devotion to our country; it measures everything, in short, except that which makes life worthwhile, and it can tell us everything about America except why we are proud that we are Americans.[5]

We take Robert Kennedy's proposition seriously. In *The Body Economic*, we focus on the choices that governments make and the implications of those choices not only for our economies, but also for our bodies. We now have extensive data that reveal which measures kill, and which save lives. As citizens, we can call on our governments to make the right decisions—decisions that protect our health during hard times.

INTRODUCTION

Olivia remembers being on fire.

Eight years old, she was scared by the sound of dishes crashing onto the kitchen floor. Her parents were having another fight. She ran up the stairs to her bedroom and hid under a pillow. Exhausted from crying, she fell asleep.[1]

She woke up with a splintering pain on the right side of her face. The room was black with smoke. Her bedsheet had erupted in flames. Screaming, she ran out of her room and straight into the arms of a firefighter who had raced up the stairs. He wrapped her tightly in a blanket. As she would later hear the nurses in the hospital whisper, her father had set the house on fire in a drunken rage.

It was the spring of 2009, during the ongoing Great Recession. Olivia's father, a construction worker, had been laid off. Millions of Americans had joined the unemployment rolls, and some turned to drugs or, like Olivia's dad, to alcohol.[2]

Olivia's father ended up in jail. Olivia required extensive treatments for her burns and undoubtedly will need years of therapy to heal the mental scars from that horrible night.

But Olivia survived. Others were not so lucky.

Three years later and half a world away, on the morning of April 4, 2012, Dimitris Christoulas set off to the Greek Parliament building in the center of Athens. At age seventy-seven, he saw no other way out. Christoulas had been a pharmacist, retired in 1994, but now he was having trouble paying for his medications. Life had been good, but the new Greek government had slashed his pension, and life was now intolerable.[3]

That morning, Christoulas went to Syntagma Square, the city's central plaza. He walked up the Parliament steps, put a gun to his head, and declared, "I am not committing suicide. They are killing me." Then he pulled the trigger.

Later, a note found in his satchel was released.[4] In it Christoulas equated the new government to the widely hated World War II government of Georgios Tsolakoglou that collaborated with the Nazis:

> The Tsolakoglou government has annihilated all traces for my survival, which was based on a very dignified pension that I alone paid for 35 years with no help from the state. And since my advanced age does not allow me a way of dynamically reacting (although if a fellow Greek were to grab a Kalashnikov, I would be right behind him) I see no other solution than this dignified end to my life, so I don't find myself fishing through garbage cans for my sustenance. I believe that young people with no future, will one day take up arms and hang the traitors of this country at Syntagma square, just like the Italians did to Mussolini in 1945.

"This was not suicide," a protester later said. "He was murdered." A mourner nailed a note to a tree near the spot where Christoulas died. "Enough is enough," it read. "Who will be the next victim?"

Olivia and Christoulas may have been 5,000 miles apart, but their lives were woven together by the worst economic crisis since the Great Depression. As two public health researchers—one at Stanford in California and the other at Oxford, England—we became concerned that the Great Recession would take its toll on people's bodies. We heard stories from our patients, friends, and neighbors who lost their health insurance but also experienced harms that went well beyond the medical clinic or the pharmacy, intruding upon the very fabric of their lives—their ability to afford healthy food to eat, avoid the high stress of losing a job, and keep a roof over their heads. We wondered what impact the Great Recession would have on the rates of heart disease, of suicide and depression, and even the spread of contagious diseases.

In search of answers, we have mined data from around the globe and from decades of prior recessions. We've found that public health can be profoundly affected by economic shocks. Some of our findings were expected. When people lose jobs, they are more likely to turn to drugs and alcohol or become suicidal. When they lose their homes, or are mired in debt, they often turn to junk food, for comfort or simply to save money.

Tragic as they are, the misfortunes of people like Olivia and Dimitris are unsurprising. More than 600 Greek citizens killed themselves in 2012. Before the Great Recession, Greece had the lowest suicide rate in Europe. Now that rate has doubled.[5] And Greece isn't alone. Suicides in the other European Union countries had been dropping consistently for over twenty years until the Great Recession.

But in our global research, we also encountered some surprises. Some communities, even entire nations, became *healthier* than ever as their economies were devastated. Iceland went through the worst bank crisis of all time, but the population's health actually improved. Health in Sweden and Canada also improved. Norway reached its highest life expectancy ever. But this had nothing to do with the cold climate. Japan, which had suffered a "lost decade" from the prolonged effects of recurrent recessions, now reports some of the best health statistics in the world.

Some economists looked at these data and concluded that recessions were "a lifestyle blessing in disguise," the cause of these health gains. Thanks to losing income in the Great Recession, they argued, people would get healthy: drink and smoke less, and walk rather than drive. They were finding that recessions correlated with a drop in death rates in many places. Looking grimly into the future, one economist predicted that an economic recovery will kill 60,000 people in the United States. Such odd and counter-intuitive pronouncements are contradicted by data from health departments around the world. During the Great Recession, life expectancy in the United States appeared to fall in some counties for the first time in at least four decades. In London, heart attacks rose by 2,000 amid the market turmoil. And suicide and alcohol death reports keep piling up on our desks.[6]

These data were a puzzle. How had some people become healthier during recessions, while others ended up like Olivia and Dimitris?

The answers could be found in the politics of the Great Recession. The 2012 US presidential election helped define a seemingly eternal debate between austerity and stimulus, services and revenue. Lo and behold, austerity lost. President Barack Obama campaigned on raising taxes on the wealthy and investing in social services, and he won. As the US climbs slowly out of recession, other countries should take note. Britain, under a Conservative Party government since 2010, has enacted an austerity regime that has, as of January 2013, shown signs of sending the country back into recession.

Over the past decade, we've looked through reams of data and reports in search of answers. Austerity or stimulus? Cuts or hikes in taxes to the rich? Cuts or hikes in services to the poor? We traveled from the coldest gulag in Siberia, to the red-light district of Bangkok, to the biggest intensive-care unit in the United States to find answers. The data we've gathered lead irrevocably to this conclusion: societies that prevented epidemics during recessions almost always had strong safety nets, strong social protection.

Disasters like Olivia's inferno and Dimitris's suicide do not always follow economic downturns. Rather, they are the consequences of a simple political choice—a choice to bail out bankers and cut safety nets for everyone else. Just a few key decisions, we've found, can stop a recession from turning into an epidemic. But our research shows that austerity involves the deadliest social policies. Recessions can hurt, but austerity kills.

The world's biggest economic adviser, the International Monetary Fund (IMF), was once a leading proponent of austerity cuts to safety nets in recessions. In a recent report, the IMF reversed its policy. Now it finds that austerity actually slows down economies, worsens unemployment, and hampers investor confidence. In Europe, businesses are now clamoring against austerity, having seen their demand dry up. The safety net policies that we advocate for not only boost people's health but help people return to work, maintain their incomes, and keep the economy going in bad times.[7]

Collectively, we have lost sight of what matters most. Debts, revenue, and growth are important. But when you ask people around the world what they value most, they don't pull their wallets out of their pockets, or talk about the new additions to their homes, or the brands of their cars, or even the latest gadget in the Apple store. In survey after survey, people are consistent about what they care about. Above all, they say they value their health and that of their families.

Suppose we reframe the debate to focus on "body economics": the health effects of our economic policies. Since our economic choices have a huge impact on health, they ought to pass the same rigorous tests that we apply to other things that affect our health, like pharmaceuticals. If economic policies had to be proven "safe" and "effective," just like any drug being approved for our patients, we might have an opportunity to make our societies safer and healthier. Instead, at the moment, in those countries where austerity is ascendant, we're undergoing a massive and untested experiment on human health, and left to count the dead.

The price of austerity is calculated in human lives. And these lost lives won't return when the stock market bounces back.

PART I

HISTORY

1

TEMPERING THE GREAT DEPRESSION

"I will never forgive them," wrote thirteen-year-old Kieran McArdle to the *Daily Record,* a national newspaper based in Glasgow. "I won't be able to come to terms with my dad's death until I get justice for him."[1]

Kieran's father, fifty-seven-year-old Brian, had worked as a security guard in Lanarkshire, near Glasgow. The day after Christmas 2011, Brian had a stroke, which left him paralyzed on his left side, blind in one eye, and unable to speak. He could no longer continue working to support his family, so he signed up for disability income from the British government.

That government, in the hands of Conservative Prime Minister David Cameron since the 2010 elections, would prove no friend to the McArdles. Cameron claimed that hundreds of thousands of Britons were cheating the government's disability system. The Department for Work and Pensions begged to differ. It estimated that less than 1 percent of disability benefit funds went to people who were not genuinely disabled.[2]

Still, Cameron proceeded to cut billions of pounds from welfare benefits including support for the disabled. To try to meet Cameron's targets, the Department for Work and Pensions hired Atos, a private French "systems integration" firm. Atos billed the government £400 million to carry out medical evaluations of people receiving disability benefits.[3]

Kieran's father was scheduled for an appointment to complete Atos's battery of "fitness for work" tests. He was nervous. Since his stroke, he had trouble walking, and was worried about how his motorized wheelchair would get up the stairs to his appointment, as he had learned that about a quarter of Atos's disability evaluations took place in buildings that were not wheelchair accessible. "Even though my dad had another stroke just days before his assessment, he was determined to go," said Kieran. "He tried his best to walk and talk because he was a very proud man."[4]

Brian did manage to reach Atos's evaluation site, and after the evaluation, made his way home. A few weeks later, his family received a letter from the Department for Work and Pensions. The family's Employment and Support Allowance benefits were being stopped. Atos had found Brian "fit for work." The next day he collapsed and died.

It was hard for us, as public health researchers, to understand the government's position. The Department for Work and Pensions, after all, considered cheating a relatively minor issue. The total sum of disability fraud for "conditions of entitlement" was £2 million, far less than the contract to hire Atos, and the Department estimated that greater harm resulted from the accidental underpayment of £70 million each year. But the government's fiscal ideology had created the impetus for radical cuts.[5]

Across the Atlantic in the United States, President Barack Obama spoke of the ongoing recession as the worst economic crisis since the Great Depression. The comparison was apt. People began looking to politicians and economists of the Depression era for guidance on how to proceed during this newest downturn. Republican President Herbert Hoover and Democratic President Franklin Delano Roosevelt had governed during the Depression in the United States, and the British economist John Maynard Keynes had championed an activist governmental policy of stimulus spending to end the Depression.[6]

In the first panicked months of 2008, few people questioned a need to act swiftly to rescue the economy. The salient question was how: increased spending or budget cuts? There was a real fear that if the banks went under, entire national economies would collapse. The financial sector had become such a large part of economic life that politicians deemed some banks "too big to fail." If we let them collapse, the damage would be even more catastrophic to the economy than the high price of helping them—there would be more panic, chaotic bank runs, and less money for entrepreneurs and small businesses.[7]

The US and European governments mobilized an unprecedented rescue package for the banking sector. Although the banks had lost private money, public funds from taxpayers would be used to bail them out—to the tune of over $2 trillion in the US and UK. Witnessing this massive rise in government spending, Martin Wolf, a journalist at the *Financial Times*, proclaimed, "We are all Keynesians now." He may have spoken too soon.[8]

In response to the massive government debt, conservative politicians in the United States and Europe launched their new economic policy: a drive to reduce spending not by lowering entitlements to private corporations like banks, but by attacking social welfare spending.

In the UK, the Conservatives' case for austerity was simple: the government had a huge debt overhang, and now that debt needed to be paid back. If it was not, it would become harder and harder to borrow money, and more costly to repay. No one, after all, wants to lend money to an entity living on credit, so interest rates would increase and make debt repayment even more difficult. If we simply printed money, our currency would be worth less because of inflation, creating hard times in an already troubled economy. So the only option left, they argued, was to cut back on welfare spending—the programs that Cameron argued were slowing down the economy.[9]

This argument was simple, intuitive, and wrong. It was, as the Nobel Prize–winning economist Paul Krugman put it, akin "to the claim that soup kitchens caused the Great Depression."[10]

Government debt isn't like personal debt. If one of us misses a mortgage payment, we risk damaging our credit rating, and possibly even losing our home. So if we owe money, we need to find a way to pay it back as soon as possible. But government debt does not need to be paid back overnight—in fact, it can be dangerous to do so. In an economy where we're all in the same boat, one person's spending is another person's income. So when the government cuts spending, it reduces people's income, leading to less business, more unemployment, and a vicious spiral of slowing down the economy.

The central goal in debt management is to keep debts sustainable. To be sustainable, government debt repayments should be kept lower than the rate of revenue from economic growth. If that happens, we will grow out of debt, as economic stimulus leads to more income and more tax revenues to reduce the debt. But budget cuts have slowed down growth—and this is precisely why, in spite of all the UK's radical cuts, the latest data show that British debt continues to rise.[11]

As public health researchers, we were shocked and concerned at the illogic of the austerity advocates, and the hard data on its human and economic costs. We realized the impact of the Great Recession went far beyond people losing their homes and jobs. It was a full-scale assault on people's health. At the heart of the argument was the question of what it means to be a society, and what the appropriate role of government is in protecting people.

Economists were studying the Great Depression for guidance on how to end the Great Recession. They were poring through historical statistics on economic growth. We went in a different direction, and started digging through the archives of the United States Public Health Service to find out how and why people died during the Depression. The patterns we found were not all ominous—indeed, we found that some people actually became healthier during the Great Depression. What determined their health had not only to do with economic cycles, but critically depended on how politicians chose to respond to the crisis. The Depression revealed that some political choices can simultaneously improve health and help the economy recover.

The first clue came from understanding how the Depression itself started. The Depression can be traced back to the panicked selling of 16 million shares of stock on Black Tuesday, October 29, 1929. But the roots of the Depression lay in a series of events that are strikingly similar to the Great Recession—stark inequality, a real estate bubble, and a banking crisis.[12]

During the late 1920s, the US super-rich—the Fords, Vanderbilts, Carnegies, and Rockefellers—were the masters of the country's financial markets. This top 1 percent of the population held over 40 percent of America's wealth, and their investments drove the rise and fall of stock prices, as well as a real estate bubble. There was an "orgy of apartment building" in Florida during the Roaring Twenties, as lots in Miami were bought and sold as many as ten times in a single day. Commercial lending banks loosened loan conditions, and mortgages were easy to get. Mortgage-related debt doubled between 1922 and 1928.[13]

Eventually the housing bubble burst, leading to the 1929 Crash. In the Depression that followed, more than 90,000 businesses went bankrupt and at least 13 million Americans—one in four workers—became unemployed. Half a million farmers lost their land. Three out of five Americans were classified as living in poverty. Shantytowns of ramshackle cardboard boxes and tents sprang up into slums called "Hoovervilles" in a nod to President Hoover. Soup kitchens and bread lines were everywhere.[14]

As we looked through these poverty statistics from the Depression, we expected the impact on people's health to be seismic, and tragic. And some of it was. After Black Tuesday, suicide rates rose. While reports of brokers and bankers jumping out of windows were rife, one of the first documented suicides was a construction worker helping build the Empire State Building: he had been laid off and jumped from it to his death. He was representative of the stress placed on the working class. The risk of suicide was actually concentrated not among those who lost their bets in the stock market, but among those with the least savings, the least opportunity to get a new job after being laid off, and the highest risk of losing their homes or being unable to feed their families if they lost their income.[15]

But we were surprised by some counterintuitive findings as well. For example, Dr. Louis Dublin, an actuary at the Metropolitan Life Insurance Company, announced in 1932: "Never before have there been such satisfactory health conditions in the United States and Canada as during the first nine months of this year." His job was to track death rates for the company's 19 million policyholders. He found that mortality among white policyholders was well below the previous minimum in 1927; among blacks, the death rate was the lowest in a decade.[16]

Perhaps our assumptions about financial crises and health were wrong. Stress alone might not explain the deaths of people during recessions. Something else might be at play. But first we had to determine if Dublin's statistics were accurate. One possibility was that statistics from people who had insurance might tell only half the story. People with insurance were probably better off, and so data from insurance companies might be hiding the full picture of suffering among poorer people who were not part of Dublin's datasets.

Digging deeper, however, we found that other data sources confirmed the insurance company's reports. Dr. Edgar Sydenstricker, a statistician for the US Public Health Service who independently examined death certificates from the entire country, came to the same conclusion. In 1933 he wrote, "1931 was one of the healthiest years in the history of the country," adding that "After several years of severe economic stress, the gross death rate has attained the lowest level on record. Infant and tuberculosis mortality have not increased in the country as a whole; on the contrary they have continued to decline."[17]

Public health experts were puzzled by the trends in the data. The US Surgeon General attributed the health improvement to a mild winter, suggesting that it might have staved off an "unpreventable epidemic," such as typhoid or whooping cough. Not everyone was convinced by this explanation, especially since a mild winter one year during the Depression was actually contrasted by harsher winters during the other years. An alternative argument was that the Depression itself was the reason for health improvements, although the reasons why were not obvious. Perhaps laboratory studies might shed light on why death rates improved during hard economic times. In 1928, the American biologist Raymond Pearl had published a classic study of fruit flies that found the flies that grew the most rapidly had the shortest lifespans. Applying these arguments to humans, some commentators proposed that society's fast pace of living during the Roaring Twenties—the fast and furious lifestyle of alcohol and cigarettes—had produced backward trends in health, which began to reverse as the Depression produced a calmer, more "normal mode of living." When people lost jobs, rather than working long hours, they might spend more time with their families or choose to exercise more. And when people lost income they would drink and smoke less, or walk instead of drive. All these changes would act to improve their health.[18]

To find out if this explanation was plausible, we turned to the most reliable source of data available from the period: death certificates compiled by the US Centers for Disease Control and Prevention (CDC). These data covered 114 cities in thirty-six states over the decade from 1927 to 1937, before and after the Great Depression. The data allowed us to compare what happened to people's health in a variety of places, and analyze the different causes of death to find consistent patterns. Moreover, they allowed us to understand what the trends in life expectancy were before the 1929 Crash, so that we could see if events during the Great Depression were changing pre-existing trends or were just part of a broader pattern of public health trends unrelated to the economic crisis.[19]

We first analyzed the CDC data to check the accuracy of the public health reports from the insurance industry and the Public Health Service.

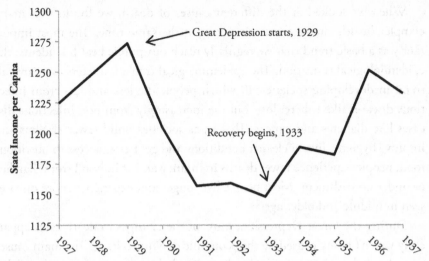

FIGURE 1.1 State Income per Capita, US, 1927 to 1937[20]

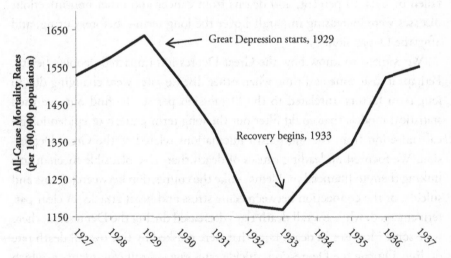

FIGURE 1.2 Trends in All-Cause Crude Death Rates, US, 1927 to 1937[21]

We were able to confirm that mortality rates fell by about 10 percent during the Great Depression across the United States. As shown in Figures 1.1 and 1.2, when the Great Depression started in 1929, average income fell by about one-third, but death rates also began to fall. And when recovery began in 1933, death rates began to rise again.

When we looked at the different causes of death, we found that many complex health changes were occurring at the same time. The most important was a basic trend that we regularly teach our public health students: the epidemiological transition. The epidemiological transition refers to an overall trend in developing societies, in which people die less and less from infectious diseases like tuberculosis but die increasingly from non-infectious diseases like diabetes and cancer. That is, as societies build sewer systems and improve hygiene, live in cleaner conditions and get better access to nutritious food, people experience fewer deaths in infancy and childhood from diarrhea or under-nourishment. Most people live longer and experience more diseases seen in middle and older age.[22]

During the Great Depression, most of the changes in death rates apparently weren't being caused by the economic downturn itself. The main causes were due to long-term trends that had already been occurring as part of this epidemiological transition. For example, rates of pneumonia and flu had fallen by over 10 percent, and deaths from cancer and other non-infectious diseases were increasing in parallel over the long term—before, during, and after the Depression.[23]

We wanted to know how the Great Depression impacted people's health. Perhaps it just came at a time when other disease rates were changing due to long-term factors unrelated to the Depression per se. To find out, we used statistical models that could filter out the long-term pattern of epidemiological transition from the short-term fluctuations related to the Great Depression. We focused on leading causes of death that have plausible mechanisms linking them to financial problems—like the connection between job loss and suicide, or the connection between acute stress and heart attacks. A clear pattern emerged: while overall death rates decreased during the Depression, there were some increases in death rates that were masked by this overall death rate decline. During the Depression, suicide rates saw a significant increase, which was hidden beneath the overall decline in death rates. As shown in Figure 1.3, starting in 1929, suicide rates rose by about 16 percent from 18.1 per 100,000 population to 21.6 per 100,000 population at the peak in 1932.[24]

Yet when we looked more closely at the data, we saw there were huge variations across the thirty-six states in the CDC database, with suicides rising to different degrees at different times. In Connecticut, suicides spiked by 41

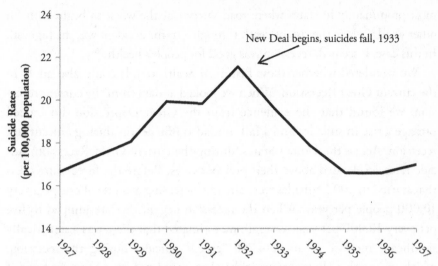

FIGURE 1.3 Trends in Suicide Rates, US, 1927 to 1937[25]

percent, but in New Jersey, they actually fell by 8 percent. Using statistical models, we found that those states, like Connecticut, that had more bank failures had larger spikes in suicides.

However, suicide is a relatively rare cause of death. So even though we found that the economic crash was associated with more people taking their lives, something else was happening to compensate and outweigh the rise in deaths from suicides, leading to an overall decline in death rates during the Depression.

A close look at the data revealed that the increase in suicide was hidden behind a large decrease in death rates from road traffic accidents. Road safety in the early decades of the twentieth century was a barely understood concept; car accidents had become a leading cause of death. Across the US, deaths from automobile accidents in the 1930s exceeded those from typhoid fever, measles, scarlet fever, diphtheria, whooping cough, meningitis, and childbirth combined. But as the Depression took hold, trends changed: the early 1930s saw the first decrease in traffic fatalities in history. Most Americans could no longer afford cars or gasoline, so there was, quite simply, less traffic. When we looked across states, we found the states where the economy slowed down the most were those states where traffic declined and traffic deaths dropped in parallel. This occurred most prominently in states where road safety was the worst to begin with (in other words, where the risk of death through a traffic accident was the highest). In this case, it seemed, recession was good for people's health.[26]

We wondered whether these historical health trends could also apply to the current Great Recession. When we looked at data from the current recession, we found that the evidence from the Great Depression did indeed presage a rise in suicides and a fall in road-traffic deaths during our current recession. Across the United States, during the current Great Recession, suicide rates accelerated above their previous rates. Before the foreclosure crisis that started in 2007, suicides were already increasing at a rate of one per every 10,000 people per year. When the recession began, the rate jumped to five per every 10,000 per year. Overall, we estimated that there was a statistically significant increase of about 4,750 "excess" suicides during the recession, which means that these were suicides that would not have been expected if the recession had not occurred. In the UK, too, we estimated roughly 1,000 excess suicides during the same period.[27]

If mental health trends from the Great Depression also applied to the current recession, then we might expect road traffic deaths would also fall. Indeed, US automobile deaths dropped by 3,600 deaths in 2010—reaching a sixty-year low. There was less traffic on the road, especially when wages dropped and gas prices increased during the recession, which statistically correlated to the drop in automobile deaths. Similar reports of reduced traffic accidents came in from Europe. Northern Ireland reported the lowest road traffic deaths on record, experiencing an unprecedented 50 percent decline in fatalities and 20 percent decline in serious injuries. Ironically, this drop led surgeons in London to complain about a lack of organs for transplant surgeries in 2008, because their usual source of supply—road traffic deaths—had dried up.[28]

Some observers have interpreted these trends quite favorably. NBC News ran the headline "Good news! Recession may make you healthier." But such interpretations were missing the bigger lessons from the Great Depression. While the Depression seemed to be a mixed blessing for health, what appeared to be far more important—both during the Depression and in the decades that followed—was how the US government chose to respond to the crisis.

We studied two major policy debates that took place in the United States during the Great Depression. The first was about alcohol. The timing of the Great Depression overlapped with Prohibition on alcohol. The Volstead

Prohibition Act, passed in 1919, mandated that "no person shall manufacture, sell, barter, transport, import, export, deliver, furnish or possess any intoxicating liquor." The act, however, divided the country. In those states that enforced Prohibition rigorously, people abstained, or were forced to buy alcohol (sometimes quite toxic homebrews of methanol or bathtub gin) at illegal underground bars, speakeasies. But other states—like Connecticut and California—were "wet" throughout. Mixing business failures with alcohol partly contributed to these wet states' higher suicide rates than dry ones. But during the Great Depression, those states with the most stringent Prohibition campaigns experienced one positive trend: significantly fewer drinking-related deaths. Wet states like Connecticut had 20 percent higher death rates from alcohol than did dry states. Thus, Prohibition prevented about 4,000 deaths in dry states from hazardous drinking during the Depression. If it had been applied equally throughout the country, Prohibition would have saved at least 7,300 lives (not that we're advocating a return to Prohibition—just gleaning a lesson from it).[29]

Perhaps the most convincing piece of evidence that Prohibition protected people from harm was revealed after it was lifted. In the early 1930s, there was public outcry against Prohibition. It was viewed as a source of rising crime, as gangsters like Al Capone operated illicit smuggling from the Canadian and Mexican borders. In addition, Prohibition had also highlighted government interference in people's lives. But the policy argument that led to the end of Prohibition ultimately had to do less with ethics or criminal justice and more with the politics of debt. President Roosevelt wanted to gain votes from the working classes, but also stimulate the faltering US economy by boosting consumer demand. His answer was for people to buy more alcohol and pay a tax on it. As shown in the Figure 1.4, alcohol-related deaths during the Great Depression didn't spike until 1933, when Prohibition was repealed. Alcohol-related deaths immediately rose sharply, a trend that continued for the next several decades.[30]

But the second policy debate had even greater implications for public health than the politics of alcohol. It centered on the appropriate role of government during an economic crisis.

In the lead-up to the 1932 election, the American electorate was polarized. The economy was in shambles, and total US debt had jumped from 180 percent of GDP in 1929 to 300 percent of GDP in 1932, its highest ratio ever

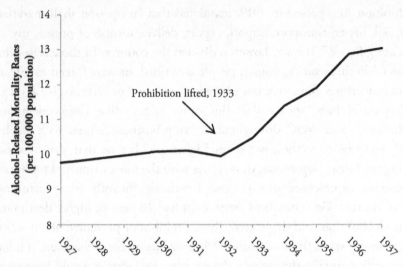

FIGURE I.4   Death Rates from Alcohol, US, 1927 to 1937[31]

(that is, until the current recession). A political war raged over austerity, with the country divided between those calling for budget cuts, and others calling for social protection programs to help the millions who had lost jobs and homes during the Depression. Should government step in to rescue the American economy with more spending? Or was it necessary to cut budgets to prevent a further collapse?[32]

The election pitted the incumbent president, Republican Herbert Hoover against Democrat Franklin Delano Roosevelt. To the millions of Americans plunged into poverty, Hoover's campaign advice that people should "pull themselves up by their bootstraps" seemed singularly out of touch. Hoover believed that if anyone should provide relief to the unemployed and homeless, it should be private charities and local governments, not the federal government.[33]

While Roosevelt was initially not far from Hoover in this opinion, he experienced enormous political pressures from the nation's left. Much of this pressure came from a groundswell of labor unrest. Between 1929 and 1931, the wages of auto workers in Michigan had dropped by 54 percent. By 1932, more than 200,000 people in the auto industry had lost jobs, a third of whom had been laid off from Ford's factories. On March 7, 1932, in Dearborn, Michigan, 4,000 unemployed workers led a hunger march. They had come together to protest their shared fate: hunger, poverty, and unemployment. The workers carried banners bearing slogans such as "Give Us Work, We Want Bread Not Crumbs" and "Tax the Rich and Feed the Poor." Their march was peaceful until Ford security guards and police tried to stop it. They fired tear gas into the crowd. Marchers responded by throwing stones. And then Ford security guards shot into the crowd, killing fourteen and wounding fifty. What had started as the Ford Hunger March had ended as the Ford Massacre.[34]

The Ford March was followed by similar battles across the country. Workers began to join together, in some cases forging new collective organizations such as the United Auto Workers Union in 1935. The super-rich came to be viewed as drivers of the crisis, given their involvement in the risky land deals and financial transactions that had precipitated Black Tuesday. This popular criticism of the rich led to a swelling of support for the US Socialist Party, largely composed of farmers who had lost their land and factory workers who had been laid off.[35]

The political left became more powerful than ever before in US history. Roosevelt grew concerned that union support for Socialist presidential candidate Norman Thomas would split the left-wing vote and give Hoover a second term. And so Roosevelt promised to implement social protection programs to help farmers and factory workers recover from the Depression. His promise tipped the balance in his favor, and he won the election. In his inaugural address, Roosevelt said: "I pledge you, I pledge myself, to a New Deal for the American people."[36]

The New Deal would eventually include such ground-breaking programs as the Federal Emergency Relief Act and Works Progress Administration, which gave 8.5 million jobless Americans work by creating new construction projects; the Home Owner's Loan Corporation, which prevented at least a million foreclosures; the Food Stamp Program, which gave vouchers for basic foods to those who could not afford them; the Public Works Administration, which built hospitals and provided immunizations for Americans who could not afford them; and the Social Security Act to combat poverty among senior citizens.[37]

The New Deal had a momentous effect on the public's health. Although it was not designed with public health in mind, its support meant the difference between losing healthcare and keeping it; between going hungry and having enough food at the table; between homelessness and having a roof overhead. In providing indirect support to maintain people's well-being, the New Deal was in effect the biggest public health program ever to have been implemented in the United States.

To study the effects of the New Deal on public health, we scrutinized the differences between death rates that emerged after the New Deal was implemented. But we could not simply look across the entire country, because health was being affected by the ongoing recession and epidemiological transition. We needed to measure variation in each state's exposure to the New Deal in order to statistically isolate the effect of Roosevelt's programs.

Here, we looked to the politics of the New Deal for clues. There were major differences among states in the extent to which they implemented FDR's programs. In general, we found that states with left-leaning governors, who were politically aligned with Roosevelt, tended to invest more in New Deal programs than their Republican counterparts did. The New Deal–supporting politicians funded more housing programs, invested more in construction projects to generate jobs, and supported food stamps and welfare aid. By contrast, conservative governors sought to minimize New Deal programs, even cutting many of their state budgets to reduce deficits.[38]

The stark contrasts between states' responses to the Great Depression created variation in the degree to which the New Deal was implemented across the country. In social science research, we call such an historical episode a "natural experiment," because it gives us an opportunity to identify the effects of a policy. While it would be impossible to randomize some US states to participate in the New Deal and others not to participate, as in a medical experiment, the choices of these politicians created a real-world laboratory where we could see whether those states that had more New Deal spending gained better health as a result. Statistically, we accounted for a number of other factors that could affect these results, like different demographics, different pre-existing health conditions, education levels, income, and a variety of other control variables that we included in our analyses.

Louisiana became a prime showcase for the New Deal. Governor Huey Long was one of its most vocal supporters, but he felt it didn't go far enough. So he launched the Share Our Wealth movement in 1934 and called for higher taxes on the wealthy and corporations in order to fund public works, schools, and pensions. Under Long's leadership, Louisiana invested about

$50 per person per year in social protection spending, whereas the governors of Georgia and Kansas devoted about half as much to such spending. Under Long, Louisiana created new programs for nutrition, sanitation, and public health education, doubled funding for the public hospital system, and provided free immunizations to nearly everyone who couldn't afford them. Long started night schools that taught 100,000 adults to read, founded the Louisiana State University School of Medicine, doubled funding for the public charity hospital system, and extended free immunizations to 70 percent of the population—all during the worst economic crisis in history.[39]

New Deal and Share Our Wealth programs made a difference. It was so big a difference that a major gap developed between states that supported the New Deal and those that did not, even among states that started out in similar public health and economic situations. People in Louisiana and other states implementing New Deal measures benefited from significantly greater declines in infectious diseases, child mortality, and suicides, particularly when compared with people in states like Georgia and Kansas that didn't implement these measures.[40]

Overall, New Deal programs not only helped avert further economic disaster but also were statistically correlated to large and lasting public health improvements. The Great Depression created conditions that public health experts expected would spread infectious diseases, but infections fell steadily—with the biggest declines in the cities and states where New Deal housing programs helped prevent excessive crowding. Across the United States, each $100 per capita of New Deal spending was, on average, linked to declines in pneumonia by about eighteen deaths per 100,000 people—a remarkable improvement at a time when effective drugs to combat the disease were not widely available.

The New Deal also helped improve children's survival, as construction and rebuilding programs prevented shantytowns from becoming slums where stagnant water and overcrowding often led to diarrhea and childhood respiratory tract infections. Across the United States, each $100 per capita of New Deal spending was on average linked to reductions in infant deaths by eighteen per 1,000 live births.

And the New Deal was associated with reduced suicide rates. As shown in Figure 1.3, the first year of the New Deal (1933) marked the turning point in the rise in suicides. Using extensive statistical models controlling for alternative explanations, we found that each additional $100 per person of New

Deal spending was associated with a significant decline in suicides by four per every 100,000 people.

At the time, the American medical community was impressed by the results. Dr. William Welch, president of the American Medical Association, maintained that government investment in public health programs was not only a matter of saving lives and improving people's quality of life, but also making sound investments that would benefit the economy. "Any undue retrenchment in health," said Welch, "is bound to be paid for in dollars and cents as well as in the impairment of the people's health generally. We can demonstrate convincingly that returns in economic and social welfare from expenditures for public health service are far in excess of their costs."[41]

Welch was right—the New Deal programs were affordable even during Depression times. By today's standards, they still offer good value for the money. The social protection programs were as cost-effective, with similar costs per life saved, as common medications.[42]

Overall, the size of these New Deal relief programs constituted less than 20 percent of the gross domestic product. And they not only reduced deaths but also sped up economic recovery. The New Deal brought an immediate 9 percent rise in average American income, increasing people's spending and helping to create new jobs. Rather than creating a vicious negative spiral of increasing debt and deficits, as critics of the New Deal had predicted, the stimulus helped the US economy grow out of debt.[43]

At the time, politicians and the public didn't have access to data that we have at our disposal. In hindsight, it is possible to see clearly the lasting benefits of the New Deal, both to the economy and to public health.[44]

Undoubtedly, many of the health effects of the Great Recession will differ from those of the Great Depression. Prohibition is no longer in place, and our investigation into alcohol-related deaths during the Great Recession has found that more Britons and Americans are choosing to abstain from alcohol to save money. But we also found that a small, at-risk group has had the opposite reaction to our current recession: when faced with unemployment, they began drinking heavily. In the UK, where most people are still employed and drinking less overall, those people who lost work during the recession were much more likely to binge drink. Similarly, most Americans are drinking less during the Great Recession, but there is a hidden group of about 770,000 who now drink more dangerously, often landing in emergency rooms. These Americans have experienced a spike in death rates from acute intoxication and alcohol-induced liver failure.[45]

Political leaders on both sides of the Atlantic now face choices similar to those confronted by Hoover and Roosevelt. Another large, natural experiment is being unleashed on the people of both countries. Under Prime Minister Cameron's austerity measures in the UK, we see more and more sad stories like that of Brian and Kieran McArdle. The UK economy has yet to recover, as its debt continues to rise. Meanwhile in the US, President Obama is constantly battling with Republican deficit hawks, but has insisted on keeping and strengthening the safety net. And while not quite going so far as a New Deal, the US stimulus has helped lead the country to a slow but real recovery so far.

What the Great Depression shows us is that even the worst economic catastrophe need not cause people's health to suffer, if politicians take the right steps to protect people's health. The Great Recession involves a fundamental political choice: whether to apply the lessons of the Great Depression and the New Deal, or to chart an altogether different path that could have dire consequences.

2

THE POST-COMMUNIST
MORTALITY CRISIS

Ten million Russian men disappeared in the early 1990s.

The Russian Republic of the Soviet Union had more than 147 million residents. Its population had been growing at the same rate as the United Kingdom in 1990 and 1991, at about 0.3 percent per year. But in 1992, Russia's population began to vanish. The United Nations had been tracking data on the populations of all nations, and when they noticed this drop, they contacted a team of researchers in Russia.[1]

The research team set out across the country to investigate. They saw signs that something was amiss when they reached the country's mono-industrial settlements (*mono-gorod*)—towns set up by the Soviets to support its military and economy, where everything was planned to the last detail. The mono-towns were so named because they had only one business; the Communist Party had forced each village to specialize. Pitkyaranta, for example, was designed to mill lumber; Norilsk was a giant nickel factory; and several Siberian cities were customized for mining coal. One mining town, Kadykchan, was deep in Siberia's Magadan region. It had been built by Stalin's prisoners during World War II to provide coal for the Soviet military. Everything in the town revolved around the mines, and after the war the Soviets thought through all that would be needed for its residents: schools and hospitals next to the factories, housing for the workers and their families, and even holiday resorts a short weekend's trip away. All of life necessities were in place, designed to support the town's sole purpose: extracting coal for the Soviet state.

When the research team reached Kadykchan and its neighboring towns, they found what looked like a post-Chernobyl disaster or a ghost town: windows broken, storefronts boarded up. A sculpture of Joseph Stalin's head that once gazed sternly atop the town hall had crumbled, his jaw eroded into a hollow cavity filled by birds' nests. Enormous Soviet steel mills had been stripped to pieces, frozen over into large, silenced blocks of ice. Inside the factory, metal tools had caked with rust, and factory floors had overgrown with tomato and potato plants, converted into a garden plot.

At their peak, the Soviet mono-towns had between 10,000 and 100,000 residents, depending on the needs of the industry. Kadykchan once had 11,000 residents. By 1989, at the time of the last Soviet census, the population numbered 6,000. In 2000, when the Russian demographers conducted their visit, there were under 1,000. The population now were mostly women, children, and *babushkas* (Russian grandmothers), peering curiously through the cracked windows.

Where had all the men gone?[2]

The answer, it turned out, was hidden in the history of Russia's turbulent transition from a Soviet Socialist Republic to a Western market economy. The missing men were indicative of a broader collapse that had come with the rapid transition to a capitalist economy. It led to a massive tragedy in its own right—a demographic crisis that still haunts Russia today, and one that was eminently avoidable. The post-communist mortality crisis resulted not from the decision to transition to capitalism, but from specific policy choices about how to manage that transition that turned out to have dire consequences.

In the early 1990s, Russia's economic system collapsed. Its GDP fell by more than a third, a catastrophe on a scale not seen in industrialized nations since the Great Depression in the United States. In terms of purchasing power, Russia's economy in the mid-1990s shrank to the equivalent of the US in 1897. While officially unemployment was zero in the Soviet era, it jumped to 22 percent by 1998. In 1995, government statistics found one-quarter of the population were living in poverty, but independent survey data revealed the poverty rate to be much higher, at more than 40 percent of the population. A decade after the transition to capitalism began, the World Bank estimated that one-quarter of the population were living on less than $2 per day, and people living in the Soviet Union's former republics reported that they didn't have enough money to cover their basic nutrition.[3]

As the Soviet Union began to disintegrate, the fall of one Soviet town's factory set in motion a domino-like chain reaction. Soviet mono-towns depended on each other for supplies and parts, materials that no other companies in the world manufactured. In time, as one firm went under, it bankrupted its dependent Soviet mono-towns. Virtually overnight, the whole purpose of the Soviet mono-town ceased to be. People were left stranded in remote corners of Siberia, thousands of miles from the large cities of Moscow and St. Petersburg. To survive, they ate potato peelings and foraged in the forests for roots and berries. And there was the boredom, endless boredom. People had nothing to do, nowhere to go, and little hope for a better future.[4]

It was during that rapid transition that men began to die at an increasing rate. During Russia's move to the new market economy, men in towns and cities began to disappear—not old or frail men, but young men who would have otherwise been the vital force of the economy. The US Bureau of the Census had forecast that the Soviet Union's workforce would grow from 149 million in 1985 to 164 million in 1998—projections that were correct until 1990, after which the actual numbers fell to 144 million in 1998.[5]

Soon after the population data became public in 1999, the UN's investigative team published their official report, warning that "a human crisis of monumental proportions is emerging in the former Soviet Union, as the transition years have literally been lethal for a great many people." As shown in Figure 2.1, life expectancy among Russian men dropped from sixty-four to fifty-seven years of age between 1991 and 1994.[6]

What became known as "the post-communist mortality crisis" turned out to be the worst drop in life expectancy in the past half-century in any country that wasn't an active war zone or experiencing a famine.[7]

But the connection between the economic collapse of the mono-towns and the soaring death rates was not immediately clear. We had learned from the Great Depression that even a terrible market crash was no guarantee of a mortality crisis. So if a crashing economy didn't necessarily equate to a mass rise in deaths, what had caused so many Russian men to die during the economic depression of the 1990s?

We set out to investigate. Our first thought, as we looked into death certificates from this period, was that perhaps these data weren't real. The Soviet regime

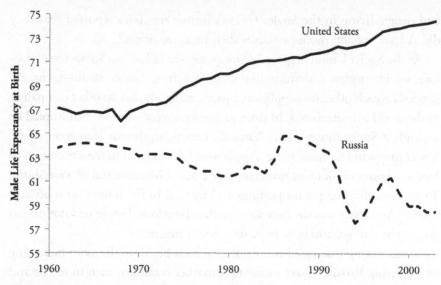

FIGURE 2.1 Post-communist Mortality Crisis[8]

was known to have kept its secrets; indeed, the KGB, the Soviet secret service police, could make a man disappear without a trace. Perhaps these men had been killed long ago and their deaths were only now coming to light, after the Russians let independent French and Russian demographers access the data to keep track. Or perhaps the Soviets had inflated their reports of the size of its male population—seeking to intimidate Western countries about their prospects for military recruitment. (This was hardly a far-fetched idea: In 1976, the Communist Party had launched a Commission on the Non-Publication of Data, whose members argued, "We must not reveal the number of boys born. Our enemies could use this information. We must make it a state secret.")[9]

To check whether the rise in death rates was genuine, we pored through troves of death certificates from before the fall of the USSR. We obtained data from the archives of the new government's demographic organization, Goskomstat. More than 90 percent of all deaths were reviewed and certified by doctors who were able to confirm each death and its cause, a rate higher than in many Western countries.[10]

An unusual feature of the Russian crisis was that the deaths were concentrated in young, working-age men. Most disease outbreaks disproportionately affect vulnerable people, such as infants and the elderly. The rate of death rose by a disconcerting 90 percent among the subgroup of men aged twenty-five to thirty-nine, in the prime of their lives.

Perhaps there was a terrible outbreak of influenza or other epidemic or widespread famine—or an as yet unknown pollutant from Soviet factories. But the death certificates that we, along with numerous other demographers, reviewed from Russia's statistical agencies did not support that theory. What the statistics showed was that many of these young men were dying from alcohol poisonings, suicides, homicides, and injuries. Such deaths seemed straightforward: men whose factories had shut down and were out of work were experiencing a high level of mental distress and anxiety, and their response was to turn to alcohol, harming themselves and others.

The young Russian men were also dying of heart attacks. This fact surprised us at first. We might have expected to see men in their fifties and sixties with clogged arteries having a heart attack, but rarely would people in their thirties and forties come to the hospitals with cardiovascular problems. The coroners' reports showed that the autopsies of the young men's arteries were clean. There was no plaque buildup. So what had caused the cardiovascular deaths?

To understand Russia's puzzling mortality patterns, we needed to look at different layers of health problems to understand their root causes. We wanted to move beyond identifying the immediate causes of death and their risk factors such as tobacco, unhealthy diets, and alcohol, to find the "causes of the causes," the social and economic changes that led people to harm themselves and others.

Since these deaths happened very rapidly, our first suspicion was that Russian men may have "self-medicated" to cope with the stress of the economic downturn—consuming huge amounts of vodka and home-brewed spirits. Russia has long had an epic drinking culture, one encouraged since the eighteenth century by the tsars to keep people from revolting. There's even a Russian word, *zapoi*, coined to describe the condition of being so drunk as to be incapacitated for days and even weeks at a time. More than three-quarters of all male industrial workers in Russia today would be considered "at-risk drinkers" by American medical criteria (that is, consuming more than four drinks on a single day).[11]

Social stress and alcohol go hand in hand; alcohol is a well-known trigger of depression, suicide, and homicide. And alcohol might also explain the rising rate of heart attacks in the young men with clean arteries. Cardiologists knew that in moderation, alcohol can reduce the risk of heart attacks; in large amounts, however, it provokes heart disease.[12]

Russian politicians had tried to curb their country's alcohol problems. In 1985, the Soviet Union's leader, Mikhail Gorbachev, launched an anti-alcohol campaign. It was remarkably effective, immediately increasing overall life expectancy by three years. Not only did alcohol deaths fall, but tuberculosis and heart disease did as well, as alcoholics often experience these two conditions from crowded living conditions and the heart disease impact of heavy alcohol use. But the campaign proved so unpopular that it was abandoned in 1987. It was repealed in part to help raise government revenues from state sales of alcohol. Drinking increased after the program ended so that by 1992, when Russia began its transition to the market, Russian deaths from alcohol were back to their high levels as before 1985.[13]

Even more troubling, it wasn't just the amount of alcohol Russian men were drinking during the early 1990s—it was the type. The form of alcohol changed, as men creatively found ways to binge without spending much money (they were, after all, mostly unemployed). Drinkers in Russia, Ukraine, and the Baltic states were drinking alcohols that were commercially manufactured using aftershave, mouthwash, and other products that contained alcohol but were not meant for consumption. These sources of alcohol were incredibly cheap and, unlike vodka and spirits, they weren't taxed. The brews from these alcohols were known as *odekolon* and were ostensibly sold as perfumes, but everybody knew what their real purpose was: they were labeled by flavor rather than scent, and had flip-top caps so that people could finish them easily in one sitting. These *odekolons* were particularly lethal: one study showed that drinking non-beverage alcohols increased the risk of death from alcoholic psychosis, liver cirrhosis, and heart disease by a factor of twenty-six over not drinking these substances.[14]

Vladimir, an *odekolon* drinker from Pitkyaranta who lost his job when the town's paper mill went bankrupt, provided an illustrative example of the drinking culture at the time. He was known for passing out drunk on the floor of the town's abandoned mill after drinking for two weeks straight, often waking up in the hospital. Vladimir binged on cheap *odekolons* (while in more rural areas people drank home-distilled brews, *samogons*). People like Vladimir drank more and more during the early 1990s, even as their income dried up. When asked by a *New York Times* reporter why he continued to drink, Vladimir said, "I can't explain it straightaway. I have a home. But I have nothing to do."[15]

Like millions of other Russian men, Vladimir had no hope for the future, no work, nothing to do, and nowhere to go—and *odekolons* were the cheapest way out. About one out of every twelve young Russian men was drinking these noxious alcohols. Only about 5 percent of men who were employed drank them, but nearly 25 percent of those who were unemployed did. These data alone couldn't tell us if the alcohol abuse caused the unemployment or the other way around, but the outcome was devastating either way; the combination of heavy drinking (*zapoi*) and *odekolons* was staggering. In Izhevsk, almost half of all deaths of working-age men were found to be attributable to hazardous drinking (when counting binge drinking and the harms from the surrogate alcohols). Across Russia, alcohol was estimated to have accounted for at least two out of every five deaths among Russian working-age men during the 1990s, totaling 4 million deaths across the former Soviet Union.[16]

To understand the full impact of this phenomenon, we looked at data from the Russian Longitudinal Monitoring Survey, which had followed men and their families from 1994 through 2006. Using a technique called survival analysis, we looked at 6,586 men who had jobs in 1994, of whom 593 had died and the rest had survived. We then evaluated what factors could predict who was most likely to have died or survived. The data revealed that the men most likely to drink vodka and nontraditional alcohols were manual workers and technicians. And they were also the most likely men to die. The gap in death rates between the factory workers and the managers had widened dramatically in the period we studied. In particular, the survey asked people about their perceptions of social standing as a measure of social stress. We found that those persons who had the least economic status, power, and respect in their communities were at a three-times greater risk of dying than those with the highest wealth, respect, and power. Overall, we found that a twenty-one-year-old Russian factory worker could expect to live fifty-six years, about fifteen years less than the factory managers and professionals.[17]

But the worst risks were seen in people like Vladimir, who were no longer in the workforce; men like him had a six-fold higher risk of dying than those who kept working. As if losing work was not enough of a shock to people's health, in the Soviet Union it also meant the ancillary loss of community and social support structures. In the Soviet era, employment was more than a paycheck and a purpose in life. Soviet working conditions were quite unlike those in Western firms. Although they were totalitarian and assembly-line-driven, they also had some uniquely beneficial aspects. Soviet planners provided their employees with on-site hospitals, diabetes screenings, childcare, and other social protection programs. While parents worked, children could play. And for the parents, there wasn't too much intensive work happening. The running joke among factory workers was, "We pretend to work, and they pretend to pay us," and it was true; people didn't earn much, but they did have stable jobs and many fringe benefits. All of these social support programs were provided free of charge to Soviet workers and their families. In the Soviet mono-towns, there was a deep sense of community, as people were, whether they liked it or not, all in it together.[18]

A key question, given the troubling rise in deaths, is how these harms could have been avoided. Many have argued that the extraordinary mortality rates in post-Soviet Russia were simply an unavoidable consequence of the necessary shift from a communist to a capitalist economy. After we published our studies showing a rising death rate among newly unemployed Russian men, one analyst for the *New York Times* asked us whether the mortality crisis wasn't "just an unforeseen and unwelcome result of the end of communism." In other words, was it inevitable that the transition from communism to capitalism resulted in terrible shocks and traumatic risks to health? That's a hugely important question. For answers, we looked at similar data across all the countries that had once constituted the Soviet Union and the Soviet bloc. If stress-related deaths were indeed an *inevitable* result of profound changes inherent to the transition from communism to capitalism, then the data would show dramatic increases in illness and death throughout all these nations.[19]

But the data didn't show a rise in deaths everywhere. Poland actually became healthier while Russia got sicker. Both Russia and Poland had experienced similar death rates in 1991, before the fall of the Soviet Union. But three years later, deaths had risen in Russia by 35 percent, while in Poland they fell by 10 percent. Kazakhstan, Latvia, and Estonia all had large jumps in mortality rates on par with Russia's experience, while Belarus, Slovenia, and the Czech Republic did not.

The key to understanding these differences is the policy choices made about how to transition from communism to capitalism. The critical decision was about the appropriate pace of reform. Those countries pursuing a very rapid transition from communism to market systems with radical privatization programs experienced a one-two punch of mass economic dislocation, together with huge cuts to social welfare. Ultimately the "rapid privatizers" suffered worse health than the "gradualists," who reformed more slowly and in so doing maintained their social protection systems and saw health improvements during the transition to capitalism.

As the Soviet Union was breaking apart, politicians and economists—both in Russia and in the West—debated about the best way to establish Western market capitalism on the ruins of communism. It was clear that the Soviet system was unviable, as could be plainly seen in the empty grocery stores and shortages of meat, milk, and matches. Some form of transition needed to occur—and indeed a gradualist one had already begun with Gorbachev's perestroika and glasnost reforms in the late 1980s. As the Soviet Union fell apart, the key question for debate was how—and how quickly.

Economists were divided about what was the appropriate pace of reform. One group of radical free-market advisers argued that the capitalist transition needed to occur as rapidly as possible. These economists pushed for Shock Therapy, a radical package of market reforms. Its proponents were mainly Harvard economists, including Andrei Shleifer, Stanley Fischer, Lawrence Summers, and Jeffrey Sachs, as well as Russian leaders such the Soviet economist and acting prime minister of Russia, Yegor Gaidar.

The rapid reformers argued that the sooner market reforms were implemented, the sooner economic benefits would accrue. That is, the Soviet factories would restructure and be successful again, and people would be more productive and earn more money, lifting Soviet society out of stagnation. Communism's fall had created a period of "extraordinary politics," according to members of the World Bank's transition economics team, during which politicians could demand great sacrifices from the population. Fast reforms would be economically painful because they would involve cutting people off from all the social protection systems they had been getting; but the reformers were, above all, concerned that if they did not act swiftly, Communists would return to power. This strategy traded short-term pain for long-term gain. This was, in essence, a deeply political plan to prevent the return of Communism and ensure that a capitalist market economy would endure in Russia. Once the market was established in the Soviet state system, it would be all but impossible to reverse.[20]

A key supporter of this theory, Jeffrey Sachs, published a landmark paper outlining his plan in January 1990. The essay, "What Is to Be Done," shared the title of Vladimir Lenin's pamphlet from ninety years prior, which had set out plans for the October 1917 revolution and the creation of Communism. The modern version argued a plan for Shock Therapy, a program to implement rapidly a combination of radical free-market reforms.[21]

Shock Therapy had two main elements. First, there would be economic "liberalization," which meant releasing the government's grip over the prices of goods in the market. The Soviet Union had controlled everything, from the wages workers earned, to the price of bread they bought in the factory towns. Such control needed to end, went the thinking of the Shock Therapists, if the market was to begin to work for the betterment of Soviet society.[22]

Next would come a massive privatization program. It would help remove the government's influence and create incentives for profit; extensive privatization would need to take place, selling off government-run projects. This was the most controversial and painful policy, but many economists viewed it as the key. Milton Friedman, the radical free-market economist and godfather of Shock Therapy, put it succinctly: "privatize, privatize, privatize"— break the Soviet state's grip on the economy as soon as possible. It was not only the economy that would be affected, however. In the Soviet Union, the state's funds for supporting public health and social services came directly from its state-owned enterprises. Mass privatization would not only dislocate workers, but also lead to huge cuts to its cradle-to-grave social protection system.[23]

Never before had anyone attempted to privatize an entire economy in such a short period of time. To put the Shock Therapists' plan into perspective, Margaret Thatcher, the great privatizer of the British economy, privatized about twenty large British utilities companies in eleven years during her time as prime minister. The Harvard economists planned to privatize more than 200,000 Soviet enterprises in less than 500 days. The reformers argued that speed was essential lest the former Soviet Union slip back into communism. As Lawrence Summers of Harvard University put it, "Despite economists' reputation for never being able to agree on anything, there is a striking degree of unanimity in the advice that has been provided to the nations of Eastern Europe and the former Soviet Union (FSU)."[24]

Yet in reality not everyone agreed with the Shock Therapists. A group of "gradualists," most prominently Joseph Stiglitz, who had been chief economist of the World Bank and in 2001 would win the Nobel Prize in Economics, concluded that capitalism could not be created overnight. Arguing that it had taken centuries for capitalism to develop in Western Europe, Stiglitz and his allies called for a slower transition, recommending that Eastern European countries slowly phase in markets and private property while allowing regulatory agencies and legal rules time to develop, to ensure that markets worked well rather than becoming manipulated by the powerful. They advocated a "dual-track" system so that former communist countries would incrementally "grow out of the plan," with the private sector eventually outgrowing an outmoded state-owned sector.[25]

As a solution to the debate, in 1991, Harvard economists proposed an idea for a grand bargain, backed by the US government. This promised as much as $60 billion in economic aid to support the Soviet workers and their families if the rapid reform plan was adopted; in exchange, the West would gain military concessions and influence over Soviet foreign policy. The US Agency for International Development led the aid effort, providing nearly $1 billion alone to the region to promote private-sector development. Soviet President Gorbachev, however, called for a slower pace of reform. His political adversary, Boris Yeltsin, approved of the US plan. After an August 1991 military coup against Gorbachev failed largely because of Yeltsin's opposition to it, Gorbachev's power and that of the Soviet Union itself were fatally compromised. Yeltsin banned the Soviet Communist Party in November, and on December 25, 1991, the Soviet Union came to an end.[26]

That political outcome tilted the balance of power in Russia to those who supported pursuing Shock Therapy, in a move away from Gorbachev's slower pace of reform. Not just Russia, but most countries in the former Soviet bloc, heeded the advice of the Shock Therapists. Shock Therapy policies were fully implemented in Russia by 1994, as well as in ex-Soviet republics like Kazakhstan and Kyrgyzstan. But politicians in other countries such as Belarus decided instead to take the gradualist path instead of Shock Therapy. A group of relatively similar countries embarked on widely different reform paths—a huge "natural experiment" in which relatively similar groups of people underwent vastly different reforms, and experienced dramatically different outcomes.

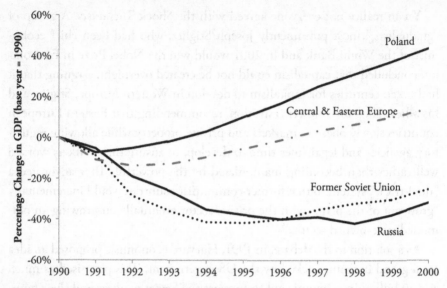

FIGURE 2.2   Economic Collapse in Russia and the Former Soviet Union, but Rapid Recovery in Central and Eastern Europe[27]

The results were disastrous in those countries that implemented Shock Therapy. As shown in Figure 2.2, between 1990 and 1996, per-capita income in Russia and most of the former Soviet Union (FSU) plummeted by over 30 percent, slightly less than the decline in the Great Depression. In purchasing-power-parity, Russia's economy in the mid-1990s fell to become equivalent to that of the United States in 1897.[28]

Mass privatization, a central plank of Shock Therapy, was supposed to break the Communist Party's influence on the economy. But, in Russia, it simply led to the mass transfer of wealth from the state to the former Communist Party elites, the *nomenklatura*, resulting in a handful of oligarchs and an enormous rise in inequality. Ultimately, it was the common public who lost out. Poverty skyrocketed—from 2 percent in 1987–1988 to over 40 percent by 1995. A running joke among families became "The worst thing about Communism is Post-Communism." In 1992, Russia's vice president, Alexander Rutskoy, denounced Yeltsin's program, calling it "economic genocide."[29]

But not all countries had the same fate. Russia's neighbor Belarus followed a gradualist path. It kept poverty rates below 2 percent during the transition. Its unemployment rate rose in the transition period to a peak of

4 percent but has remained below ever since and, today, has a rate of less than 1 percent. Across the region, the macroeconomic data from twenty-five post-communist countries covering the years 1989 to 2002 revealed that that those countries that implemented rapid mass privatization suffered increased male job losses by 56 percent compared with those that pursued a gradualist path.

Poland's experience made clear that privatization wasn't inevitably bad; rather, the problem was that its rapid pace in other countries had often left firms without strategic owners. Poland, held up as the poster child for Shock Therapy, did liberalize quickly in the early 1990s, but in fact delayed large-scale privatization under pressure from trade unions and angry protesters. In the Czech Republic, too, mass privatization was proposed, and even attempted, but then partly reversed after revolts by unions in the mid-1990s. This slower pace of privatization made a lasting impact on economies. Those countries that privatized their biggest steel mills more slowly were better able to attract foreign investors to take them over. Unlike Russian managers who took over firms and stripped their assets through mass privatization schemes, some foreign investors had a strategic interest in the firms they purchased. Poland was able to attract Volkswagen, along with $89 billion worth of foreign investment between 1990 and 2005. Similarly, the Czech Republic had the French car-maker Renault and Volkswagen Group competing to take over the state-run company, Automobilovézávody, národnípodnik, Mladá-Boleslav (now known as Škoda). Volkswagen won the bid in 1991, in a joint-venture partnering agreement with the Czech government. Škoda was once the laughing stock of the car industry, but with Volkswagen's help, it soon became one of the country's most important sources of economic growth, and today sells more than 875,000 cars each year.[30]

Transitions weren't painless in any countries of the former Soviet bloc, but they were far less dire and less sustained where the transitions took place more gradually. The Central and Eastern European countries that privatized more gradually to gain foreign investors also had an initial economic recession just like all the former Soviet states, but averted a full-scale economic depression like the one in Russia and the other rapidly-privatizing economies.

Rapid mass privatization was intended to break the Soviet state's grip on the economy, which was perceived by the West as corrupt. Ironically, however, corruption increased after rapid privatization. Many of the insiders who took over firms in shady privatization deals didn't invest in companies but simply stripped down their assets, sold them, and deposited the money in Swiss bank accounts. To look at what happened to firms, we investigated surveys of managers in 3,550 companies operating in twenty-four post-communist countries. We found that privatization to foreign owners led to increased restructuring of firms into competitive ones, with boosts to both investment and employment. This was precisely the pattern we had seen with Volkswagen in Eastern Europe. But mass privatization to Russian owners wasn't actually followed by the expected economic boom; instead it led to an economy in free fall, with more bribery and asset-stripping than before privatization. The economic impact of mass privatization was to perpetuate economic stagnation, dropping the affected economies' output by 16 percent—a fall equal in size to the countries experiencing the Great Recession of the present.[31]

The former Soviet countries' very different economic responses to the collapse of communism had distinctly different effects on the health of their populations. When we compared the data between these countries from 1989 to 2002, before and after transition, we found that rapid privatization carried two chief risks to people's well-being: people losing their jobs and their social safety nets all at once—a one-two punch.[32]

The World Bank, the leading development agency supporting mass privatization, recognized the health risks. The Bank argued in 1997 that "The central premise is that before long-run gains in health status are realized, the transition towards a market economy and adoption of democratic forms of government should lead to short-run deterioration."[33]

Jeffrey Sachs argued that a speedier transition would improve economic growth and, as a result, minimize health damage. But despite such adamant declarations, data from Russia showed a stark picture of human suffering and increasing poverty. As Sachs himself would acknowledge in 1995, the reforms did generate enormous stress and anxiety for the workers, creating winners and losers, but he maintained that the situation would improve in the longer term: "The reforms have surely created a rise in anxiety levels, even if they have not resulted in a fall in actual living standards. In a quite tough sense, economic reform in the early years is a bit like a society-wide game of musical chairs. Once market forces are introduced, a significant proportion of the population must search for new forms of economic livelihood. The result of that search, to be sure, will be highly positive in the longer term for most of the workers, but the process of change can be deeply upsetting during the transition, and some workers will also end up as economic losers from the changes."[34]

Consistent with the Shock Therapists' predictions, mass privatization led to short-term increases in unemployment and more than 20 percent cuts in government spending, including to health budgets. The consequences were the most severe in the Soviet mono-towns. There, a large rise in unemployment left people without savings to pay for food, housing, medications, or even access to healthcare. Contrary to the Shock Therapists' predictions, however, it also led to an economic depression. Those countries that implemented mass privatization had steeper declines in economic growth, slower recoveries, and more cuts to government spending on healthcare. We found that people living in those countries that pursued mass privatization had substantial drops in access to healthcare.[35]

Russia and its southwestern neighbor Belarus serve as an illustrative comparison. Belarus was long part of the Soviet Union, but declared independence from Russia in 1991, just before Russia began pursuing mass privatization programs. One leading advocate for the Russian Shock Therapy approach, the Swedish economist Anders Åslund, called Belarus a "Soviet theme park" for its resulting slow pace of privatization. But even though Russia was much larger than Belarus, since the 1960s both countries had followed similar economic and mortality trends. The differing policy choices between Russia and Belarus created a type of natural experiment where we could identify the health effects of mass privatization by comparing two countries with similar histories, cultures, and past mortality trends, which differed mainly in their choice of Shock Therapy.[36]

As we can see from Figure 2.3, these two countries had experienced roughly similar trends in death rates in the past decade. Russia then underwent mass privatization, selling off over 120,000 companies within two years. On the other hand, Belarus was slow to privatize. Russia experienced skyrocketing poverty and mortality rates, while Belarus kept poverty at less than two percent of its population and continued to have its usual rates of death.[37]

This comparative pattern recurred throughout the region. Countries embracing economic Shock Therapy—such as Kazakhstan, Latvia, and Lithuania—experienced a sudden and emphatic drop in life expectancy over the course of

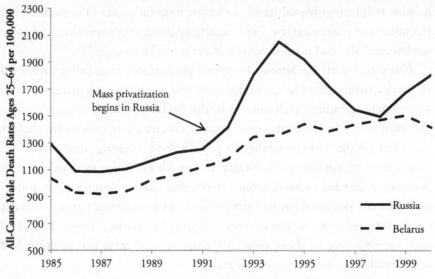

FIGURE 2.3   Mortality Trends in Russia and Belarus[38]

five years, while neighboring gradualists like Belarus and Poland fared much better in terms of public health outcomes.[39]

But it was possible that factors such as the size of the economy could be confounding the picture. We used statistical models to adjust for the differences in a country's economic performance, its past economic crises, its experience of ethnic and military conflict, its current level of development, the portion of people who lived in cities, other Shock Therapy policies including liberalization of markets, the level of foreign direct investment, and other social and economic factors that could come into play in twenty-four post-communist countries. Even after these multiple control variables, we found that countries such as Russia and Kazakhstan, which had implemented radical mass privatization schemes, had experienced, on average, an 18 percent rise in death rates after the policy went into effect, which was not seen in the more gradualist privatizers like Belarus and Poland. As a check on the validity of our findings, we looked at causes of death that should not fluctuate rapidly because of austerity—such as lung cancer, which would take several decades to develop. There we found no effect. But we did find that mass privatization increased male suicides by five per 100,000, heart disease by 21 per 100,000, and alcohol-related deaths by 41 per 100,000. Overall, mass privatization was correlated with a significant drop in life expectancy by two years.[40]

This short-term pain was, of course, foreseen by the Shock Therapists. But they had predicted that short-term suffering would lead to long-term economic growth, which would compensate for the human costs. If that were the case, it could be argued, the sharp increase in mortality could be seen as collateral short-term damage en route to a brighter future. A general rule of thumb is that "wealthier is healthier": people with larger incomes are more able to pay for healthcare and lead healthier lives by living in cleaner and more hospitable environments, eating more nutritious food, and taking up residence in safer neighborhoods. So was the economic benefit of Shock Therapy to the Russian people sufficient to neutralize the short-term rise in death rates? That was, after all, the theory of the Shock Therapists. In other words, did short-term pain lead to long-term gain?[41]

When we looked at the actual data, we unfortunately found that mass privatization did not speed up the economy. Quite the contrary, it led to a drop in GDP by a further 16 percent, making the full impact of privatization about equivalent to a 2.4 year loss in life expectancy.[42]

Eventually, even some of those who had initially advocated Shock Therapy came to acknowledge its negative health consequences. Milton Friedman later admitted an error. "In the immediate aftermath of the fall of the Soviet Union, I kept being asked what the Russians should do. I said, 'Privatize, privatize, privatize.' I was wrong. [Joseph Stiglitz] was right."[43]

Of course, not everyone was pleased by the finding that mass privatization was correlated with a large rise in deaths—predictably, the former advocates of Shock Therapy rushed to defend their actions. We published a peer-reviewed paper on the health effects of Shock Therapy in January 2009 in the British medical journal *The Lancet*, and the week after it came out, Sachs attributed Russia's dramatic increase in poor health to unhealthy diets rather than the impact of Shock Therapy. But Russian diets high in red meat and saturated fat had been on the increase since the 1960s, and had not suddenly changed for the worse during the few years of the early 1990s. Others who had recommended mass privatization to the Soviet bloc wrote that the crisis might have been from "disease stemming from some past exposure to pollution." Yet no major pollution exposures could account for a rapid spike in deaths concentrated among only the young men. Searching for further explanations, other economists then claimed that the alcohol deaths were just from the ending of the Gorbachev alcohol prevention program, but neglected to mention that the

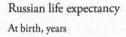

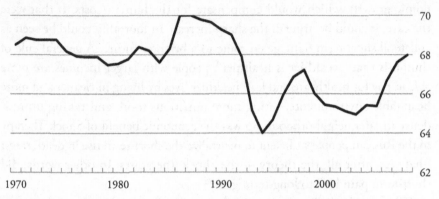

FIGURE 2.4   Russian Life Expectancy: Real Data, Our Graph[44]

program had ended long ago, and the number of people whose lives were saved were vastly outweighed by the rise in deaths after Shock Therapy.[45]

The attacks next turned into outright manipulation. Two weeks after our article was published, *The Economist* magazine, which backed Shock Therapy, wrote an opinion article dismissing the health effects of rapid privatization, concluding that "mistakes were made but Russia's tragedy was that reform came too slowly, not too fast." The editors of the magazine manipulated the mortality crisis data in a manner that made it look like the deaths had disappeared. By averaging the data over five years—and selectively choosing some survey years rather than others—they smoothed the death rate curve in 1990s Russia. This made the dramatic increase in mortality look like a steady decline—an easy way to "lie with statistics." If our university students had committed that kind of statistical manipulation on their term papers, they would be sent to the Dean. While Stalin doomed millions of people with the stroke of a pen in the 1930s, *The Economist*, it seemed, managed to bring millions of the dead back to life with a click of a computer mouse.[46]

What got lost in all the desperate attempts to deny the data was one of the most important findings from the research: how to prevent economic shocks from impacting people's health.[47]

Today, two decades after Russia began its transition to capitalism, the health of Russian men is still worse than it was before reforms began in 1991. Over-

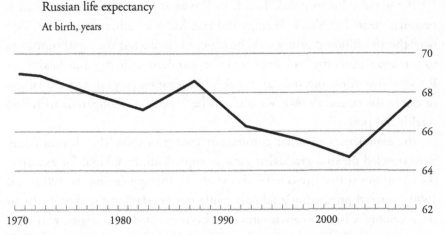

Russian life expectancy
At birth, years

FIGURE 2.5 Russian Life Expectancy: Our Graph, as Re-engineered by *The Economist*[48]

all life expectancy for men and women was sixty-eight years in 1991; in 2012 it was sixty-six years. The death of millions of Russian men continues to haunt the nation. Even the mighty Russian military has now faltered, unable to find sufficient healthy recruits to replenish its ranks.[49]

While men began dying in greater numbers following Shock Therapy, the whole nation suffered. Those left behind now feel the brunt of the death of a breadwinner. In Russia, it's not just the elderly but a generation of young women who now face hardship. Russia's women face the disheartening prospect of having to shoulder the burden of debt and household expenditures alone, after their husbands died too young.

Although Russia has now concluded its painful transition to capitalism, the lasting effects of this journey continue to impact health. After the shocks of privatization, Russia's crumbling system of workplace-associated medical clinics was no longer able to control infectious diseases. Once thought to be a disease of the past in Russia, tuberculosis has returned with a vengeance, with a rise starting in 1992. Together with sub-Saharan Africa, the former Soviet bloc is now one of only two regions in the world that are losing the fight against tuberculosis. The failures to curb tuberculosis are so grave in Russia that it has become the epicenter of new, mutant variants that resist nearly all antibiotics. This advance of "multi-drug-resistant" tuberculosis poses serious threats worldwide.[50]

The massive hit to public health in Russia is particularly tragic when it becomes clear that Shock Therapy didn't achieve its other stated aims. Perhaps the 10 million deaths would be easier to stomach if the rapid transition to a market economy had improved the standard of living and health for Russians over time. But instead, Russia's privatization programs served largely to create the country's own version of "the 1 percent"—oligarchs with vast wealth and power.

The experiences of other communist countries show that Russia could have traveled down a gradualist path to capitalism. In China, for example, the Communist Party rejected calls for Shock Therapy during the 1980s and 1990s, instead privatizing gradually while slowly relaxing the state's grip on the economy. China's growth rates have been in the double digits, year after year, even amid the recession that started in 2007. And its population's health has benefited from China's model of economic growth; China now boasts health statistics that rival some Western nations. While China's life expectancy for both men and women in 1985 was sixty-seven, it is now seventy-three.[51]

Russia wasn't the only victim of Shock Therapy. Through a series of debt crises in the 1980s and 1990s, the International Monetary Fund and World Bank pushed radical economic policies onto countries in Latin America, sub-Saharan Africa, and Asia. The vast nation of Indonesia was the next unfortunate guinea pig for the Shock Therapists, who stepped in to advise the country about how to respond to the threats to its economy and health wrought by the East Asian Financial Crisis of the 1990s.

3

FROM MIRACLE TO MIRAGE

Kanya was just sixteen when she started coughing up blood. It was 2001, and she was one of hundreds of farmers' daughters around Kanchanaburi, an area of Western Thailand, who were experiencing strange symptoms: rashes, weight loss, and chest infections including pneumonia and tuberculosis.

At the time, Sanjay was helping the Thai government's "mobile clinics"— pickup trucks and cargo vans that the Ministry of Health in Thailand had converted into roaming medical clinics. The backs of the trucks were stocked with drugs and bandages, and the drivers—two nurses and a local doctor— would drive between villages near the Thai-Burmese border, stopping at each house along the way to offer free basic healthcare services to farmers and their families who otherwise couldn't afford it.

The farmers were suffering from the worst financial crisis since Russia's debacle. Since 1997, Thailand and its neighboring countries had experienced a dramatic rise in poverty after a real estate bubble burst, plunging East Asia into a deep recession. The International Monetary Fund, an international bank that was the "lender of last resort," had offered bailouts, but on the condition that countries implement massive austerity on health and social services. The funding cuts could not have come at a worse time. Hundreds of thousands of farmers in rural areas around Kanchanaburi had lost their ability to sell goods on the common marketplace, as fluctuations in the prices of rice and vegetables had left them on the losing end of trade deals. Austerity meant that there was no buffer, and the farmers struggled to make enough money to avoid starvation.[1]

Kanya told the clinic's director what had happened. After the crisis hit, she had been recruited by "city men" who said that she could get a good job in Bangkok—waitressing at restaurants or manufacturing clothing in factories. With her earnings, she could send money back home to her family who couldn't afford food or medicine. But rather than being brought to riverside restaurants or factories to work, she was taken to one of Bangkok's red-light districts. There, a German tourist repeatedly raped her.

After hearing her story, the mobile-clinic doctor tested Kanya and others for HIV. Like all of the young Kanchanaburi women who presented with unexpected weight loss, rashes, pneumonias, or tuberculosis, Kanya tested HIV positive. Left undiagnosed for several years, HIV had weakened her immune system, leaving her susceptible to tuberculosis.

Kanya had managed to escape Bangkok to her family, but by that point her family could do little to help her. She had been diagnosed far too late. Her immune system weakened, she died from complications of tuberculosis.

Kanya was not alone. In 1998, Thailand's death rate from infectious diseases began to rise. In the next five years, there were more than 50,000 excess deaths from pneumonias, tuberculosis, and HIV—deaths that followed a large dose of austerity.

Kanya's story begins with the financial boom that started in the 1980s. International investors were thrilled with the "emerging markets" in East Asia. Nearly half of the world's foreign investment flowed there. Investors reaped windfall profits. Thailand and many of its neighboring countries like Indonesia and Malaysia were experiencing remarkable economic growth at rates near or above 5 percent each year. As real estate boomed, employment rose, and poverty levels dropped. For the first time, many Asian children (including girls) not only got the opportunity to go to school, but started achieving math and science exam scores higher than children in the West.[2]

The World Bank labeled several countries in the region "Asian Tigers." The Bank called it the "Asian Miracle," a "model" for the rest of the world to follow.[3]

If this seemed too good to be true, that's because it probably was. Before the crisis began, the international finance community had been working suspiciously hard to preserve the image of the Asian Miracle. An exposé in *The Wall Street Journal* reported that the World Bank, at the insistence of the Indonesian government, had "softened reports on Indonesia's economy, reports that helped the government win better ratings and draw in capital." Dennis de Tray, an economist who ran the 150-person World Bank mission in Indonesia, admitted that "in every country that we operate in there is a trade-off between, shall we say, being pure and helping people"—essentially noting that the World Bank thought it was helping people by promoting the Asian Miracle.[4]

The inflated reports did not fool all observers; some saw through the hype and recognized that a full-blown crisis was brewing. In 1994, the oft-prescient Paul Krugman warned of the "myth of the Asian miracle." He noted that Asia's rapid development was powered by extraordinary boosts in foreign capital rather than by investments that were enhancing technology or more efficiency at work, a tell-tale sign of an economic bubble. A glut in real estate had developed, and, by 1996, $20 billion of residential property remained unsold. Many buildings stood empty.[5]

By early 1997, investors had become jittery about whether these real estate deals were simply inflating a housing bubble. Never missing an opportunity, the investor George Soros and his Quantum Fund placed bets that East Asia's currencies were overvalued and would fall in price. His move stoked feelings of panic. Throughout the region, markets and currencies crashed. In 1997 and 1998, the Thai baht and the Indonesian rupiah lost, respectively, 75 percent and 80 percent of their value. As the dominoes fell, the entire region was soon engulfed in the financial panic of devalued currencies. All the capital that had been pouring into the Asian economies soon started to flood out. Foreign investors withdrew $12 billion of investments from real estate and other industries, further reducing the value of the region's currencies. By mid-January 1998, the currencies of all "emerging" market economies in Southeast Asia had lost half of their pre-crisis value.[6]

East Asians now experienced an economic catastrophe analogous to the Great Depression in the US. The price of food doubled, with rice and other staple food prices increasing the most because the currencies in these countries had become worth less. To make matters worse, an El Niño weather cycle contributed to a massive drought in October 1997, leading to rice and cereal shortages and further increases in the prices of basic foods. The poverty rate in Indonesia jumped from 15 percent to 33 percent in just over a year.[7]

That is why Kanya's parents had sent her to the "city men" to help support the family.

Faced with starvation, people across East Asia took to the streets in protest. In May 1998, riots broke out in Jakarta, ultimately leading to the fall of President Suharto's dictatorial regime. The violence terrorized the nation, as communities descended into chaos. Its victims were often women: at least 168 rapes were documented. A Chinese ethnic minority, seen as the privileged business class, were also targets of mob attacks.[8]

The injuries and trauma from the violence foreshadowed a more significant public health crisis that would emerge in the region. East Asian countries—Thailand and Indonesia in particular—had far less extensive healthcare infrastructure than Russia, particularly in rural areas like Kanchanaburi. There was a real danger that a human catastrophe would emerge as seen in the postcommunist crisis. It was unclear whether East Asia would respond by protecting its people, or pursue the post-Soviet one-two punch of privatization and austerity.

As with Russia in the early 1990s, there was no shortage of advice for the governments of the Asian Tigers. The IMF offered its prescriptions for recovery. The Fund was established after World War II, when Europe was struggling to recover from economic devastation. Its Founding Charter called for this specialized bank to "promote economic stability" and contribute "to the promotion and maintenance of high levels of employment"; in other words, to tame volatile global markets and protect ordinary people from the harms of instability.[9]

Before the East Asian crisis, the IMF had become widely known as an economic driving force of US policy in the region. It offered loans directly to governments to help them balance their books. Like all international banks, the IMF placed conditions on its loans. Toward the mid-1980s, during the age of Ronald Reagan and Margaret Thatcher, these conditions began to include strict targets for privatizing state-owned enterprises, liberalizing markets to remove regulations on prices and trade, and cutting government spending on health and education. The rationale for these policies was to boost the role of private industries in poor countries, increase the influence of market forces over government intervention, reduce dependency on foreign aid, and prevent inflation. Many policymakers and investors in high-income countries argued that these policies were good for development. Because these theories came from policy advisers in Washington, DC, they were referred to as the Washington Consensus.[10]

During the East Asian Crisis, the IMF found itself in a quandary. The countries it was now being asked to help had followed economic advice the IMF had given them during the boom years. Indeed, that advice was commonly believed to have fueled the economic boom and to have precipitated the subsequent financial crisis. Now the IMF was forced to argue that the very same Asian countries needed to make a dramatic change in policy. As with its approach to Russia's crisis in the 1990s, for Asia the IMF advocated the Shock Therapists' one-size-fits-all prescription: trade short-term pain for long-term gain.[11]

The IMF's prescriptions may have found a consensus in Washington, but they worried health experts in East Asia. Rather than allowing countries to imitate the New Deal, the IMF called for extensive budget cuts, particularly to the health sector. The cuts were premised on the idea that countries should maintain a budget surplus during a recession rather than engage in deficit spending. According to the theory, running a budget surplus would inspire confidence in investors, ultimately bringing about a faster economic recovery and staving off a human catastrophe. However, significant data had refuted the theory that this was necessary or wise. The theory was based more on repeated assertion than on actual practical success—as seen in Russia, the consequences were disastrous, for both the economy and public health.[12]

Not all East Asian countries decided to take the same paths in response to the crisis. Some followed the advice of the IMF to cut budgets, but others chose to invest in social protection programs to support their people. So the crisis provided a kind of natural experiment, something scientists seldom observe across entire countries. Such an experiment happened in the US in the Great Depression when some states adopted the New Deal and others did not to the same extent. It again happened with the fall of the Soviet Union, as similar populations took different policy paths toward privatization and the resulting austerity.

The natural experiment in East Asia began with a common economic shock. All countries faced serious threats to health—a combination of unemployment, rising food prices, and debts. In response, on November 21, 1997, the South Korean government made an official request to the Fund for an emergency rescue loan. Indonesia and Thailand signed up next. Yet Malaysia did not. Amid mass demonstrations, the Malaysian prime minister, Maha-thir Mohamad, refused IMF "assistance," since it had so many strings at-tached that many felt would be harmful to Malaysians. So Malaysia served as the "control group" in this experiment. It implemented a fiscal stimulus of 7 billion ringgit, including a boost to social safety net measures to mitigate the impact of the crisis.[13]

Those countries that cut social protection programs had greater rises in poverty. Gross domestic product in 1998 fell by a dramatic 30 percent in South Korea, 27 percent in Thailand, 56 percent in Indonesia, and 34 per-cent in Malaysia. But these economic shocks tipped more people into poverty in South Korea, which had weaker social protection systems and also had implemented the harshest austerity. In 1997–1998, poverty in South Korea doubled from 11 percent in 1997 to 23 percent in 1998. Indonesia and Thai-land also experienced significant increases. Malaysia, by contrast, had avoided the harsh austerities of IMF-borrowing countries, and experienced a much smaller rise in poverty, from 7 percent to 8 percent.[14]

As austerity worsened poverty during the recession, people's mental health suffered. In South Korea, the IMF soon became known as "I Am Fired." Men's suicide rates, which had decreased during the previous decade, sud-denly increased by 45 percent. In Thailand, the suicide rates rose by over 60 percent, against a background rise in death rates from all causes.[15]

Without a strong safety net, rising poverty and escalating food prices led to mass hunger in Thailand and Indonesia. In 1998, there was a 20 percent rise among mothers in the rate of "wasting," a state of malnutrition where muscle and fat tissue are lost. Mothers were sacrificing their food in order to feed their children. In Thailand, the number of pregnant women who were anemic, lacking sufficient iron, vitamin B12, and folate, rose by 22 percent in 1998. Imported powdered milk had tripled in price since the start of the cri-sis, and some poor families fed infants sweetened green tea instead of milk. There was a subsequent drop in infant weights, increased risk of infant mor-tality, and a rise in underweight primary school children during the crisis, given the low nutritional value of these substitute infant formulas.[16]

Under the circumstances, the countries desperately needed an emergency food delivery program. President Roosevelt had introduced such a program in the United States in 1939, and it had helped 20 million people. It provided income and food support and an agriculture program to ensure a steady domestic supply of food during the Dust Bowl drought in America. Yet the IMF enacted the opposite strategy—cutting food subsidies during East Asia's drought in 1998. It further advised opening up the countries even further to private trading markets. Such a move perversely left the currencies of Thailand and Indonesia more exposed to currency speculators, who quickly seized the opportunity to move their investment money out of the economy.

The currencies of Thailand and Indonesia continued to collapse, plunging people deeper into poverty and hunger. In January 1998, a few months before the May 1998 riots, protesters gathered in Jakarta's central market. Dozens of women, enraged by the escalating price of food, shouted at Jakarta's Governor Sutiyoso, a former military general. "The price of rice has soared to 4,000 rupiah per kilogram," one woman said. "I cannot possibly afford to buy more than two kilograms. I don't have that much money." Another woman asked, "Where's the sugar and flour, sir? There is not even any milk for our children." The governor, who had been trying to keep public spending low to meet the IMF targets, capitulated to the women and ordered his troops to provide milk.[17]

Meanwhile, the IMF, in an effort to curb budget deficits, responded to the crisis by further taxing kerosene by 25 percent for Indonesians. Kerosene is the main fuel the poor use for cooking their food. The IMF's chief economist, Stanley Fischer, tried to show regard for the working class by noting that the price of rice was kept unchanged. But given the increased price of fuel, the stable yet still high price of rice was little consolation—people were unable to cook raw rice without fuel.[18]

Malaysia took a dramatically different approach, and reined in rising food prices. In 1997 Prime Minister Mahathir claimed that the source of the currency crisis was "currency trading," which he called "unnecessary, unproductive and immoral." It should be stopped and made illegal, he said. Malaysia introduced controls on market speculation and fixed its exchange rate to the dollar. As a result, speculative investors had difficulty betting on the rises and falls of Malaysia's currency. In addition, Malaysia expanded its food support programs for impoverished citizens. Unlike Indonesia and Thailand, Malaysia experienced no significant rise in malnutrition among mothers.[19]

In short, the East Asian Financial Crisis was a natural experiment that put to the test multiple theories about how to respond to a recession. The recession itself put millions of people at risk of poverty; but it was the policy decision to cut food and unemployment support that turned the crisis into a public health disaster. The alternative to austerity could be seen in Malaysia, where, under political pressure, politicians chose to control the money flowing out of the economy and increase investments in social protection programs. Those choices helped prevent Malaysians from suffering the fate of Thailand, Indonesia, and South Korea whose politicians chose to swallow the bitter pill of austerity.

Across East Asia, the collapsing currencies caused massive increases in the costs of importing painkillers, insulin, and other essential medicines. As drug prices increased, the cost of medical treatment at public healthcare centers in Indonesia shot up by 67 percent.[20]

As healthcare prices rose, people needed help from their governments to be able to afford care. But instead of increasing health spending, those countries borrowing from the IMF implemented steep budget cuts. On IMF advice, the Thai government in 1998 cut health expenditures by 15 percent. In Indonesia, total public-sector health spending fell by 9 percent in 1997 and another 13 percent in 1998. All in all, Indonesia saw a 20 percent reduction in per-person spending, and a 25 percent cut in government funding for primary healthcare services between 1996 and 2000.[21]

These spending cuts caused people to lose access to care. Women and children increasingly stopped attending clinics and hospitals as the cost of care became unaffordable. Healthcare use by Indonesian children aged ten to nineteen years dropped by a third. In several communities, the supply of medicines also evaporated as funds to government clinics were cut. About half of the health clinics in one large neighborhood of Jakarta closed because of rising prices. Throughout Indonesia, government health facilities experienced shortages of antibiotics, iron supplements, and contraceptive pills as government budgets were slashed. The 1998 Indonesia Family Life Survey found that 25 percent of public hospitals and clinics exhausted their stocks of penicillin, and that 40 percent of clinics ran out of the critical antibiotic ampicillin.[22]

Austerity also reversed progress in the fight against HIV by cutting some extremely effective public health programs. Before the crisis, in the early 1990s, Thailand had been the epicenter of Asia's HIV epidemic. It reported some 100,000 new cases of HIV in 1990; three years later, the figure had jumped to over a million cases. Dr. Wiwat Rojanapithayakorn, head of the

World Health Organization's East Asian headquarters, watched aghast as the virus spread from Thailand's cities to the countryside and back again. His investigations helped reveal that 97 percent of all cases were linked to transmission from sex workers, a third of whom were HIV positive in 1994. Yet his was an optimistic finding. It meant that a solution could be worked out. A key way to prevent new cases was to direct interventions at specific sites, by entering brothels and encouraging sex workers and their clients to use condoms.[23]

Such a campaign was beyond Dr. Rojanapithayakorn's area of expertise. So he teamed up with a social activist, Meechai Viravaidya—who became known as Mr. Condom—to promote a "no condom, no sex" message. The duo traveled throughout the country, distributing free condoms to massage parlors and brothels, insisting that sex workers and their clients use them. If they refused, the operations would be closed down by police.[24]

The results were stunning. In less than two months, the "100% condom use" program cut new HIV infections from 13 percent among sex workers in Ratchaburi province to less than 1 percent.[25]

Armed with this evidence, Rojanapithayakorn approached the Thai government for help. It agreed to broadcast HIV prevention messages every hour on the country's radio stations and television networks. Of course, all this required funding, and the annual HIV prevention budget increased from $2 million in 1992 to $88 million in 1996. Within three years, condom use among sex workers rose from 25 percent to more than 90 percent.[26]

But then the Asian financial crisis struck. To meet IMF austerity-driven budget targets, the Thai government made sweeping cuts to funding for condom distribution and related public health measures. Overall, the nation's health promotion budget was slashed by 54 percent. Authorities tried to protect the budget for HIV treatment and prevention, but in 1998 it too was cut by 33 percent at the behest of the IMF. By the year 2000, domestic funding for HIV prevention was less than a quarter of what it had been before the crisis.[27]

When we looked at the Thai health system's data, we found that condom distribution to brothels dropped from upwards of 60 million condoms in 1996 to 14.2 million in 1998. As a result, Thailand's HIV prevention program began to falter. The rate of AIDS patients reported in Thailand increased from 40.9 per 100,000 in 1997 to 43.6 per 100,000 population in 1998. The pharmaceutical budget for preventing mother-to-child transmission could only meet 14 percent of the estimated total need after the cuts.

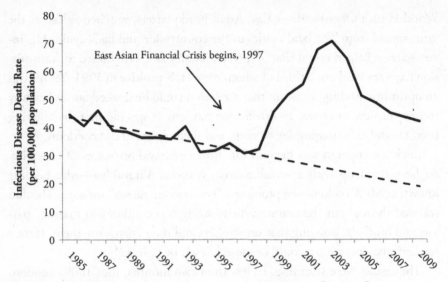

FIGURE 3.1 Thailand's Large Increase in Death Rates from Infectious Diseases[28]

The number of orphans with HIV rose from 15,400 in 1997 to 23,400 in 2001. Half of those infected children who received no medical treatment died by the age of five.[29]

Thailand's progress in preventing infectious diseases such as HIV was all but erased, as shown in Figure 3.1. Between the 1950s and 1996, infectious disease deaths had been falling at a rate of 3.2 deaths per 100,000 population per year. This progress began to reverse in 1998, when infectious disease death rates started to rise at a rate of 7.6 deaths per 100,000 population each year. The main cause of the rise in deaths was untreated HIV, and its complications, pneumonia and tuberculosis.[30]

To fill the gaping holes in Thailand's public health system left by austerity, medical volunteers like Sanjay had stepped in to help support Thailand's HIV prevention and treatment programs. They were able to save some lives. But for others—like Kanya, the sixteen-year-old girl from Kanchanaburi—they were too late.

In contrast to Thailand, Malaysia chose to ignore IMF advice to cut budgets, and instead increased real healthcare spending by about 8 percent in 1998 and 1999. The boost to healthcare funding translated into a rise in patients who were treated in the public health system by about 18 percent. The increased HIV control budget enabled Malaysia to introduce a mother-to-child transmission prevention program, modeled on Thailand's. In other words, just as Thailand's flagship public health programs were being wiped out, Malaysia put identical ones into place. And during the crisis, there was no significant rise in HIV in Malaysia even as control of the disease began to falter in Indonesia and Thailand.[31]

Meanwhile, the IMF's partner organization, the World Bank—which oversees social well-being and poverty relief—evaded questions from reporters and researchers about how health had been affected by the crisis and the IMF's programs in the region. In South Korea, the Fund became known as the "Infant Mortality Fund," because the infant mortality rate rose in association with the Fund's austerity program. When asked, "Has health worsened in Indonesia?" Bank officials replied that it was "difficult to get a complete and consistent picture of the health impact of the crisis and the effectiveness of policy responses. Some standard barometers suggest catastrophic results were averted. For example, infant mortality rates seemed to have continued a 'downward trend'." Yet an analysis published in the prestigious British medical journal *The Lancet* by independent health researchers found that the Bank's reports were "inaccurate" and "groundless." The Bank, usually meticulous in citing data sources, failed to cite any for its assertion that infant mortality decreased. In reality, the Indonesian Central Statistics Bureau reported in the United Nations Human Development Report that infant mortality had increased, rising in twenty-two of its twenty-six provinces of Indonesia by an average of 14 percent.[32]

Despite these results, not all IMF programs were disastrous. A few IMF measures helped prevent disease, mostly by reducing alcohol use. In 1998, to meet the IMF demand for budget surpluses, Thailand's government was forced to increase sales taxes on alcohol. According to the National Tax Administration data on alcoholic beverages, the reforms worked: consumption of alcoholic beverages fell by 14 percent over two years.

Recession in East Asia did not have to spell a health disaster. But massive budget cuts corresponded to real rises in hunger and forgone access to doctors and clinics. Cuts did not just occur to a few poorly performing programs, but were made without regard for Thailand's internationally acclaimed HIV program. The health disaster that followed set back progress in fighting hunger and infectious diseases. East Asia had become the next textbook case of what can happen when austerity politics are placed before people's health. As in Russia, the large dose of austerity harmed the ultimate source of East Asia's progress: its people.

In the years following the crisis, an economic divide emerged between IMF borrowing- and non-borrowing countries. Malaysia, having rejected the IMF's directives in pursuing its own path of state intervention, avoided mass misery and suffering, and accelerated its economic recovery. Malaysia was, in fact, the first country in the region to experience economic recovery. Although average incomes declined in 1998, Malaysia's recovery began the following year. Food prices had risen 8.9 percent in 1998, but two years later back to a mere 1.9 percent above their pre-crisis levels. South Korea was an intermediate case; as a bigger economy than Malaysia's, with greater government spending prior to the crisis, it had more "policy space" in which to maneuver and could better negotiate with the IMF to avoid the most painful budget cuts. It was the second nation to recover after Malaysia.[33]

In 2000 Joseph Stiglitz summed up the role of the IMF in the East Asian Financial Crisis: "All the IMF did was make East Asia's recessions deeper, longer, and harder. Indeed, Thailand, which followed the IMF's prescriptions the most closely, has performed worse than Malaysia and South Korea, which followed more independent courses."[34]

Ironically, of the four countries examined here, only Malaysia was able to meet the IMF's ultimate economic targets even though it didn't participate in the IMF program. Malaysia ended up with a budget surplus in 1997, even though it was the only country that avoided cutting social protection spending.[35]

Those within the IMF were beginning to admit their errors. In a confidential report leaked to the *New York Times*, IMF staff members agreed that their lending conditions worsened the crisis. "Far from improving public confidence in the banking system," the report stated, "[our reforms] have instead set off a renewed 'flight to safety'," referring to continued withdrawal of investment from the region that prompted banking closures. In other words, the IMF's programs had worsened the sense of panic, not only because of its dire warnings which scared investors, but also because high interest rates and budget cuts slowed down the economy.[36]

The natural experiment in East Asia had striking results. When Malaysia refused to cut its public health budgets, immunization programs and food assistance projects were preserved, and the country did not experience a marked rise in malnutrition and HIV, unlike its neighboring countries that slashed health budgets. As one UNICEF report concluded, "In Malaysia, unlike in Indonesia, the Republic of Korea and Thailand, there is little doubt that the social impact of the crisis has been contained." An independent analysis of the data by Australian public health experts summarized the situation: "These results strongly suggest that social protection programs, adapted to meet the needs of the most threatened population groups, are necessary and important tools to protect against the adverse effects of an economic crisis on health and health care." Researchers at the Johns Hopkins School of Public Health agreed, concluding that "social protection programs play a critical role in protecting populations against the adverse effects of economic downturns on health and health care."[37]

Ten years after the East Asian Financial Crisis, the worldwide Great Recession hit Indonesia. It brought the country an opportunity to learn from its mistakes; this time the Indonesian government increased some subsidies to poor people. Thus, the poor could still afford cooking oils amid rising food and fuel prices in 2008 and 2011 (which were due in part to the movement of investors out of mortgage-backed securities and into food commodities investments).[38]

It was only in this current Great Recession crisis that the IMF issued a formal mea culpa for its shortcomings during the East Asian Financial Crisis. In October 2012, the Fund admitted that the economic damage from its austerity and liberalization recommendations in East Asia may have been as much as three times as great as it had previously assumed. While the IMF had predicted its measures would grow Indonesia's economy by 3 percent, the economy actually contracted by 13 percent. The director of the Fund issued a formal apology. Such apologies were of little use to the millions of lives destroyed by the IMF's "help." Many East Asian countries will not go back to the Fund if they can avoid it; these countries together have amassed $6 trillion in savings accounts filled with foreign exchange investments in case of another economic downturn. "People learn from what happened in the past," said Indonesia's Trade Minister Gita Wirjawan. "Certainly what we went through in 1998 was painful.

I lived through that, and hopefully the difficulties we went through served as lessons."[39]

The lessons of history—the New Deal, Shock Therapy in Russia, and the IMF programs in the Asian Financial Crisis—are clear. They present us all with a clear decision. Will we continue to balance budgets on the backs of the most vulnerable members of society? Will tens of millions of people like Olivia in California, Dimitris in Athens, the McArdles in Scotland, Vladimir in Russia, and Kanya in Thailand have to suffer for misbegotten austerity programs? Or will we finally recognize that economic health and human health go hand in hand?

PART II

THE GREAT RECESSION

4

GOD BLESS ICELAND

"Gud Blessi Is'land."

The three words appeared in blocked white letters on television screens all over Iceland on October 6, 2008.

"Fellow Icelanders," a voice began. "I have requested the opportunity to address you at this time when the Icelandic nation faces major difficulties."[1]

Most people in this island nation of 317,000 refer to each other by their first names. This was Geir Hilmar Haarde, the prime minister, speaking. The block letters on the screen were replaced by his image: he stood behind a cluster of microphones, wearing his signature blue blazer, next to the country's flag. His cheeks sagged with worry.

"There is a very real danger, fellow citizens, that the Icelandic economy, in the worst case, could be sucked with the banks into the whirlpool and the result could be national bankruptcy," he said, adjusting his glasses nervously.[2]

The stress was palpable. In 2008, financial crisis had spread like a virus across the Atlantic, from the American mortgage crisis to the European stock market, and now to this tiny island nation. In December that year, *The Economist* reported that "Iceland's banking collapse is the biggest, relative to the size of an economy, that any country has ever suffered." The crisis came as a massive shock to the peaceful nation of Iceland, and many commentators predicted doom. All its biggest banks failed, the stock market crashed by

90 percent, and investments worth nine times the country's annual economic production disappeared within one week in October 2008. The Icelandic Public Health Institute asked local journalists to write more positive stories in an effort to curb the risk of suicide. As Bloomberg financial news reported, "This was no post–Lehman Brothers recession: It was a depression."[3]

As a result, Iceland's people now faced their biggest health threat since World War II. With a large rise in debt, the universal healthcare system faced bankruptcy. The entire system was publicly funded and run; there were virtually no private hospitals, clinics, or insurance. So if government funding dried up for the health service, people's access to healthcare would be directly impacted. Another threat was that if Iceland's currency, the krona, depreciated, the cost of importing essential medicines would soar—making medicines unaffordable at a time when government budgets were already overstretched. Adding to the risks, the possibility of major job losses and home foreclosures threatened to provoke depression, suicides, and heart attacks, placing pressure on Iceland's public health service.[4]

Geir continued his speech. "I am well aware that this situation is a great shock for many, which raises both fear and anxiety. If there was ever a time when the Icelandic nation needed to stand together and show fortitude in the face of adversity, then this is the time. I urge you all to guard that which is most important in the life of every one of us, protect those values which will survive the storm now beginning."

Iceland stood apart from other nations battling the Great Recession. While most people were focusing on the US, UK, Greece, and Spain, Iceland served as a miniature laboratory to examine how the recession affected public health. First, by studying a sparsely populated island of people with similar culture and diets, it was possible to pinpoint the impacts of economic policies in a way that is much more difficult within larger nations or whole regions like the European Union. In Iceland, nearly every person had the same health insurance coverage, and it was possible to keep track of every person in terms of their visits to the doctor, their hospitalizations, and their death. By contrast, Europe had varied healthcare coverage and access, and people were often lost from the system (especially the most vulnerable groups, like the homeless), so pinpointing what factor caused certain people to be ill was difficult to investigate. Second, Iceland had developed a strong, Nordic-style system of social protection programs—programs including food support, housing assistance, and job re-entry programs. Its people had a high degree of trust in the government, at least until the crisis began, and a remarkably high degree of social inclusion—membership in organizations and clubs. For all of these reasons, the World Values Survey, run by a network of social scientists across the globe, consistently found that the island was "the happiest" country in the world (in contrast with the Russians, who were the most unhappy) since the late 1990s. Hence, Iceland was a good place to test our hypothesis that the country's strengths—notably, its democratic participation, social support, and inclusive social protection system—could make it more resilient to an economic meltdown, preventing a public health disaster despite experiencing a terrible financial crisis.[5]

To understand what happened in Iceland, and properly test our hypothesis, it was essential to understand why this island was affected by the US mortgage foreclosure crisis. That connection provides a critical lesson on how Iceland's government faced a choice about whether or not to cut social protection programs during the crisis, and why it made the choices it ultimately did.

The story begins with the history of Iceland's boom, bubble, and bust.

Sitting outside the Eurozone, Iceland is a proud and independent nation with its own currency, the krona. But it was not, historically, a wealthy nation. Discovered by Irish monks, rediscovered by Norwegian Vikings, and later colonized by the Danes (who ruled until the early twentieth century), Iceland had been one of the poorest Western European countries through the 1940s, when its main economic product was fish. Since World War II, the economy grew at a modest pace, partly by attracting tourists to its famous blue lagoons and steamy thermal baths.[6]

In the mid-1990s, the island's government decided that the economy needed to expand beyond fish and tourism. Their strategy, like that of other micro-states such as the Caymans, was to become a private offshore banking center. Iceland reinvented itself as a tax haven for the world's ultra-rich. In the early 2000s, commercial and investment banking merged together, paving the way for new methods of loaning money and investing it in high-yield commodities. In scenes reminiscent of the period leading up to the East Asian Financial Crisis, Iceland's city planners boasted about exponential growth of grandiose buildings in the capital city: "If Dubai, why not Reykjavik?"[7]

One of the most popular of these new investment vehicles would also prove the riskiest. IceSave, an Internet-based banking program run by the private bank Landsbanki, offered 6 percent interest rates to attract foreign investors. The BBC branded it a "best buy." IceSave was soon inundated with foreign investments. Over 300,000 Britons, for instance, put their retirement savings into the IceSave program, enticed by high interest and the promise of a stable economic environment. Even Cambridge University's investment office and the UK Audit Commission—an independent financial watchdog—transferred large portions of their endowments to Iceland. Seeing Landsbanki's success, other Icelandic banks also set up high-interest-rate investment schemes to woo depositors. As a result of these deposits, the country's three largest banks (Landsbanki, Kaupthing, and Glitnir) moved up into the list of the world's top 300 investment trusts.[8]

By the beginning of 2007, Iceland had become the fifth richest country in the world, with an annual per-capita income 60 percent higher than that of the United States. Masses of capital flowed into the country, as economists labeled Iceland's situation a "capital inflow bonanza." Stimulated by easy loans, business was booming. Unemployment fell to 2.3 percent, the lowest in Europe.[9]

Everyone was quick to praise Iceland's meteoric rise. *The Wall Street Journal* trumpeted the "Miracle on Iceland" as "the greatest success story in the world." The economist Arthur Laffer, once a member of President Ronald Reagan's economic advisory board, agreed: "Iceland should be a model to the world."[10]

Behind the scenes, however, Iceland's economy balanced on a precipice. In order to maintain a high level of payouts to its bank investors, the country was running enormous deficits from high levels of imports and vast borrowing of foreign currency, a situation reminiscent of East Asia in the 1990s. Businesses and new building construction were relying on loans from Icelandic banks. These banks in turn were paying out the loans from dangerous investments overseas, mostly investments that promised a high return that had not yet materialized (for example, the mortgage-backed securities in the United States). Then came the first warnings of impending doom: in 2006, the Danske Bank of Copenhagen labeled Iceland a "geyser economy," on the brink of exploding because of the heavy reliance on foreign financial flows. In August 2007, Robert Wade of the London School of Economics gave a public lecture warning Icelanders about their risky economic strategy, but business and government leaders dismissed him as "alarmist." When Robert Aliber, an expert on financial systems, came to Iceland in 2007 and 2008 and also warned of the dangers, his statement that "You've got a year before the crisis hits" was ignored by the business community. As the prime minister reported in March 2008, five months before the crash, "Negative reports on the Icelandic economy, as published in several foreign newspapers recently, come as a surprise to us. All indicators and forecasts are consistent that the prospects are good, that the situation in the economy is by and large strong and the banks are sound."[11]

Just a few months after the government denied that there was a problem, a shockwave from the United States hit Iceland's economy. The country's finance minister announced, "It all went down the drain." Across the ocean in the United States, "mortgage default swaps"—bundled investments of mortgages sold by American banks, often under false premises—had whirled up a price bubble that burst. Iceland's banks had invested much of their money in the mortgage investments and US stocks. In the midst of American home foreclosures and stock market crash, the Icelandic banks lost substantial parts of their investments, and were no longer in a position to pay back their own investors. Consumers started to withdraw their funds from IceSave, worried that the bank would not be able to pay back their money given the stock market crash in America.[12]

They were right. In October 2008, IceSave began to implode, as customers rapidly withdrew their investments and Iceland's stock market fell by 90 percent. The country's GDP fell by 13 percent, and unemployment rates rose from 3 percent to 7.6 percent between 2008 and 2010. Nearly 40,000 homeowners were unable to make their mortgage payments as a result of income losses; over a thousand homes were foreclosed. With a shrinking tax base due to higher unemployment, would Iceland be able to pay for public healthcare care, unemployment support, pensions, and other social protection programs?[13]

To help pay for the government's mounting debt, the Central Bank of Iceland asked Europe for help. But the island had quickly become a pariah. No one wanted to give money to a country that had just lost all of its investments. After tens of thousands of Brits lost their life savings in IceSave, Icelanders became so unpopular that some living in Britain began pretending that they were from the Faroe Islands. "They treated us like terrorists," said one Icelander to a BBC reporter, commenting on the public jeers being received by those who identified themselves as being from Iceland. A BBC headline read: "Iceland: Britain's Unlikely New Enemy."[14]

So it was clear that Iceland wasn't going to receive much help from its neighbors. The politics of the crash were also creating internal rivalries within

Iceland. A small group of bankers in Iceland—less than 1 percent of the population—had seen their wealth grow as the country's currency strengthened during the banking boom. The Icelandic banking elite became like Russia's oligarchs—using this new wealth to buy SUVs, expensive tuna from Japan, caviar, and private jets. They also found it relatively affordable to borrow from banks abroad with such a strong and rising currency, and total debt grew to 9.5 trillion Icelandic kronas—over 900 percent of the value of domestic industrial production, the second highest ratio in the world. But when the krona then dropped from 190-per-euro to 70-per-euro over just a few months, disaster hit home. More than a third of Icelanders lost a major household item, typically their home. Anger focused on the government as riots rocked this once-peaceful island nation. People were divided about whether they should pay back the debts from IceSave and other collapsed investment schemes. An immigrant community of Poles, who worked in fishing, became the target of hatred and blame. "Incompetent government" was another oft-heard phrase. In the midst of the chaos, a Swedish filmmaker, Helgi Felixson, sensed an opportunity to capture a nation falling apart, and started making a documentary about its recession and social strife, entitled *God Bless Iceland*.[15]

Desperate to find a way to manage its debt, the government turned to the lender of last resort. In October 2008, Iceland called on the IMF to develop a rescue package for the country. It was the first time since 1976 that the Fund been asked to bail out a European country (in 1976, the United Kingdom had requested a bailout). As usual, the financial plan for Iceland came with recommendations for austerity. Iceland would get $2.1 billion in loans, but the government would have to slash public spending by 15 percent of GDP. It would have to implement strict austerity measures in order to quickly pay back IceSave's private investors, even though the IceSave program was operated by a private bank rather than by the government. IceSave's debt was several times the country's entire economy, and the IMF was calling for 50 percent of Iceland's gross income to be paid to private investors over a seven-year period, between 2016 and 2023: in other words, in very short order.[16]

Icelanders were now faced with a profound moral question. To what degree if any were they as a people and a country responsible for the malfeasance of their business class? Iceland's public taxpayers were being asked to pay for a private bank's bad investment decisions. This was serious news in a country where there was already a vast disparity between a rich few who had amassed great debt through a lavish lifestyle and the rest who were now being asked to pay. Of the country's 182,000 families, some 100,000 had little or no debt, while 244 wealthy families had each accrued investment debts exceeding $1 million. Even though only a few Icelandic bankers had bet on high-risk investments, the entire Icelandic community would now have to shoulder their debt, and suffer the consequences.[17]

The burden of budget cuts was set to fall heavily on areas not viewed by the IMF's economists as central to economic recovery—particularly on the public health system, which faced a 30 percent cut. Incredibly, the IMF considered healthcare a "luxury good," and compared with continental European countries, Iceland had relatively high public health spending, indicating to some IMF economists that government spending on health could be cut to encourage privatization.[18]

In protest to the proposed plan to pay back IceSave's debt and cut budgets, Iceland's health minister resigned. He refused to cut 30 percent of the nation's health budgets as the IMF required. Such a cut would be more than twice the average budget cut proposed for other budget sectors like education or the military. Our colleague Dr. Guðjón Magnusson, next in line to be appointed to as Iceland's chief medical officer, joked with us at a meeting of the European Health Forum in Gastein, Austria, in September 2009: "What's the difference between the IMF and a vampire? One stops sucking your blood after you have died."[19]

As in other countries, the bad financial news from this economic recession was no guarantee of a public health disaster—only of the potential for one. We were keeping a close eye on the health data of Iceland, hoping it would go down the path of the New Deal under FDR, but concerned that the IMF was pressuring it toward Russia's fiasco. Dr. Magnusson shared our concerns about the health of Iceland's population, and stressed the importance of maintaining Iceland's public health system. He invited us to attend a conference that he was planning in Reykjavík in October 2009 to discuss what might be done to prevent a health crisis. His research team and Iceland's public health and social affairs ministry would host it. He had numerous questions for us that people were asking in Iceland: How would the health system cope with large budget cuts proposed by the IMF? Which policies could prevent people from experiencing a rise in depression and mental health problems? What other health risks were known to have occurred in past economic crashes? Sadly, he had a heart attack a few days after the Gastein conference, and died.

In honor of Dr. Magnusson's wishes, we presented our data on the health impacts of previous recessions at the Reykjavík conference. We showed the historical evidence of how recessions increase the risks of suicides, the calamitous events that we had seen in the post-Soviet countries, and the divergent fortunes of East Asian nations. While Iceland had many strengths, the data suggested that if it implemented deep budget cuts to vital social protections—the very cuts in healthcare and social services that were being advised by the IMF—the risks to the health of its population would potentially be multiplied.

At the conference, arguments were put forward on both sides. Those who advocated austerity argued that it would inspire confidence in investors, who would bring money to help Iceland escape a further plummet into depression and prevent a public health disaster. But the data from prior recessions did not support this conclusion, which seemed more ideological than evidence-driven. There was no evidence from prior recessions that extensive austerity would stave off depression, but rather the opposite: austerity tended to increase unemployment, reduce people's spending, and slow down the economy.

The way to resolve this austerity debate was with data. The critical question was whether austerity or stimulus would improve public health and aid overall economic recovery. The debate hinged on a calculation called the "fiscal multiplier." The multiplier is an estimate of how many dollars of future economic growth are created for each dollar of government spending. When a fiscal multiplier is greater than 1, it means that government spending has a multiplicative effect—each $1 of government spending creates more than $1 in future economic growth. When the multiplier is less than 1, it means that each $1 of additional government spending is destroying the economy, creating inefficiencies or taking away money from the private sector that would better boost the economy.

The IMF economists had assumed, without hard data, that the fiscal multiplier had a value of about 0.5 for all countries, meaning that government spending would shrink the economy. Hence, cutting budgets would boost growth. But their assumption was made without actually calculating the multiplier from real data. The IMF had also assumed that all forms of government spending were the same—that spending on elementary schools would have the same economic impact as spending on the army. This made little sense. Without data on the sector-specific effects of budget cuts, even if the IMF promoted austerity, how would it know which cuts would be the most detrimental and which would do the least harm to the economy and maximize the prospects for recovery?

This situation called for a reality-based, data-driven approach, not theoretical mathematical models based on untestable assumptions. We recalculated the IMF estimates from real data, and disaggregated the data by different types of government programs. That enabled us to study the details of what spending or cuts actually did in each major area of government spending. We used over ten years of data from 25 European countries, the United States, and Japan, and found that the IMF's assumed multiplier value for Iceland was too low. The real multiplier had a value of about 1.7 in the overall economy: thus, austerity would have a recessionary effect.

Not only did the IMF underestimate austerity's economic harms, but it overlooked the even greater damage that resulted from cutting public health. Health and education had the largest fiscal multipliers, typically greater than 3. In contrast, defense multipliers were significantly less than 1, and so were bailout packages for banks. These figures made sense, because much of the money spent on defense doesn't actually build jobs in manufacturing and technology domestically anymore, unlike in previous years. Much of it actually leaves the economy, going to foreign contractors and to pay for non-recoverable costs like fuel for fighter jets. Nor do banker bailouts tend to stimulate the economy, as funds are more likely to end up stashed in offshore bank accounts and less likely to get reinvested into providing jobs or technology. Health and education programs, by contrast, conferred both short- and long-term economic payoffs. In the short term, these sectors were able to better absorb funding and turn it into productive work for teachers and nurses and technology firms. In the long term, the products of investments in education and health services were smarter and healthier workforces.[20]

When Icelandic journalists invited David to explain these findings in 2009, he described them this way: "It doesn't make sense to pull the engine out of a sinking plane. Now is the time to hit the accelerator, not the brakes." Many economists echoed these concerns on financial grounds. Joseph Stiglitz, on Icelandic television, said: "If the IMF tells you to do austerity, kick them out." But that advice would not be easy to follow. Like many of the East

Asian countries following the crisis there, Iceland had few options for getting capital, given its small central bank and a national debt already leveraged to over eight times its gross domestic product. Ultimately, it was forced to turn to the IMF as the lender of last resort.

But just before the government completed its IMF review of the loan agreement in early 2010, which would pay back IceSave and carry large austerity measures, something unusual happened: the president of this modern democracy rejected the plan and asking the nation's people what they wanted.[21]

It was a move triggered in part by the riots that began in early 2009. In January, upwards of ten thousand Icelanders took to the streets in protest, clashing with riot police around the parliament building. All things considered, the protest was relatively peaceful, resembling something closer to a street party than a clash with tear gas and Molotov cocktails. People hurled eggs, old shoes, and tomatoes at Parliament, while others pounded drums and started a bonfire to keep warm. Protesters called for a stop to budget cuts to pay for bankers' gambling, and an ousting of the "corrupt" government. Inside Parliament, the political leaders tried to shrug off the protesters as vagrants. But the protesters themselves made it clear who they really were. As one of them, Sturla Jonsson, told reporters, "I want to tell you that the people gathered here are not 'activists' or 'militants.' They are just ordinary adults of all ages."[22]

Prime Minister Haarde was eventually forced out of office. "We very clearly noticed the protests," said one member of parliament, "and we get the message that people want change." A protest of ten thousand people may seem small; but for Iceland, it is staggering—amounting to 3 percent of the population. A proportionally sized protest in the United States would involve 10 million people.[23]

The protests prompted a major democratic move. In March 2010, a public country-wide referendum was held, the first since Iceland had voted on independence from Denmark in 1944. The choice of how to proceed with the bankers' debts was posed to voters: Shall we absorb the private debt to compensate the bankers and their risky investors in the IceSave scheme, drastically cutting our government budgets and sending our tax dollars to them? Or shall we say no to paying for the bankers' gambling and avoid a large dose of austerity, instead investing in rebuilding the economy? Ninety-three percent of Icelanders voted against paying for the bankers' debts.[24]

Stock markets were quick to react negatively to the vote. The attitude on Wall Street reflected the thinking of everyone from the seventeenth-century philosopher John Locke to the ubiquitous Milton Friedman. Locke, whose writings underpinned the American Constitution, worried that democratic voting on policies about government spending could be risky; "tyranny of the majority" risked an angry mob seeking only to serve itself, knowing little about the complexities of economics, which were understood by an elite intellectual minority. Milton Friedman, the free-market economist, famously argued that economic decisions should be left to a computer, which would be willing to make tough, painful decisions. Perhaps ordinary people would be unwilling to make hard decisions about debt and budget cuts that were being advised by the International Monetary Fund—decisions that were vital to saving their own futures. If this perspective was correct, then Iceland's politicians had doomed the country by letting its people decide.[25]

Not all experts were critical of the democratic move, however. Robert Wade, who had warned of an impending global economic crisis before it happened, shared his advice with the Icelandic media. He recommended that money be put into public work programs (a là the New Deal), so that people who lost jobs could do real work again, rather than simply be given unemployment benefits. These people would then boost the economy by generating income to spend. Indeed, having too many unemployed young people could create a "lost generation" of youth who had never worked, or who might even emigrate and never come back. Wade encouraged businesses not to fire people but to move them to short-time work in order to keep them engaged with the labor market. He also called on the government to protect the pensions of those who relied on them, to ensure that the elderly were not cut off from basic needs.[26]

So the loud Icelandic "No" (Nei in Icelandic) was a true test of a major debate: were the voters of Iceland wrong, selfish, and ultimately ignorant of what was best for them when they followed the advice of Wade? Or should they instead have absorbed the bankers' debts and swallowed the bitter pill of austerity and the recommendations of Wall Street, Friedman, and the IMF?

We examined both the economic and the public health data to keep track of what happened after the vote—and compared that data to what was predicted to happen. We looked at Iceland's death statistics, which are collected by the World Health Organization's European Office. Over the period from 2007 to 2010, the worst years of crisis, death rates continued to fall steadily throughout the country. There had been a slight rise in suicides after the market crash, but not a statistically significant one: in 2007, there were 11.4 suicides per 100,000 people, rising to 12.1 in 2008 and falling in 2009 to 11.8. In an overall population of about 300,000, these were not meaningful changes, corresponding to thirty-seven suicides in 2007, thirty-eight in 2008, and thirty-six in 2009.[27]

Looking at another more sensitive indicator of stress, heart attacks, we examined data on hospital admissions. Given Iceland's organized healthcare system, it was possible to track every person in the country who was admitted to an emergency room, and to identify the health problem that had landed them there. In researching past European recessions, we found that heart attacks tended to have a short-term increase during banking crises. But we didn't find any increases in the heart attack rates in Iceland. There was a slight increase in the total number of people admitted to the cardiac emergency room, but only in week 41 of the year 2008, and only among women, not the working-age men among whom we tend to see a stress-related rise. Nor was this blip statistically significant when we looked at week-to-week fluctuations in Iceland's small population.[28]

Had we missed something that might indicate an increase in stress among Icelanders that is commonly observed in recessions? Was it too soon to see longer-term health effects? While it was possible that some people might forgo healthcare during recessions because they cannot afford it, this seemed unlikely. Iceland had maintained its universal healthcare system. Unlike the Russian people experiencing Shock Therapy, everybody had their healthcare costs covered, and hospitals and clinics hadn't closed, so access was not a concern.

To look for other health impacts of the crisis and Iceland's response to it, we turned to other sources of data about health and well-being in Iceland. To our surprise, we found that there had been an increase in upper airway respiratory problems. Perhaps there had been a rise in stress-related smoking, which would have been very possible given that one in three people in Iceland smoked. But, investigating more closely, we found that these respiratory problems had nothing to do with the financial crisis, but rather the eruption of the Icelandic volcano, Eyjafjallajökull, in April 2010. The population was exposed to toxic fumes that had covered the island for days.[29]

So we turned to data on mental health problems—perhaps these figures had risen? Again, we found no sign of a rise except for a mysterious blip in week 41. What had happened in week 41? That week, there were two stressful events. Prime Minister Geir gave his "God Bless Iceland" speech, leading people to fear for the worst. And in the UK, to recover the British depositors' investments in IceSave, Prime Minister Gordon Brown invoked the UK's Anti-Terrorism Act of 2001, the same law that was applied to freeze and gain back British assets from Colonel Gaddafi of Libya. While we cannot disentangle which stressors may have triggered a short-term burst of hospitalizations of patients with extreme psychological distress, the correlation reinforced the idea that the stresses and anxiety had not only to do with the crisis per se, but also with whether policymakers responded to economic threats to reassure their people that they would be protected come what may.[30]

From a public health perspective, a rise in psychiatric admissions is also considered the tip of the iceberg. Only a few people with depression and mental health problems actually end up in psychiatric hospitals or seek help at doctor's offices; the rest are hidden away from the healthcare system. We evaluated two Icelandic Health Surveys, each of which had kept track of 3,783 people who came from the various social strata of Iceland's population: the first survey was conducted in 2007, before the meltdown, and the second in 2009, after it. Based on a standard measure of depression symptoms from the World Health Organization, we found that among men, there was a slight increase of 1.5 percent in symptoms of depression; again, however, these were so small that they were not statistically significant based on standard international criteria. Of note, more vulnerable groups—those with lower education, those who were single, and the unemployed—were also not at higher risk of symptoms according to the surveys. In contrast, women did appear to be more vulnerable to depression symptoms; their rate of symptom reporting increased by 2.4 percent, but this rise was again not large enough to be statistically significant. Overall, we could not find any compelling evidence that depression had significantly increased in Iceland as a result of the crisis.[31]

In fact, we found that people increasingly reported "positive" symptoms in spite of the economic crisis—for example, that they more frequently woke up feeling fresh and rested. These positive symptoms seemed to be explained by people working less, and having more leisure time. To double-check the quality of these survey data and make sure they were credible, we took the data to Cambridge University, where depression expert Felicia Huppert evaluated it and replied, "These are beautiful data!"

All of this corresponded with the first UN World Happiness Report in 2012, presented by the "happiness economist" Richard Layard. In terms of "gross national happiness" and "the happy index," among other measures, Iceland had maintained its position as number one in the world. It had both the highest quantity of "positive affect" (good moods) of any country surveyed, in spite of the ongoing economic crisis.[32]

So how had Iceland managed to remain happy and healthy despite a massive economic meltdown?

A team of Icelandic economists analyzed data from around the country and reached the same conclusions as we did from our studies of the Icelandic Health Survey. They found that some of these positive trends, like having more free time, were likely to have been linked to the recession itself. The Icelandic Health Survey also contained questions about people's diets, as well as their drinking and smoking behaviors and other major public health risk factors in 2007 and 2009. The research team found that, during the period of crisis, Icelanders reduced their frequency of smoking, heavy drinking, and consumption of unhealthy fast food. These changes were in part driven by changing prices and lower incomes. When prices go up, people tend to buy fewer cigarettes and less alcohol, and eat at home instead of in restaurants. Icelanders also got more sleep than before the recession, an increase linked to less time at work. While the study wasn't able to show decisively that the recession *caused* these changes in health behavior, it did find further evidence that health statistics were moving in a positive direction during the recession.[33]

Health appeared to improve, in part, from a better diet and lower alcohol use. In October 2009, McDonald's pulled out of the country, blaming Iceland's "unique operational complexity," as the price of tomatoes and onions skyrocketed when the krona's value fell. "For a kilo of onions imported from Germany," reported one local franchise owner, "I'm paying the equivalent of a bottle of good whisky." But after McDonald's left, people increasingly turned to cooking at home with local foods instead of going out for imported fast food, with the result that the consumption of locally caught fish also rose as fast food consumption fell. Indeed, the eventual economic recovery in Iceland was driven by in part by the return of the traditional fishing industry, leading in due course to an export boom.[34]

Iceland also upheld its state monopoly on alcohol. It rejected the advice of the IMF to privatize alcohol stores as a means for boosting the economy. In the 1980s and 1990s, it was difficult to find spirits on sale. Iceland's combination of high alcohol prices and tight regulation, at a time when the imports of spirits became prohibitively expensive because of the falling currency, made alcohol a costly option for coping with stress.[35]

So, overall, some of the key factors in the recession actually seemed to keep people healthier during the economic crisis. But what about the democratic referendum—did deficit spending, and delayed payment to IceSave's investors, critically harm the future economy and public health of Icelanders?

Iceland took two important steps that protected people's health and well-being. By first rejecting the IMF's plan for radical austerity, it protected a modern-day equivalent of the New Deal. In the decades before the recession, Iceland had put in place a strong social protection system. After the public referendum to maintain that system, the government bolstered supports to those in need even further. In 2007, Iceland's government spending as a fraction of GDP was 42.3 percent. This increased to 57.7 percent in 2008 and has remained about ten percentage points above pre-crisis levels at the time of this writing. This increase didn't lead to inflation, runaway debt that has been impossible to pay back, or foreign dependency—the predicted disasters that austerity advocates claim will result from stimulus programs.[36]

Iceland didn't balance the budget through massive cuts to its healthcare system. While its currency devaluation meant the National Health Service had less money to import drugs and medicines, the government offset this threat of unaffordable pharmaceutical imports by increasing health budgets between 2007 and 2009—from 380,000 kronas per person to 453,000. The result was that essential services were protected, so that patients did not lose access to care.

Iceland also maintained its social protection system—programs to help people maintain food, jobs, and housing. It boosted key labor market programs to help people get back to work if they were recently unemployed. It implemented a new policy allowing small and medium firms to apply for debt relief; if they could show positive cash flow in the future, the debt or part of it would be forgiven. As a result, employers were not only able to retain employees but to hire new ones during the crisis. "The government has substantially boosted expenditure on public employment services to offer appropriate job matching and training services," reported the Paris-based technical economic institute, the Organization for Economic Cooperation and Development (OECD). The OECD had aligned itself with the IMF's advice for austerity, but strongly recommended it be done with a "human face"—to maintain social protection.[37]

Overall Iceland's social protection spending rose from 280 billion kronas ($2.2 billion) to 379 billion ($3 billion) kronas, from 21 percent of GDP to 25 percent of GDP between 2007 and 2009—a rise that went beyond benefits to the unemployed and healthcare coverage. The additional spending also helped fund a series of newly instated "debt relief" programs. For example, to homeowners who had negative equity, the country wrote off debt that was above 110 percent of the property value, and offered money to those who qualified as poor to help reduce mortgage payments. This was a radical step. Other countries hit by the Great Recession were not so supportive of their citizens. In Spain, for example, even when people were evicted from their homes and declared bankruptcy, they had to continue paying their housing debts and many became homeless. In Iceland, by contrast, the debt relief programs helped people stay in their homes, and there was no significant increase in the number of homeless. The number of houses receiving income support rose from about 4,000 in 2007 to 7,000 in 2010. Thanks to these kinds of supports, the percentage of households at risk of poverty was unchanged despite Iceland's crisis. Had these social protection supports not been maintained, a third of Iceland's population would likely have been plunged into poverty. Iceland's Ministry of Welfare also implemented a "Welfare Watch" group, which would publicly respond to the government about how people's health and well-being were being impacted by the downturn. Many of their recommendations were implemented.[38]

In addition to keeping the safety net, the other critical factor in Iceland's response to the crisis was national solidarity. Despite early tensions between wealthy debtors and the rest of the population, the national referendum sparked a new period of unity. The people of Iceland felt that they were all experiencing the crisis together. Iceland maintained its position as having some the highest rates of "social capital" in Western Europe: meaning that it's common for people to have strong groups of friends in their neighborhood, at work, and at church. Unlike the Russian situation where people were left in isolation and desolation in mono-towns from the Soviet era, the Icelanders had strong community networks. When we arrived at the country's airport, we were surprised that practically everyone knew each other on a first-name basis. People regularly went to saunas and steambaths with their families after work—not only making it easier to relax and alleviate stress, but building a sense of community and togetherness (if also a bit of indecent exposure)—

all which may have contributed to a heightened spirit of democracy in a time of crisis. And Iceland's level of inequality, which had jumped prior to the crisis, fell sharply after the economic collapse to levels on par with its Nordic peers.[39]

The collapse of the Icelandic economy, then, did not lead to much of a health crisis—in fact, the impact of the crisis as a whole didn't even make for an exciting movie. When the reviews rolled in for Helgi Felixson's documentary *God Bless Iceland*, critics carped; one complained that there was "not enough mustard" for the movie to build much drama. The film's problem, from a theatrical standpoint, was that Iceland hadn't fallen apart as predicted.[40]

The response of Iceland's government to the crisis reminds us how important it is to safeguard democracy, even at a time when extraordinary responses are needed. Even if hard decisions need to be made, a bitter pill is easier to swallow if you administer it yourself.

It was Iceland's heavy "financialization" of its economy during the 1990s and early 2000s—relying on high-risk investments by banks, rather than on industries that actually produced real, useful goods and services, or developed new technologies—that put its people at risk in the first place. But when managed with care, the crisis became an opportunity for the Icelandic people to rediscover their values, enabling the nation to rebuild an economy that is now thriving on its fundamentals. In 2012, Iceland's economy grew 3 percent and unemployment fell below 5 percent, while the UK's economy, under the Conservatives' austerity programs, continued to sink. In June of that year, Iceland made repayments on loans, ahead of schedule. Fitch Ratings—one of the big three ratings agencies, along with Standard and Poor's and Moody's—had initially called Iceland's economic choices an "unorthodox crisis policy response," but in early 2012 it restored the country's high investment status, rating Iceland as "safe to invest."[41]

Even the IMF later admitted that the unique Icelandic approach led to a "surprisingly" strong recovery. The IMF's reform proposals, followed by a retreat on its previous position, was history repeating itself. This time, in its ex-post evaluation, it concluded that one key lesson was that "social benefits were safeguarded in line with the authorities' post crisis objective of maintaining the key elements of the Icelandic welfare state. This was achieved by designing the fiscal consolidation in a way that sought to protect vulnerable groups by having expenditure cuts that did not compromise welfare benefits and raising revenue by placing greater tax burden on higher income groups."

While couched in bureaucratic language, the admission that social protection programs were vital to economic recovery and well-being was a revolutionary statement for the IMF.[42]

While these reports emphatically validated Iceland's approach, not everyone was pleased. The UK and Netherlands ramped up their pressure for Iceland's people to pay back IceSave's private investors with public tax dollars and implement strict austerity in Iceland. In April 2011, the Icelandic people turned out for another vote. This time, 60 percent of the population rejected a deal between Iceland and its main creditors, the Netherlands and UK, under which the IceSave investors would be immediately paid back. As the *Financial Times* reported, Icelanders had "put citizens before banks." Larus Welding, the former bank chief of Glitnir, was later convicted of fraud as part of national reconciliation. Iceland's president, Ólafur Ragnar Grímsson, said, "The government bailed out the people and imprisoned the banksters— the opposite of what North America and the rest of Europe did." Iceland's banks had been deemed "too big to fail," and the government let them fail. The consequences were clear in the data showing Iceland's successful recovery while most of the rest of Europe continued to suffer.[43]

At the time of this writing, the terms of austerity plans to pay back Ice-Save's creditors are making their way to international courts. Prosecutors in the UK and Netherlands sued the Icelandic government to speed up debt repayment. In the meantime, it appears that avoiding a deep austerity program, and making smart investment choices in critically important social protection programs, has spared lives. So even though Iceland had allowed its bankers to engage in reckless betting with people's money, citizens stepped in to determine how to clean up their mess. They chose wisely, protecting people from further harm, while simultaneously restoring the economy to growth.

The people of Iceland are also learning lessons from the IceSave disaster— taking proactive steps to ensure another crash never happens again. In July 2011, twenty-five of the country's citizens put together a crowd-sourced constitution designed to give the people greater control over their natural resources and break up cronyism between the banks and political elites. Using social media applications, all Icelanders could respond to six questions about constitutional changes. On October 2012, two-thirds of Iceland's population voted to replace the Icelandic constitution with a new one based on this crowd-sourced constitution.[44]

FIGURE 4.1   Rapid Economic Recovery in Iceland but Slow Meltdown in Greece[45]

Iceland's social benefits were safeguarded because its political leaders made democracy a priority, and its people voted for social protection programs, which in turn bolstered a strong society. As then Prime Minister Geir said in 2009, "No responsible government takes risks with the future of its people, even when the banking system itself is at stake." Rather than pursuing a path of deep fiscal austerity, Iceland supported key social programs that were vital to maintaining public health, including housing assistance, job re-entry programs, and healthcare coverage.[46]

We would love to be able to claim that the people of Iceland had heeded our advice, but it was they themselves who read the public health data and chose to put in place clear and necessary safeguards to protect health in hard times. God didn't save Iceland, its people did. By contrast, as shown in Figure 4.1, one of Iceland's distant European neighbors did not do so well. In the next chapter, we will see what happened to Greece when the European Central Bank (Europe's central bank for the euro) and IMF suspended Greek democracy—imposing radical austerity, with completely different results.

5

GREEK TRAGEDY

A handsome former Air Force officer in his fifties, Andreas Loverdos was looking for prostitutes—but not for himself.

On the morning of May 1, 2012, Loverdos, a medical doctor and the Greek Minister for Health, joined a squad of officers from the Greek Police Enforcement and Justice Department on the streets of Athens' downtown Omonia neighborhood. Ten days before a very tense Greek general election, Loverdos had decided to take action.

In April 2012, the Greek government had passed a law allowing Loverdos's Health Department to test anyone for sexually transmitted diseases—with or without their consent. The new law came in response to STD reports from hospitals and clinics all over Greece. New cases of HIV infection had jumped 52 percent between January and May 2011 alone. This was an astounding increase. HIV, often thought of as a disease most prevalent in developing countries, had been stable in Greece since the turn of the century. It hadn't risen so drastically in any Western European country in over ten years.[1]

The news of Greece's HIV epidemic made international headlines, and was taken as a sign that the country was falling behind the rest of Europe. Loverdos was in an awkward position—running for re-election just as the news of Greece's failing public health system drew the world's attention.

When in late 2011 the BBC began describing Greece as the "sick man of Europe," Loverdos felt compelled to respond. The Greek government had made radical cuts to the public health budget, under pressure from the IMF and European Central Bank. HIV prevention programs were among the first to be axed. So Loverdos called a meeting with his top campaign strategists. The group came up with a plan that has, historically, worked in almost all countries in which sexually-transmitted disease rates have spiked: scapegoat the most vulnerable people.[2]

Casting himself as the new protector of "unsuspecting family men," Loverdos appeared on national television pledging to restore morals and virtue to a Greek society that had lost its way in the recession. He vowed to arrest prostitutes, calling them a "menace to society" and an "unsanitary bomb." His Department of Health fed the Greek media a stream of photos of HIV-positive prostitutes, branding them a "death trap for hundreds of people."[3]

As the prostitution sting continued in Athens's seedier neighborhoods, the police also surrounded the elite five-star Hotel Grande Bretagne in Constitution Square, in the heart of Athens close to the Parliament. They were shielding the hotel's guests from the crackdown, and from the rising numbers of homeless people—beggars, drug users, and street children—who had taken up residence in the alcoves of abandoned shops, subway grates, and doorways surrounding the square. Homelessness had jumped by 25 percent between 2009 and 2011, as a spike in foreclosures and a shattered social protection system left people with nowhere to go. Meanwhile, homicides doubled in Greece between 2010 and 2011, with a marked rise in Athens' downtown area surrounding the Hotel Grande Bretagne.

The police were also protecting the Bretagne's guests from the angry protesters camped outside its doors. The hotel was one of the unofficial residences for the "troika," the foreign technocrats from the European Central Bank, European Commission (the executive body of the European Union), and the IMF, who were locked in heated discussions about Greece's future. In May 2010, as the negotiations about a potential bailout dragged on, protesters gathered in the square. A few turned into a hundred, then a few thousand, starting skirmishes with the Athens police, who met the protesters' calls for democracy with tear gas, police dogs, and riot tanks.

The narrative of this Greek tragedy was essentially the opposite of the story of Iceland. At the behest of the troika, Greece's democracy was suspended. A brutal dose of austerity, unlike any seen in Europe since rationings during World War II, threatened the lives of the poorest and most vulnerable, who were now paying for errors made by the government and banking sectors. As more and more news of public health crises came in, government officials repeatedly met the evidence with open denial, failing to acknowledge, let alone respond to, what was a growing catastrophe.

Greece alas served as an unwitting laboratory for testing how austerity impacts health. The roots of this extreme case of disaster can be traced to a tsunami of financial failures, corruption, tax evasion, and ultimately a lack of democracy. The popular will was not able to express itself in Greece as it had in Iceland.

To understand how Greece got into such a mess, we need to go back at least four decades. At the fall of the country's military junta in 1974, which seized power in 1967, Greece's economy was among the poorest in Europe. After Greece transitioned to democracy, the economy was rebuilt on tourism, shipping, and agriculture. Tourists flocked to white sand beaches on Greek party islands like Mykonos and Santorini, and Greek farmers supplied Europe with cotton, fruit, vegetables, and olive oil. Overall, Greece's economy grew slowly, but steadily, at less than 1.5 percent each year on average in the 1980s and 1990s.

Then, Greece's admission to the European Union in January 2001 set the country on course for an economic boom. EU capital began flooding into Greece, fueling a construction bonanza. Over the next five years, European Structural Funds provided $24 billion for infrastructure projects. The Greek government matched the EU funds with heavy borrowing, supporting large-scale construction projects such as new ports for shipping and sport facilities to host the 2004 Olympics in Athens. The government even built a large museum in order to reclaim the Parthenon Marbles, which had been snatched by an English aristocrat and installed in the British Museum. The Greek museum was one of the biggest cultural projects in Europe, at a cost of $200 million.[4]

Thanks to a combination of EU funds, foreign investments, and low tax and interest rates, by the mid-2000s Greece's economy was red hot. In February 2006, George Alogoskoufis, Greece's minister of finance, said, "We are in a position to achieve an economic miracle." That June, the Greek economy hit a peak of 7.6 percent GDP growth. (Portugal and Spain, the other EU countries that had started in similar economic positions to Greece, continued growing at less than 2 percent per year.[5])

Beneath the surface, however, the economy was in trouble. The Greek government was running 5 percent deficits each year to maintain infrastructure projects, which could only be sustained because of its high growth rate. Part of the problem was excess spending, but deficits were also rising because the government had cut corporate tax rates from 40 percent in 2000 to 25 percent in 2007 in an effort to attract companies to set up business in Greece. The bottom line was that Greece had enacted the opposite of sound macroeconomic policy: spending too much in good times rather than saving money in case of future needs. This dangerous economic pattern of development would soon have devastating effects on the health of Greece's people.

When US banks started to melt down in 2008, Greece's financial sector was caught in the ensuing storm. Unlike Iceland, Greek citizens experienced not one, but a series of financial earthquakes. The first was a "demand shock," or loss of demand for Greek goods and services, as well as less construction. Then came a "real numbers shock" in which Greece's economic data were revealed to have been fabricated. Finally an "austerity crisis" hit the country: the shock from the measures that the IMF and European Central Bank imposed on Greece in return for financial bailouts—despite data (and plenty of evidence, even from within the IMF) that such measures were neither necessary nor smart for helping economic recovery or preventing a public health disaster.

The demand shock in Greece came after the US mortgage-backed securities crisis. Between May 2008 and May 2009, the Athens Stock Exchange fell by 60 percent. While less directly exposed than Iceland's largest banks to shady international investment transactions, Greece's economy was indirectly at risk because it was on the receiving end of the risky investments. As Europe's investors lost their fortunes, lavish trips to Greek islands stopped, imports of Greece's fruits and vegetables declined, and construction projects came to a halt, leaving cranes dangling in mid-air. While Europe's and North America's bankers were bailed out, these bailouts did little to shore up the ripple effects on the Greek economy. The average Greek household income fell by 0.2 percent in 2008 and another 3.3 percent in 2009, in what began Greece's slow descent into an abyss of financial despair.[6]

This initial tremor was then followed by a financial earthquake, the real numbers shock, in which it was revealed that Greece's economy was far weaker than the government had claimed. In the years before the crisis, the European

Union's statistical agency, EuroStat, had flagged a number of concerns with Greek economic reports. One audit by the European Commission's accountants, for example, found that Greek authorities had wrongly classified certain debts as being outside the government budget. A group of German auditors also used a computer algorithm to detect what looked like fraud: it suggested that someone in the Greek government had cooked the books and had typed in a bunch of inflated numbers to add up to a better budget result.[7]

Investors had seen the signs of financial fragility and a bubble forming, but had ignored the warning signs—that is, until the crisis opened Greece's economy to global scrutiny. In early 2010, Greece's real financial situation was revealed to be a great deal worse than even the EU auditors had thought. Reporters discovered that Greek leaders had paid the investment bank Goldman Sachs hundreds of millions of dollars in fees to arrange transactions that helped hide the country's real level of borrowing from the EU throughout the past decade. The country's debt data had been manipulated to look good enough for the nation to enter the Eurozone; Goldman Sachs had done such a good job of covering up the fraud that the data passed a detailed financial review by European Union auditors. In reality, Greece's debt levels had grown from 105 percent in 2007 to 143 percent of GDP in 2010.[8]

In early 2010, when news broke of Greece's real economic situation, panic ensued. Credit ratings agencies downgraded Greece's bonds to "junk" status in April 2010. This frightened investors who might have otherwise sensed a business opportunity in Greece and could have helped the economy recover. The interest rates on Greek government bonds began to spiral out of control as investors, having no idea what the real situation was, feared investing in the country. Greek interest rates jumped from 2 percent in 2009 to 10 percent in 2010, making government debt even more costly to repay.[9]

This real numbers shock was followed by even more suffering in Greece than the demand shock. Greece's GDP sank further, falling by 3.4 percent in 2010. The super-rich had stashed funds in offshore bank accounts; it was ordinary people who paid the price. Unemployment rates rose from 7 percent in May 2008 to 17 percent in May 2011. Among young people seeking their first jobs after high school or college, unemployment rose from 19 percent to 40 percent. A generation of newly educated people was starting adult life out of work.[10]

Now Greek society stood at the brink of collapse. With uncertainty hamstringing the country's ability to pay back debts, and its currency tied to the rest of Europe, the Greek government had few options to pay for basic needs like garbage collection and fire stations. It was forced to turn to the IMF for help. In May 2010, the IMF offered loans with the usual strings attached: privatize state-owned companies and infrastructure and cut social protection programs. If the Greek government agreed, the IMF and European Central Bank would provide 110 billion euros in loans as part of a three-year bailout plan that would go toward paying off Greek debt. Greece's creditors—including the French and German banks that had helped fuel Greece's construction bubble—took a so-called haircut, agreeing to write off half of their debts and to lower interest rates on their loans to the country.[11]

Whether to accept this IMF package was a matter for public debate, but Greece's leaders felt there was no alternative. At first, Prime Minister George Papandreou, who headed the major party, PASOK, the Panhellenic Socialist Movement, tried to convince fellow Greeks that this would be the only way forward. In May 2010 amid the negotiations, he portrayed the decision as black or white, between "collapse and salvation." No one else was willing to lend money to Greece. But he recognized the pain the IMF bailout would bring. On approving the IMF's plan, he said: "With our decision today our citizens will have to make great sacrifices."[12]

Overall, the IMF's aim was to make cuts totaling 23 billion euros in three years, about 10 percent of its entire economy, and sell off state enterprises for 60 billion euros to reduce Greece's deficit from 14 percent to less than 3 percent of GDP by 2014. The troika's lending documents revealed that public-sector workers would bear the brunt of the cuts, facing mass layoffs, wage cuts, and pension reductions. The bailout also included conditions to raise taxes on fuel and related commodities by 10 percent, further emptying people's pockets and reducing their buying power.

Protests against the troika plan began in May 2010 with a series of strikes and demonstrations. Led by the Direct Democracy Now! Movement, thousands of protesters from every political party filled Syntagma Square. The protests started peacefully, but soon turned violent, leaving three protesters dead. Fires from Molotov cocktails lit up the Athens skyline at night. Amid the turmoil, one budget sector managed to avoid cuts: the police. Two thousand new police officers were hired and given extra training in riot control. Tear gas, riot gear, and tanks were brought in for use by the police and military.[13]

As in Iceland, the Greek protesters called for a nationwide referendum on the agreement. Prime Minister Papandreou promised that the government would protect the most vulnerable: "It is not going to be easy on Greek citizens, despite the efforts that have been made and will continue to be made to protect the weakest in society." Nevertheless, the first IMF austerity package went into effect in May 2010, without a vote.

We had been studying how economic change impacted public health since 2007, before the financial situation deteriorated in Greece. We had pulled together all the data we could lay our hands on from the Greek health system—from hospitals, non-governmental organizations, the health ministry, and household surveys. We could see early warning signs of trouble brewing: rising unemployment, mass foreclosures, increasing personal debt—all which were risk factors for declining health. Greece's badly weakened social protection programs were ill-prepared to cope with a sudden rise in the number of people needing support, especially after being crippled by radical austerity measures.

Exact figures on the health impacts of austerity were hard to come by. Government reports on the subject seemed to be perpetually delayed or otherwise unavailable. When they did come, they suggested that the health system was improving. One official government report praised the healthcare system's progress as a result of improvements in efficiency. But anecdotal reports from doctors in both Greek and international newspapers made us concerned that serious problems were looming.

When healthcare systems collapse, good Samaritans sometimes come forward to pick up the slack. One *New York Times* investigation reported on a Greek underground Robin Hood network of doctors who used donated medications and supplies to treat patients no longer covered by the Greek public healthcare system. Dr. Kostas Syrigos, chief of oncology at Sotiria General Hospital in central Athens, described one patient as having the worst breast cancer he had ever seen. She had been unable to get medical care for a year because of the troika's healthcare reforms. When she arrived at the underground clinic, her tumor had burrowed through her skin and started weeping fluid onto her clothing. She was in excruciating pain, and mopping up the ulcerating wound with paper napkins. "When we saw her we were speechless," Dr. Syrigos said to the reporter. "Everyone was crying. Things like that are described in textbooks, but you never see them because until now, anybody who got sick in this country could always get help."[14]

The stated goal of the troika's austerity plan—"to modernize the healthcare system"—sounded like it would avoid these catastrophes. Who wouldn't want to modernize their healthcare system? Greece's system was indeed in need of reform, a point that was well-known among European public health researchers. The problem is that the troika plan wasn't drawn up by healthcare experts or even based on their recommendations. Rather, it was constructed mainly by economists with little or no input or guidance from healthcare experts. It was as if a government had set out to modernize the automobile industry without talking to anyone who understood how a car was produced.[15]

The IMF's "recovery" plan was based on the fuzziest math. Its goal was "to keep public health expenditure at or below 6 percent of GDP, while maintaining universal access and improving the quality of care delivery. In the short-term, the main focus should be on macro-level discipline and cost-control." Where that 6 percent target came from was never mentioned, but it was puzzling, since all other Western countries spend far more than that to maintain basic healthcare. For example, the German government, a premier advocate of the austerity plan in Greece, spends more than 10 percent on healthcare.

The IMF rolled out a series of risky ideas that sounded like good deficit-reduction measures. But in practice they led to people losing access to healthcare. One such idea was to cut spending on medications. The IMF's agreement with the Greek government specifically called for "a target to reduce public spending on outpatient pharmaceuticals from 1.9 to 1 and 1/3 percent of GDP." As with many IMF programs, these cuts looked even riskier once one delved into the reasons for Greece's rising healthcare costs.

After Greece joined the EU in 2001, the country's spending on pharmaceuticals soared. Quite why was at first unclear, although corruption was a main suspect. There were numerous reports of patients and pharmaceutical companies giving doctors a *fakelaki* (small envelope) or directly depositing large sums into doctors' bank accounts, in exchange for prescribing more pills. Pharmaceutical companies also used creative ways of building relationships with doctors, taking them on lavish Hawaiian vacation-conferences and funding their membership in company advisory committees.[16]

But while the IMF had correctly spotted a trend of rising costs, its solution made matters worse. Rather than regulating pharmaceutical marketing and sales, it cut hospital budgets, preventing hospitals from obtaining medicines and medical supplies. Hospitals started to run out of antibiotics. Waiting lines doubled and then tripled. Many patients were unable to find a doctor in even the largest city hospitals. In May 2010, just after the first IMF bailout package took effect, the pharmaceutical company Novo-Nordisk pulled out of Greece because it was no longer being adequately paid after the troika's price cuts; the Greek state owed the company $36 million. That pullout not only cost jobs but also deprived 50,000 Greek diabetics of insulin.[17]

Meanwhile, Greeks were reporting that their health was worsening. In 2009, compared to 2007, they were 15 percent more likely to report that their health was "bad" or "very bad." These self-reports tend to correlate with overall death rates, making them a widely used indicator for a society's health when other data are unavailable. (Here was another contrast to Iceland, where people reported that they were feeling just as good during as before the economic crisis.[18])

We looked for more detail as to why these reports showed people's health worsening during the crisis. We found that in 2009, people were 15 percent less likely to go to a doctor or dentist for treatment of medical problems, compared with 2007 (before the crisis). People were losing access because of long waiting times and excessive treatment costs. Fewer people could afford private care, so they turned to public hospitals and clinics. As private hospital admissions dropped, public hospitals filled the gap, with admissions rising approximately 25 percent. Then, instead of boosting support to meet the new demand, the government's austerity budget cut the jobs of 35,000 clinicians, doctors and public health workers. As a result, waiting times became intolerably long. On top of all this, doctors, whose salaries were cut, reportedly turned to a longstanding practice of taking bribes from desperate patients trying to jump the queues, leading to more inefficiency and making it more difficult for impoverished Greeks to access healthcare.[19]

The combination of recession and austerity was creating a perform storm of misery: budget cuts, clinic closures, and more "hidden" costs. The elderly were among the least resilient to these changes in the systems they had relied on for care. Overall, we estimated that at least 60,000 people over the age of sixty-five have so far forgone necessary medical care during the period of recession and austerity.

Apart from physical health, mental health was also worsening. Suicide rates were rising, most greatly among men—by 20 percent between 2007 and 2009. Consistent with this picture, mental health charities found that calls for help doubled. And this was likely the tip of the iceberg. Many Greeks didn't seek help because of the stigma that still surrounds mental illness there; the Greek Orthodox Church denies funerals to those whose deaths are classified as suicides. Perhaps predictably, therefore, Greece also experienced a rising number of "undetermined injuries" and other mysteriously unidentified causes of death that many doctors suspected were suicides disguised to save the honor of ashamed families.[20]

With public health programs collapsing because of austerity, the incidence of infectious disease suddenly skyrocketed. The Hellenic Centre for Disease Control and Prevention detected a series of outbreaks immediately after large cuts had been made to infectious disease prevention programs. For forty years, insecticide spraying programs had effectively prevented mosquito-borne diseases from spreading in Greece. After funding had been cut for the southern part of the country, an outbreak of West Nile Virus occurred in August 2010, killing sixty-two people in southern Greece and central Macedonia. Then, for the first time since 1970, there was a malaria outbreak in the southern Greek regions of Lakonia and East Attica. The European Centre for Disease Prevention and Control recommended that travelers to southern Greece stock up on anti-malarials and take other precautions like mosquito spray and nets. It was a special warning that had previously been reserved for travelers to sub-Saharan Africa and tropical parts of Asia.[21]

But perhaps most strikingly, an HIV outbreak—the only one to occur in Europe in decades—emerged in the center of Athens. At first, the sex trade was suspected to be the sole source. But a closer look at the data revealed that twenty-eight of the twenty-nine sex workers whose pictures Loverdos published online were also intravenous drug users, so drug use was likely also a major factor.[22]

Epidemiologists at the Hellenic Centre for Disease Control and Prevention were tracking the source of HIV spread. In Greece, as in many other parts of Europe, a significant fraction of all HIV transmission came from sharing infected needles. So the epidemiologists routinely monitored data from street clinics and studies of drug users' blood, to trace outbreaks and respond rapidly when they occurred. In 2011, the epidemiologists identified 384 new

HIV cases from street clinics and studies of drug users. They found little or no change in HIV infection rates from either homosexual or heterosexual activity. Instead, they verified that the bulk of the new HIV cases came from people using infected needles, who suffered a tenfold increase in new infections between January and October 2011.

"I've never seen so many drug users on the streets of Athens," noted a colleague of ours, who lived most of her life just a few blocks from Parliament Square. Figures from the Athens police department confirmed her perception. Heroin use had risen by 20 percent between 2010 and 2011, as desperate people—particularly youth facing a 40 percent unemployment rate—now lived on the streets and turned to drugs.[23]

The World Health Organization had a solution to the needle-driven spread of HIV. It recommended that in every country, each drug user should have about 200 clean needles per year available in order to avoid spreading HIV infections. This estimate was based on data from extensive studies in the 1990s showing that needle exchange programs effectively reduced HIV transmission without increasing drug use. But just as the Greek epidemiologists warned of a drug-related HIV outbreak, the budget for Greece's needle-exchange program was slashed. As a result, the Hellenic Centre for Disease Control and Prevention estimated there were only about three needles for every drug user. Moreover, a survey of 275 drug users in Athens in October 2010 found that 85 percent were not enrolled in a drug-rehabilitation program, despite high demand to participate. In Athens and other major Greek cities, waiting times for rehab programs had risen to more than three years under austerity.[24]

In this situation, there were few options left for Greece's Health Ministry. Its health budget had been cut by 40 percent. But there was a political alternative—the democratic option. One way to protect citizens even when foreign investors clamor for their money is to follow the path set by Iceland. There the public voted to delay the IceSave debt repayments and pay them back slowly over time, protecting essential budgets like public health, sanitation (the garbage hadn't been collected in many parts of Athens for weeks), and other essential services.[25]

And so, in November 2011, at the time the HIV outbreak became clear, Prime Minister Papandreou tried the Icelandic solution. He announced a referendum on a second round of austerity measures from the IMF and the European Central Bank. It was plainly apparent to the Greek public that the austerity program was not working. In spite of all the budget cuts, government debt continued to rise—to 165 percent of GDP in 2011. But under pressure from the troika and other European political leaders to pay back German and other investors quickly, Papandreou was forced to call the referendum off. While the referendum initially had support from the Greek cabinet, EU leaders voiced their opposition, and the prime minister faced a no-confidence vote in the Greek Parliament. Papandreou was forced to resign. Ironically, just as Europe praised democracy on the southern shore of the Mediterranean, having helped oust Libya's dictatorial Colonel Muammar Gaddafi, it was blocking democratic voting on the northern shore in Greece, the birthplace of democracy.[26]

Unlike Iceland, where the health minister resigned in protest at the IMF's proposed budget cuts to the health system, the Greek health minister, Loverdos, tried to weather the storm. The challenge was immense. In 2009 alone, the public health budget fell from 24 billion euros to 16 billion euros, and the next bailout was set to cut even more. And that was why the Greek Health Ministry had no spare funds to deal with the emerging HIV and malaria outbreaks.

At a conference in Athens in March 2012, we presented the Hellenic Centre's data to the Ministry of Health on the alarming rise of HIV. We called on the government to expand their needle-exchange programs. To our surprise, the ministry's representatives seemed entirely unconcerned. Their view was that these statistics were just due to North African and Eastern European immigrants who had traveled into Greece with HIV. When we then pointed out that the data showed that the majority of those affected were people of Greek origin, they had no comment.

In the subsequent weeks, we saw this pretense of ignorance morph into outright denial. When our research on health in Greece was published in *The Lancet* in March 2012 (after peer-reviewers had found the data analysis appropriately conducted, important, and alarming), Greek health system officials attempted to dismiss it. After we reported that overall suicides had risen by 17 percent, for example, a member of the health minister's staff wrote that this was a "premature overinterpretation" of the mental health crisis in Greece, even though the data had actually come from the Health Ministry itself. Our findings were then replicated by independent scientists from other universities. Meanwhile, suicide and depression rates continued to rise significantly, as verified by many Greek and international sources.[27]

In the week before the May 2012 elections, Minister of Health Loverdos himself responded publicly to concerns about the country's worsening health problems. But his response seemed to have little to do with the nation's health and much to do with the election. He resorted to xenophobia and scapegoating, arguing that immigrants were the country's major problem, a "burden" on the healthcare system. He would clamp down on "welfare fraud," claiming his plans would save Greek taxpayers 230 million euros.

Both immigrants and ordinary Greek citizens suffered from the large dose of austerity that followed Loverdos's remarks. Budget cuts in 2009 and 2010 had already eliminated a third of the country's healthcare services for immigrants. Further cuts from the second bailout in 2012 left the programs crippled. These programs were being overrun by demand: not from the immigrants for whom they had been designed, but from Greeks. The "street clinics" run by the Greek chapter of Médecins du Monde (which normally operates in low-income countries) estimated that the proportion of Greeks seeking medical attention from their clinics rose tenfold from 3 percent before the crisis to 30 percent. And to pick up the pieces of the crumbling Greek healthcare system, another international organization, the Nobel Peace Prize–winning Médecins Sans Frontières (Doctors Without Borders), launched emergency relief programs for the Greeks, even though they normally devote themselves to operating refugee camps in war-torn regions of the world.

In our eyes, the Greek austerity crisis was undermining the ultimate source of the country's wealth: its people. But not everyone agreed. In November 2012, the economist Lycourgos Liaropoulos wrote a letter to the editor of the *British Medical Journal* to report that there was "no tragedy in health" in Greece. He acknowledged that "Many are without cover" and the churches, non-governmental associations, and others are "rallying to help" but claimed that there was "no evidence of denial of services to patients." But he was ignoring substantial evidence: the continuing results of HIV surveys, the EU Statistics on Income and Living Conditions surveys, the malaria control reports, the suicide data, and, as we found, the data his team reported.[28]

Liaropoulos's letter was published shortly after Dr. Samuel R. Friedman, director of HIV/AIDS research at the National Development and Research Institutes in New York, described the situation in Greece in July 2012 as alarming: "What they [the Greek government] are doing is creating an epicenter for the spread of the virus [HIV] in Greece and beyond." Liaropoulos's letter also coincided with the visit of Dr. Marc Sprenger, director of the European Centre for Disease Control and Prevention, who had just ended a two-day trip to Greece's hospitals and clinics. His conclusions made international headlines. "I have seen places where the financial situation did not allow even for basic requirements like gloves, gowns and alcohol wipes." Dr. Sprenger's conclusions were damning: "We already knew Greece is in a very bad situation regarding antibiotic resistant infections, and after visiting hospitals there I'm now really convinced we have reached one minute to midnight in this battle."[29]

When we looked into Liaropoulos's background, we began to understand why he was defending the indefensible. He was one of the troika's chief Greek advisers on austerity implementation, receiving numerous large grants from Minister Loverdos in the process. He was also responsible for reporting Greek health data to the Organization for Economic Cooperation and Development (OECD). Ironically, the reports his own subordinates submitted to the OECD came to rather different conclusions than he did: that there had been a 40 percent rise in infant mortality and a 47 percent rise in unmet healthcare needs between 2008 and the latest available year of data in 2010 and 2011, respectively. Liaropoulos' team was responsible for the reports, but he appeared not to have agreed with the data inside them.

More official denials came from the Ministry of Health. Following reports that Greeks were having difficulty getting healthcare and giving up necessary doctors' visits because of long waiting lines, distances to clinics, and excessive treatment costs, the ministry proudly claimed the hospital budget reductions were "a positive result of improvements in financial management efficiency." In theory, this might have meant that it cost less to treat more people. In practice, it cost less because fewer people were receiving care.[30]

People on the front lines knew that austerity was hazardous to health. A mayor of one of the malaria-affected towns, the physician Jannis Gripiotis, responded in frustration at the Ministry of Health's prevarications. He said ministry officials hid data about the malaria outbreak until independent international authorities observed the spread of disease and reported it. Instead of acting, Greek officials "decided to cover it up," said Dr. Gripiotis. "They called me crazy." Doctors Without Borders program director Apostolos Veizis was enraged by the health situation and the failure of the Ministry of Health to respond: "What do you have to do to ring the alarm bell?"[31]

The Health Ministry continued to avoid collecting and publicly disclosing many standard health statistics, so investigative journalists began filling the gaps. They broke stories that drug users were deliberately infecting themselves with HIV to get access to public subsidies of 700 euros per month, that some parents were abandoning their children because they could no longer afford to care for them, and that for the first time in decades there were cases of mother-to-child transmission of HIV, as routine screens for maternal HIV were no longer being conducted on pregnant women.[32]

Investigative journalists also exposed another assault on the Greek people's health, in a move we had encountered with the McArdle family in Scotland. The government was rewriting eligibility rules for disability and welfare support to exclude more and more Greeks—addressing "welfare fraud," in the words of the health minister. Tucked away in a small note on p. 129 of the July 2011 IMF report was a provision designed to reduce government spending: "The objective is to reduce the disability pensions to not more than 10 percent of the overall number of pensions. For this purpose, the definition of disability and respective rules will be revised by end-August 2011." Andrew Jack of the *Financial Times* translated what this revision meant for those in Greece with long-term disabling health conditions. He interviewed a Greek restaurant worker named Mrs. Zoi Gkezerva. Before the crisis, she had received 4,500 euros each month to help treat her daughter's rare genetic disorder, *epidermolysis bullosa*. The condition, which leaves a child with extensive skin blistering similar to burns, requires frequent and costly treatments using sterile needles and advanced dressings to prevent wound infections. Mrs. Gkezerva was cut off from any assistance for her daughter's care under the new welfare and disability "fraud" rules. "We don't have much time left; we've already used up almost all our savings," Mrs. Gkezerva said. Responding to her case, Dimitrios Synodinos, director of the Greek Alliance for Rare Diseases, noted that "Quite a number of rare disease patients have had their disability percentage reduced so much that they are in very, very difficult situation."[33]

Austerity was wreaking havoc on the health of the Greek people. The city of Athens was trying to cut health spending from 10.6 billion euros in 2009 to 7 billion in 2012—in the middle of an HIV outbreak, a massive increase in homelessness, and a rise in suicide, among other problems. In February 2012, doctors held a one-day strike to protest the massive cuts. George Patoulis, head of the Athens Medical Association, explained that the radical government reforms to the healthcare system created chaos. No one even knew which patients would be covered for which services. Pharmacists went on strike for two days over arrears from social insurance funds, arguing government cuts to social welfare meant that they would close their doors.

The IMF's attack on the Greek body economic continued as the Greek government ignored the mounting misery. As collecting and analyzing public health data were clearly not a priority, the troika continued enforcing new austerity policies. In late November 2012, the IMF and its European partners agreed to its third austerity program with Greece—with 2 billion more euros being cut from the nation's healthcare system.

With austerity came 28 billion euros in bailouts, yet Greece was still not recovering. Government debt levels continued to rise, reaching more than 160 percent of GDP in 2012. It seemed inconceivable that all that money wasn't achieving the intended stimulus to the economy or shoring up government debts. The *New York Times* investigated and found that the IMF and European Central Bank were funneling money through Greece and straight back to the United Kingdom, France, the United States, and Germany, to creditors there who had contributed to Greece's disastrous bubble. Greece's bailout was using public funds not to help Greece but to rescue the poorly invested private money of the world's banking elite.

As in the crises in East Asia and Iceland, the IMF finally admitted, in 2012, that it had underestimated the harms that austerity could cause. One of the central arguments for austerity was the IMF's assumption about the fiscal multiplier, the statistic describing how much economic stimulus is produced by each dollar of government spending. The IMF had assumed the multiplier was about 0.5—meaning that bigger budget cuts would help spur economic recovery. But the actual economic data from the austerity program turned out to be far worse than the IMF predicted, and the Fund was forced to admit its calculations had been wrong. In February 2012, the IMF set their chief economists to the task of re-estimating the multipliers. Those economists ended up getting the same results as we did, finding that the fiscal multiplier was greater than 1. In the words of the Fund's chief economist, "we underestimated the negative effect of austerity on job losses and the economy." So all this "help" from the financial community was followed by a negative spiral of worsening job losses, less money to spend at businesses, and declining investor confidence throughout Europe—ultimately the foundation for a public health disaster.[34]

Not only was austerity a mistake, but the worst possible kind of austerity was implemented. Public money invested in healthcare can be put to good use much more quickly than money invested in many other sectors. Indeed, healthcare is one of the few economic sectors that have been growing amid the economic downturn in Europe and North America. Healthcare investment leads to new jobs (nurses, doctors, technicians) and technological development (laboratory research, innovation), providing a much deeper stimulus to the economy than almost any other kind of government spending.

Imposing hardship on Greece wasn't an economic recovery strategy as much as a political strategy. Such a message sent a warning to the rest of Europe, indeed to the world: play by the rules of the banking elite, or else. The German Chancellor, Angela Merkel, talked of the Greek bailout package as a lesson to the rest of Europe. "These countries can see that the path taken by Greece with the IMF is not an easy one. As a result they will do all they can to avoid this themselves."[35]

Greece's tragedy has shown that austerity will not save a failing economy. Rather than being part of a solution, it is part of the problem.

There are alternatives to austerity. The most notable is the Icelandic solution. That country said no to radical austerity, increased social spending, and its economy began recovering. Iceland increased its health spending by 20 percent in the middle of the worst banking crisis in history. Ironically, even some German political leaders, though demanding that Greece immediately repay German investors, recognized the economic folly of cutting social welfare budgets. In 2009, Germany had implemented a 50 billion euro stimulus to its economy, totaling 1.5 percent of GDP. At the 2012 World Health Summit in Berlin, the conservative German health minister Daniel Bahr praised the results, arguing that investing in social protection systems was vital to helping a country's economy grow.[36]

Conversely, while Europe was bailing out the banks that drove markets to the worst crash since the Great Depression, it imposed penalties on the Greek citizens who had little control over their government's accounting frauds or economic strategy. The economist James Galbraith called the treatment of the Greek people a form of "collective punishment." This level of punishment was unprecedented in Europe. Even Germany after World War II had benefited from large-scale investment as part of the Marshall Plan to reconstruct its broken economy.[37]

Unsurprisingly, the Greek people are furious and desperate. One of the most dramatic riots in the country, in October 2012, was sparked by the arrival of Chancellor Merkel. Six thousand police were mobilized for her protection, firing pepper spray and stun grenades at protesters who threw stones, burned Nazi flags, chanted "No to the Fourth Reich!" and hoisted banners reading "Merkel out, Greece is not your colony," "This is not a European Union, it's slavery," and "They've turned our lives into hell." The irony of Germany's insistence on austerity in Greece even though Germany itself had been "bailed out" by the US and the rest of Europe after World War II was not lost on the Greeks.[38]

Beyond the economic damage, the harms wrought by austerity policies also destroyed Greece's social cohesion (a factor vital to Iceland's health stability). The Greek political scene witnessed a return of radical far-right parties, just as the politics of austerity did in post-Depression Europe. The neo-Nazi Golden Dawn Party stepped in to plug the hole in safety nets left by the troika. On the streets of Athens, they began serving hot meals to the hungry, at least to people who could show a Greek national identity card. Racist attacks have risen, as troops of Golden Dawn members prowl the streets to "purge" immigrants. The purges have now expanded to include gays and lesbians. The circumstances are eerily reminiscent of the Depression-era politics that paved the way for fascism and World War II in Europe. Blaming foreigners for the crisis became so popular that Golden Dawn claimed twenty-one seats in the 300-seat parliament in the May 2012 election.

Unquestionably, Greeks are not merely the victims of foreign mistakes. Many lived beyond their means, evaded taxes, and cooked their books. But the Greek government's response to the recession turned a bad economic situation into a public health disaster. Whereas Iceland's health looks more like that of the US in the New Deal, Greece's health has begun to resemble that of Russia in the aftermath of Shock Therapy and mass privatization.

And so it was that on the morning of April 4, 2012, Dimitris Christoulas, age seventy-seven, whom we met at the beginning of this book, killed himself in front of the Greek Parliament. He had paid into his pension for years, running his pharmacy. But ironically, he could no longer afford medicines for himself. His pension was cut, and his retirement benefits slashed. He saw no other way out.

PART III

RESILIENCE

For want of a nail the shoe was lost.
For want of a shoe the horse was lost.
For want of a horse the rider was lost.
For want of a rider the message was lost.
For want of a message the battle was lost.
For want of a battle the kingdom was lost.
And all for the want of a horseshoe nail.
(Proverbial rhyme)

6

TO CARE OR NOT TO CARE

Diane was forty-seven years old when a splinter ruined her life.[1]

She had been a teacher at a charter school in California. Because of $8.1 billion in education budget cuts the state enacted in 2009, she lost her job. Without her job, Diane lost her health insurance, so she had to purchase an individual coverage plan and pay the monthly premiums out of pocket. Diane signed up to the best plan she could afford, but that came with a high deductible: typically she would have to pay $5,000 before her insurance company covered any significant medical bills, making her think twice about whether she really had the money to seek medical help.[2]

One afternoon, about a year after she lost her job and signed up for this high-deductible health insurance plan, Diane was walking on the floorboards of her old apartment and got a large splinter in her foot. Because Diane has diabetes, her minor wound became a large gash, then an ulcer that wouldn't heal.

Diane felt that she couldn't afford to pay the fee for a doctor's office visit, nor for prescription antibiotics. So she tried to treat her leg herself—hoping that the redness creeping up her leg would go away if she strictly followed instructions she had found online: hot baths, soap, scrubbing, and over-the-counter antibiotic creams.

After a few weeks, Diana started to feel feverish and sweaty. Then she passed out. Luckily, a neighbor heard the shatter of glass when Diane's head broke the coffee table. The neighbor called 911, and the police broke down Diane's door and called an ambulance.

That's when Sanjay met Diane—in the intensive care unit of the local hospital. Her leg was so badly infected it had to be amputated—something that could have been avoided if the infection had been treated earlier. Worse still, the infection had spread to her bloodstream. It was so overwhelming that it was causing her to become septic—causing her blood pressure to drop below 80 over 40. To stop it from dipping any lower and leading to a potentially fatal cardiac arrest, Sanjay inserted a catheter through her jugular vein and into the right side of her heart, so he could pump intravenous fluids into her system and give her medicines that increased her blood pressure. Her kidneys were failing because of the infection, so a dialysis port had to be sewn into her groin. But the dialysis machine created its own problems. Diane suffered a stroke when the dialysis caused a second precipitous drop in her blood pressure.

Diane now lives in a nursing home. At the age of forty-seven, she is unable to speak or walk or move the right side of her body. Like hundreds of uninsured or underinsured patients, she delayed medical care because of fear of the cost. But ironically, her one hospitalization cost over $300,000. Her stroke left her disabled, and she will cost the state of California tens of thousands of dollars a year for the rest of her life. She requires twenty-four-hour nursing care to turn her in bed, clean her when she soils herself, and spoon her food into the left side of her mouth so she won't choke on it.

Diane's story is an extreme, tragic example of an everyday occurrence in the United States: the deferral of essential medical care among Americans who simply can't afford it.

Her case is particularly tragic because if she had encountered that splinter a few years later, Diane might have been covered under the new healthcare law, the Patient Protection and Affordable Care Act (PPACA), passed by Congress and signed into law by President Barack Obama on March 23, 2010. Before the law, about 20 percent of Americans with high-deductible healthcare insurance plans like Diane skipped preventive doctor's visits because of the cost. The new legislation helps ensure that everyone has affordable healthcare coverage, even if they are unemployed. While it is impossible to say with certainty that Diane's tragedy could have been avoided, had she been covered by an affordable plan, she probably wouldn't have let cost come between her and her doctor. That meant she would have been able to go out and seek work again in an economy slowly recovering from the Great Recession.

While the United States under President Obama began taking urgently needed steps to help prevent the Great Recession from leading to more avoidable tragedies like Diane's, the UK's National Health Service (NHS) began doing the opposite. Initially its universal healthcare system had been a great protector of its people—and no one lost healthcare access due to the economic crash. But now, under the politics of austerity, the UK Tory government is trying to mimic the US model by introducing competition, markets, and private contractors into the NHS. To understand what these privatizing reforms are likely to mean for the UK, it's first necessary to trace why the US healthcare system was in such dire straits during the recession.

Before the Great Recession, the US healthcare system failed to provide coverage for many of its people. Although two-thirds of Americans received health insurance through their employer, the rest—those whose employers wouldn't cover them, part-time workers, and the self-employed—were on their own, if they couldn't qualify for federal insurance programs. These Americans had to buy health insurance on the private market, but many could not afford the high monthly payments (premiums) and high deductibles. What's more, before the passage of the PPACA, insurance companies were able to restrict coverage on the basis of pre-existing health conditions, like diabetes or high blood pressure—so many who could afford private insurance were nevertheless not fully covered. All in all the US system left about 40 million Americans—almost 13 percent of the population—without health insurance.

The Great Recession turned this bad healthcare situation into a full-blown crisis. When Americans lost their jobs in the recession, another 6 million people lost their health insurance. Losing healthcare coverage is extremely dangerous. A 2009 study found that people who lacked medical insurance were 40 percent more likely to die prematurely than those who had it. During the Great Recession, before the PPACA came into effect, there were approximately 35,000 avoidable deaths due to the lack of healthcare insurance.[3]

Americans who lost insurance through their jobs had few options during the recession. Some tried to seek insurance on the private market, but about a third of them were refused coverage for a variety of reasons, including pre-existing medical conditions. Others simply couldn't afford the cost of a private healthcare insurance plan, which could be up to $25,000 per year for a two-person family. The recession exaggerated these costs further. Across America, on the pretext that the recession made it harder to operate, insurance companies were increasing their premiums—the monthly amounts people paid in to their insurance plans. Anthem Blue Cross in California, a subsidiary of WellPoint, raised its premiums by as much as 39 percent. The American Medical Association, the largest association of doctors in the country, officially condemned this practice (commonly known as purging), but they could do nothing to stop it.[4]

Some people were eligible for public insurance (if they earned under about $23,050 household income for a family of four). These people could qualify for Medicaid, the US government health insurance program for the very poor. But as enrollment in the program jumped 8.3 percent every year since 2009, some politicians and officeholders, mostly Republican, grew increasingly vocal about "out-of-control" government spending on Medicaid.[5]

All over the US, state officials began finding ways to cut Medicaid budgets. They introduced higher deductibles and co-payments (out-of-pocket fees) for prescriptions and doctor's visits, cut benefits, levied new taxes on care providers, and instituted hiring freezes, furloughs, layoffs, and salary cuts to Medicaid workers. Since the peak of the recession in 2009, forty states have cut their Medicaid budgets in at least one fiscal year. Twenty-nine of these states subsequently cut their budgets a second time, and fifteen states did so a third time.[6]

While it is too early to determine the full extent of the long-term impact of these cuts, there are already signs that people's health is suffering. Among the Americans who switched to high-deductible plans to save money, many began forgoing medical care as Diane had done. Families on health insurance plans with high deductibles were 14 percent less likely to see a doctor when they needed to, compared with those who stayed on lower deductibles.[7]

Much of the care that people stopped paying for was preventive in nature. For example, about 500,000 fewer Americans who had health insurance undertook colonoscopy screening for colorectal cancer during the recession. A survey conducted between March and April 2009 found that of those Americans who had a chronic illness, two-fifths did not fill a routine prescription to keep their illnesses under control because of cost pressures.[8]

Just as in Greece, recession and austerity in the US resulted in people having to wait longer to see doctors and access necessary treatment. Emergency rooms in the United States were already operating at or over capacity before the recession. Patients increasingly used emergency rooms more than outpatient clinics as they ended up in situations like Diane's—avoiding preventive care when they could no longer afford it. Doctors described being "overwhelmed" or "close to the breaking point." For patients, overcrowded emergency rooms meant longer waiting times, inattention to real emergencies, and lower overall quality of care.[9]

In short, the US healthcare system failed to protect its people during the Great Recession. Americans were doing without needed care that they could no longer afford—and sometimes, like Diane, they suffered tragic health consequences.

But there was one group that benefited. Profits of health insurance companies soared during the Great Recession. In 2009 the top five US health insurance companies reported $12.2 billion in profits, a staggering increase of 56 percent over the figures for 2008. In 2009, a year that saw 2.9 million people lose coverage, insurance companies' profits rose by 56 percent. And again, during the first nine months of 2010, profits increased by an average of 41 percent, breaking all-time industry records despite the recession. These windfall profits came at the expense of patients. As insurance companies were purging people from their ranks, they were paying out less for patient care, making more money in the process. While it was once thought that high enrollment was the key to successful insurance, WellPoint's CEO Angela Braly rephrased the new objective in 2008: "We will not sacrifice profitability for membership."[10]

So, the rich got richer, and the sick got sicker. That in a nutshell was the perennial problem of the US healthcare market.

It has long been well known that markets don't work well in healthcare. The Nobel Prize–winning economist, Kenneth Arrow, had found in a seminal 1963 paper that markets often fail to deliver affordable, high-quality healthcare. That's because healthcare is different from other market goods like cans of tuna. One major reason is that healthcare needs are difficult to predict and extremely expensive. People do not know when they might have a heart attack and need a coronary bypass surgery, for example. So they can't anticipate when to save money and, even if they could, a major operation would break the bank for most people. That means people have to buy insurance—and in turn that means having someone else make decisions about what care is available and what is not.[11]

But private insurance companies are in the business of making profit. There are only two ways to increase profit: take in more revenue, or cut costs. Revenue comes from people's monthly premiums, while costs come from paying for people's healthcare. So insurance companies have perverse incentives to sign up the healthiest people who need the least amount of care, and purge from their ranks the sickest people who need the most care.

This creates a situation that public health researchers commonly refer to as the Inverse Care Law. First identified in 1971, the law can be summed up succinctly as: those who need care the most get the least, while those who need care the least get the most. The Inverse Care Law was found to operate most strongly in healthcare systems where people's ability to access care depended on their ability to pay—the market principle that underpinned the US healthcare system.[12]

And despite common misperceptions, the market-based system isn't more efficient. Although the US healthcare system excludes large swaths of the population, the US spends more on healthcare than any country in the world—totaling 19 percent of its GDP during the recession. Other advanced industrialized nations spend anywhere from 7 to 11 percent. It is a situation that continues to get worse and worse. In 1970, total healthcare spending in the United States was $75 billion, or just $356 per person. In 2010, those numbers reached $2.6 trillion and $8,402 respectively. That increase was over four times the rate of the inflation. If the price of a dozen eggs had risen at the same rate, they would cost $15 today; a gallon of milk would fetch $27.

All this excessive healthcare spending is not because the United States has an older or sicker population. Rates of smoking, for example, are higher in Europe and there are more elderly people per capita in Japan. Obesity, technology, or higher utilization didn't explain the historically high costs either, nor did prescription drug research and development.

Rather, the US simply gets less bang for its buck. Instead of spending wisely on preventive care, it runs a more expensive "sick care" system. Those able to afford it can get high-quality care—but their doctors don't necessarily use the most cost-effective treatments. Instead, they often prescribe expensive tests and procedures, like CT scans and knee replacements, that are not always medically necessary but are highly profitable. The prime beneficiaries of the US healthcare system may not be, as it turns out, the patients, but the providers—insurance companies, hospital corporations, and drug companies.[13]

Despite ranking first in the world on healthcare spending, the US healthcare system is underperforming on nearly all measures of quality. Compared with Europe, Americans tend to have higher rates of in-hospital infections, deaths from medical mistakes, and avoidable hospital visits. US avoidable mortality death rates are 40 percent higher than the European average—amounting to almost 40,000 extra deaths per year because of poor healthcare quality for Americans. Overall, the World Health Organization ranked the US healthcare system among the worst in developed countries in terms of death rates and reducing suffering.[14]

That was the healthcare system in America before the Patient Protection and Affordable Care Act, Obamacare, passed in 2010. And it was woefully inadequate in the face of an economic crisis.

Other countries' approaches to healthcare made them more resilient to economic shocks like the Great Recession. Canada, Japan, Australia, and most European countries rejected market-based approaches to healthcare, providing state-sponsored care for all. They recognized the trappings of the Inverse Care Law, and the evidence that markets don't work well in healthcare.

While millions of Americans were losing access to healthcare during the Great Recession, there were fewer signs of people skipping doctor's visits or preventive care in the UK, Canada, France, and Germany. That's because these countries did not treat healthcare as a market good but as a human right—so losing a job or income had no effect on a person's access to healthcare. When the Great Recession struck their economies, people were not forced into choosing between bankruptcy and their health.[15]

The evidence can be found in the data on healthcare access across countries. One survey compared people's access to healthcare during the recession in the US, UK, Canada, France, and Germany. Using representative samples of people from each country, the survey asked more than 5,000 people whether they had increased, decreased, or had no change in their use of routine health care since the crisis. Sadly, but unsurprisingly, about one in five Americans reported neglecting routine medical care during the recession. The figures were rosier in Europe. Healthcare systems that were funded by taxpayers rather than employers were better able to protect their populations from losing access to medical care during the recession. In Canada, for instance, there was no change in people's access to healthcare during the recession, and in the UK there was even a slight (0.3 percent) increase in access to medical care.

Countries whose healthcare systems had patients pay more out-of-pocket for their healthcare were more exposed to the shocks of the Great Recession. France and Germany were two examples. While everyone had state-provided health insurance, people were responsible for co-payments of 10 euros per doctor visit in Germany and 16–18 euros per hospital visit in France. Meanwhile, in the UK people could visit the doctor or hospital free of charge. Even this modest amount made a difference. Germany and France saw a 4 percent and 7 percent drop in access, respectively—worse than the UK, but still better than the United States, because no one was left uncovered.

During the Great Recession, the British health system performed the best at preventing people from losing access to care. This is exactly what the founding fathers of the UK National Health Service had designed it to do: provide healthcare not based on people's ability to pay, but according to their healthcare needs.

At the time of the NHS's establishment, UK public debt stood at over 400 percent of its GDP, a level far higher than any country in Europe today (apart from Iceland). Britain was rebuilding its economy after World War II had devastated its infrastructure. It had set up an emergency wartime national healthcare service, in part because private insurance was unable to meet the health needs of the British troops. The service became highly popular. After the War, the Labour party expanded the emergency service to the entirety of Britain, and so the NHS was born on July 5, 1948. As the pamphlet explaining it to the general public put it, "It will provide with you all medical, dental, and nursing care. Everyone—rich or poor, man, woman or child—can use it or any part of it. There are no charges, except for a few special items. There are no insurance qualifications. But it is not a charity. You are all paying for it, mainly as taxpayers, and it will relieve your money worries in time of illness."[16]

From its very foundation, critics of the NHS said it would bankrupt the country. Yet it did not—instead it helped to boost the UK's economic recovery, just as the New Deal had done in the Great Depression.

For over half a century, the NHS has been the world's strongest model of a universal health care system. The National Health Service provided care for everyone, free at the point of service. To keep costs down, everyone paid in a little, spreading the costs over entire society, not placing the burden just on those who were ill. The NHS also negotiated directly with pharmaceutical companies on behalf of the UK's citizens, often purchasing medicines in bulk to negotiate better prices. The UK National Institute of Clinical Excellence ensured that doctors prescribed the most cost-effective medications, rather than overcharging patients for pills that were being promoted by drug companies through fancy trips and gifts to physicians. Doctors earned high but fixed annual salaries, instead of being paid per patient or on commission, so that they didn't rush appointments or have perverse incentives to conduct batteries of unnecessary tests and procedures.[17]

There is a lot more to say about why the NHS worked, but the bottom line is the data: the UK system saved more lives with less money during the Great Recession.[18]

Today the NHS's founding principles are being forgotten, as the conservative Tory government seeks to make the NHS more like the American profit-driven, market-based system. When the Tory government came to power, they revisited a pamphlet developed under the previous Tory government of John Major that called the NHS a "bureaucratic monster that cannot be tamed" and in need of "radical reform." In 2004, Oliver Letwin, the pamphlet's lead author, said the "NHS will not exist" within five years of a Tory election victory. Indeed, after the Tories came to power they proposed the Health and Social Care Act, which embodied the free-market principles of the radical pamphlet.[19]

It was difficult for us to understand this decision. Overall in 2010, before the Tory government began dismantling the NHS, the UK spent less of its GDP on health (8 percent) than Germany (10.5 percent), France (11.2 percent), or the United States (19 percent). Ultimately, the Tories' position was not based on evidence but ideology—the idea that markets, competition, and profits would always be better than government intervention.[20]

A highly divisive public debate over the Health and Social Care Act ensued. Over staunch opposition from the Royal College of Nursing and almost all of the medical Royal Colleges (the UK equivalents of the American Medical Association), Parliament approved the Act in 2012. Thus began what many regard as a major move toward privatization of the NHS. Repeatedly, David Cameron promised the British public that the Act was not "privatizing the NHS" and that he would "cut the deficit not the NHS." The Liberal-Democratic leader Nick Clegg said, "There will be no privatization." The Department of Health website even stated that "Health Ministers have said they will never privatise the NHS." But the data tell a different story: increasingly, the government is transferring large swaths of healthcare provision to private contractors.[21]

Private profiteers are replacing dedicated doctors. In October 2012, the government awarded 400 lucrative contracts for NHS services, worth a quarter billion pounds, in what was called "the biggest act of privatization ever in the NHS." Virgin, for example, won lucrative contracts to deliver reproductive care (no pun intended). But the result was not the efficiency of private enterprise, but what had already been seen in the US market model—profits at the expense of patients. One journalist found this to be the case at health clinics in Teesside, northeast England. After Virgin won contracts to take over the services, the clinic repeatedly missed targets for screening people for chlamydia. It was a simple task that the NHS had fulfilled easily. The journalist found a memo that revealed "staff were asked to take home testing kits to use on friends and family to help make the numbers up." In Oxford, patients complained about increasing wait times to see their doctors after Virgin took over a local practice. Virgin responded that the practice had been underperforming when it was taken over, and that "there are still improvements to be made but we're pleased that progress so far was recognised and applauded by councillors." And so began what continues to be a highly sophisticated public relations campaign.[22]

The UK's next step toward US-style market-based medicine is moving forward at the time of this writing. It encourages patients to spend out of their pockets for healthcare rather than use the government-funded NHS. The Tory government is extending pilot projects to offer those with chronic illnesses "personal budgets" so that they themselves can make choices about how to manage their care, with few safeguards against profit-seeking swindlers or predatory insurance companies despite a government evaluation that highlighted many problems with this approach.[23]

Early evidence suggests the Health and Social Care Act may in fact be hazardous to the health of the citizens and residents of the United Kingdom. Just before the Coalition government came into power, the NHS had the highest patient approval ratings in its history, over 70 percent. Within two years, approval fell to 58 percent, the largest decline in three decades.[24] There are already warning signs that the healthcare situation in Britain may come to resemble that in the US before Obama. Patients are being turned away from privately managed clinics, some of which simply close their doors after meeting a daily quota to fulfill their contractual obligations. And in the first year of reform, emergency room visits jumped to the highest in a decade— perhaps because more people are neglecting preventive care, like Diane.[25] As the editor of *The Lancet* warned, "people will die."[26]

Whether the British people will fully accept this radical privatization of their healthcare system remains unclear. But once market incentives take hold of a public system, it becomes difficult, if not impossible to reverse course. In the UK, the recession-fueled combination of austerity-and-privatization seems to be creeping into every dimension of the social protection system. But evidence of its harms should give us all pause.[27]

The UK is not the only country to go down the path of healthcare privatization and cuts. Greece was perhaps the most extreme example of intentional and large cuts to healthcare, as the IMF targeted healthcare as a key budget area from which to save short-term costs. Spain had a National Health Service, similar to the British. But as its public health budgets were cut, it began to shift care to the private sector. Fees were added to basic services, so that people had to pay more out of pocket—despite clear-cut evidence that these "user fees" reduced access to necessary care and didn't save money in the long-run.[28] Spain also redefined its eligibility criteria from "residents" to "citizens," purging immigrants from the system as a means to save money. Medicines that were once included in insurance packages were carved out. And in other cases, they simply became unavailable—as in Valencia, Spain, where pharmacies stood empty after the central government cut their funding.

There is an alternative—one that the UK itself had proven during its period of tremendous hardship and enormous debt after World War II. As Italy, Spain, and Greece, under pressure from the troika, are also now pursuing radical privatization and austerity reforms to their National Health Services, they would do well to recall the words of the NHS founder, Aneurin Bevan, who back in 1948 put this moral question in ringingly simple terms: "We ought to take pride in the fact that, despite our financial and economic anxieties, we are still able to do the most civilized thing in the world—put the welfare of the sick in front of every other consideration."[29]

7

RETURNING TO WORK

On May 4, 2012, a crowd of women waving white flags marched to the entrance of the Italian government's Equitalia tax office in Bologna. They were the *vedove bianche,* the White Widows. Following Italy's austerity drive in response to the Great Recession, their husbands hadn't been able to find enough work or pay their tax debts. And so the men had chosen to end it all by taking their lives. Saddled with debt, and left to pick up the pieces, the widows were angry and frustrated that the government wasn't helping them.[1]

"Non ci suiciderete!" they chanted: "Don't suicide us." Tiziana Marrone, the leader of the protest, said, "The government must do something. It is not right what is happening in Italy." They were upset that the government had turned a blind eye to tax evasion by Italy's super-rich, but done virtually nothing to support those who had lost everything in the Great Recession. She continued, "My battle is not just mine, it is of all the Italians who find themselves in my condition, and most of all of the widows of those families, who don't know where to turn to pay all these debts."[2]

It was the second protest at the Equitalia building. Five weeks earlier, on March 28, Giuseppe Campaniello, a self-employed bricklayer, and the husband of Tiziana Marrone, went to the same office. He had just received a final notice from Equitalia doubling a fine he reportedly couldn't pay. So in front of the tax offices, he doused himself with gasoline and set himself on

fire. He had left a note for Tiziana: "Dear love, I am here crying. This morning I left a bit early, I wanted to wake you, say goodbye, but you were sleeping
so well I was afraid to wake you. Today is an ugly day. I ask forgiveness from
everyone. A kiss to you all. I love you, Giuseppe." He died nine days later.

In the Great Recession, suicide rates rose as unemployment rates jumped by
39 percent across Italy between 2007 and 2010. While the White Widows'
protest drew public attention to their private suffering from the mental health
consequences of unemployment in Italy, not everyone agreed with their interpretation of events. Some commentators said that Italy's economic suicides
were just "normal fluctuations."[3]

To find out whether this was true and if so why, we looked into the country's mortality datasets. Italy has a uniquely detailed system for tracking
each of its suicides. The death certificates include contextual details about the
causes. One example was a certificate of a sixty-four-year-old bricklayer who
had lost his job at Christmas. He left a note that said in part, "I can't live
without a job," then shot himself. In Italy, as in Russia during the early 1990s,
unemployment had left people demoralized, hopeless, and ultimately prone
to self-harm.[4]

We found that there was a large rise in suicide death certificates labeled
"due to economic reasons" during the recession, well above pre-existing trends.
Notably, rates of suicides attributable to all other causes remained unchanged.
Overall, we estimated that Italy suffered at least 500 new cases of suicide and
attempted suicides beyond what would have been expected if pre-recession
suicide trends had continued. Figure 7.1 shows the jump in excess suicides
and suicide attempts due to the combination of the Great Recession and the
Italian government's austerity response.

Across the Atlantic, the US suicide data were also on the rise during the
recession. In the lead-up to the recession, suicides had already been increasing. For Figure 7.2, we projected the rate of suicides if those trends had continued, as shown in the dashed line. What we found is that the recession
made a bad situation worse, as suicide deaths accelerated (Figure 7.2's solid
line), rising by an additional 4,750 deaths during the recession over and
above the pre-existing trend.[5]

There was little doubt that the recession was a major cause of the increase
in suicides. But it was neither a necessary cause, nor a sufficient cause of these

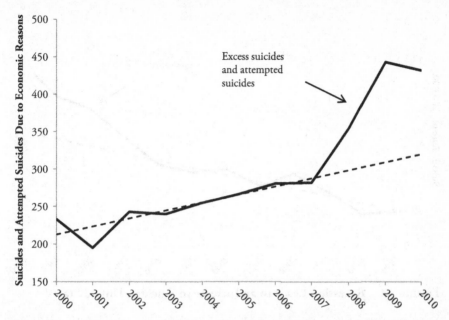

FIGURE 7.1   Recession and Austerity Increase Italy's Economic Suicides and Suicide Attempts[6]

tragedies. In countries that weren't helping to buffer families against unemployment, suicides often correlated with job losses, as in Italy and the United States. But in other countries, politicians chose to invest in social programs that helped people return to work. Sweden and Finland experienced large recessions at various times during the 1980s and 1990s, but had no significant rise in suicides despite experiencing large spikes in unemployment. Sweden and Finland found ways to prevent a crashing economy from taking a toll on people's mental health. Unemployment may be a common shock during recessions, but increased rates of suicidality are not.

Since the nineteenth century, it has been known that recessions and unemployment correlate with significantly greater risks of suicide. With advances in data collection, public health researchers and sociologists were able to establish that unemployment is a major risk factor for depression, anxiety, sleeplessness, and self-harm. Losing a job can tip a person into depression, especially in people who lack social support or are alone. People who are looking for work are about twice as likely to end their lives than those who have jobs.[7]

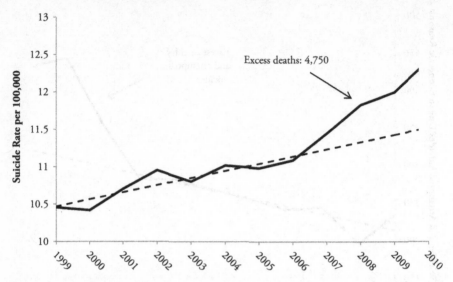

FIGURE 7.2   Recession Leads to an Increase in Suicides, United States[8]

During the early 1980s, some British economists began to question this conventional wisdom, asking whether unemployment was actually causing mental health problems per se or whether instead those who lost jobs were more likely to have been depressed in the first place. It was only possible to address this important question with large studies that tracked people over time, enabling researchers to disentangle which came first—job loss or depression. The answer, it turned out, was both: some people became depressed because they lost their jobs, while some were more likely to lose their jobs because they already suffered from depression, and their depression worsened because of unemployment.[9]

Hence, soon after the start of the Great Recession in 2007, doctors in Spain and the UK began to see a large rise in the number of patients coming to their clinics with acute depressive symptoms. As Peter Byrne, director of public education at the Royal College of Psychiatrists in the UK, said, "In 2009 all of us—whether we work in general practice, general hospitals or specialist services—are seeing an increase in referrals from the recession. The stresses of the downturn are the last straw for many people."[10]

With more patients showing signs of depression, doctors began to prescribe more antidepressants. In the UK, antidepressant use rose 22 percent between 2007 and 2009. A survey in 2010 found that 7 percent of those seeking help for "work-related stress" began pharmacological treatment for depression. Doctors gave out 3.1 million more antidepressant prescriptions in 2010 than they had just two years earlier.[11]

Spain and the United States also saw rises in antidepressant prescriptions. Between 2007 and 2009, the number of people taking daily antidepressants jumped by 17 percent in Spain. In the United States, use of antidepressants rose during the Great Recession to where 10 percent of the adult population were prescribed antidepressants during the recession. A study by Bloomberg Rankings found that rates of antidepressant prescriptions had a very strong correlation with unemployment rates.[12]

From a statistical perspective, these data demonstrated only that more people were seeking medication for depression during the Great Recession. They did not, in and of themselves, prove that unemployed people were uniquely affected. In theory, it is quite possible that people were simply more stressed and unhappy during the recession for other reasons: the general atmosphere of malaise, increased workloads, anxiety surrounding the possibility of being laid off, etc. These numbers alone did not prove that unemployment per se was the driver of worse depression in this recession.[13]

We set out to study which people were showing up to doctors' offices with depression symptoms. We looked at data on 7,940 patients from doctors' offices across Spain before the recession (2006) and during it (2010). Spain continues to grapple with one of the largest global increases in unemployment during the recession, but also had kept good track of mental health through a series of standardized depression surveys. Those surveys revealed that the number of patients showing up at the doctor's office with clinical symptoms of major depression rose from 29 percent to 48 percent between 2006 and 2010. Minor depression rose from 6 percent to about 9 percent, reports of panic attacks went up from 10 percent to 16 percent, and even alcohol abuse rose from less than 1 percent to 6 percent. Recent unemployment was a key statistical predictor of these mental health problems. This remained the case after we controlled for a number of other possible factors, including pre-existing depression and access to mental healthcare.[14]

Of course, there are other ways to address the problem of unemployment than with antidepressants. As Dr. Geoffrey Rose, the father of preventive medicine, put it: "What good does it do to give a patient medicine but send them back to the environment that made them sick in the first place?" The real question that we, along with many other epidemiologists, are now trying to understand is how we can prevent these problems from happening when large numbers of people lose work.

While millions of new prescriptions were being written in the US, UK, and Spain, not all countries facing big spikes in unemployment witnessed such large rises in the use of antidepressants. In Sweden, prescriptions rose by only 6 percent between 2007 and 2010, much less than the rise in Spain or in the UK. Instead of treating symptoms with pills alone, the Swedish response during the Great Recession, and earlier, was to address a root cause of depression—unemployment itself.

Long before the Great Recession, Swedish policymakers had been acting as doctors to the masses. The country's innovative social protection plan is called the Active Labor Market Program (ALMP). "Active" is the crucial word here. ALMPs are different from typical social safety nets for the unemployed more commonly found in countries such as the US, Spain, and the UK. Those "passive" programs usually provide cash benefits to the unemployed to replace their lost income (of course, the recipients had contributed every month to their unemployment insurance while they were working). While there is little doubt that unemployment checks help unemployed people to continue to support their families and make ends meet, the Swedes designed their programs to be "activating"—to help people get back into new jobs as quickly as possible.[15]

Since the 1960s, Sweden had been developing ALMP programs that provide workers with support, skills, and a plan to get back to work. While there is a lot of variation in how countries organize their ALMPs, Sweden's were particularly well-developed and comprehensive to help keep workers active. In Sweden, when people lose their jobs, both they and their firms register at a government job center. So people participate by default. Within the next thirty days, the center creates an "individual action plan" with the person who has become unemployed. This individual has an interview with a job trainer every six weeks to see how the job search is going. The program also requires that the participant continue their job search (and it verifies their efforts) during their participation in the ALMP. In order for people to access cash benefits, they have to take part in a guided, step-by-step plan to get back into work.

Sweden's ALMPs placed a much greater emphasis on activating workers than the US or Spain. The unemployed in Sweden were not just having their hands held, but were being actively reached out in order to help them stay economically active, and program managers worked with companies to get new jobs generated for their recently laid-off workers. That is not to say that unemployment offices in the US and Spain didn't provide job search opportunities—they did, but their programs were far less active in their outreach and aims than the Swedish ALMPs. One of Sanjay's patients, for example, encountered a US version of an "ALMP"; he had to wait three hours to get a pamphlet that told him to prepare a resumé, take a shower, and wear a suit.

Before the Great Recession, ALMPs had played a critical role in preventing unemployment from causing depression in those countries that deployed them. In Finland, a randomized controlled trial in 2002 tested the effectiveness of the country's ALMP program, Työhön (meaning "let's go to work"). Researchers assigned 629 people who had lost their jobs to a job-training program with skilled caseworkers. A control group of 632 people received printed information about finding a job (the same printed information provided by the ALMP program) but did not receive the actual help of a Työhön trainer. The results were remarkably different between the two groups. Within three months, the researchers found, workers who were enrolled in the Työhön program experienced significantly fewer symptoms of depression and anxiety, with the greatest benefits seen in those previously at high risk of depression. The researchers found that two years later ALMP participants had significantly fewer depressive symptoms and higher self-esteem, were less likely to have given up hope on finding a job, and were more likely to have successfully returned to work than the control group.[16]

In practice, ALMPs provided mental health resilience to job loss in at least three ways. First, they helped people who lost their jobs find new ones as soon as possible—eliminating a key source of depression and anxiety. Indeed, studies of depression showed that symptoms of short-term depression often disappeared once an unemployed individual returned to work. Second, ALMPs helped reduce the mental health risks that accompanied job loss by providing formal social support through a trainer, as opposed to leaving people to cope with job loss on their own. Third, the data showed that these programs could even help people who were not unemployed but worried they might be; those at risk of losing their job knew they would get assistance to find a new one, and this appeared to prevent depressive symptoms among those at high risk for unemployment. If properly implemented,

ALMPs were a classic win-win situation: improving the economy and pre-venting depression.[17]

Sweden had been learning from these data since the 1960s, and by the 1980s began operating some of the most highly sophisticated ALMPs in the world. One reason was that their politicians invested in well-resourced pro-grams. Each year, Sweden spent a total of $580 per capita to help the unem-ployed get back into work. The US, UK, and Spain were spending less than half of this figure. Not only did Sweden invest more, but it invested propor-tionally more in active programs rather than passive paychecks. In the mid-1980s, Sweden spent about three-quarters of its funds to help the unemployed on active programs, whereas the US spent about one-third, the UK one-quarter, and Spain about one-tenth of their budgets on active programs. In 2005, the Organization for Economic Cooperation and Development pub-lished a comprehensive report comparing unemployment programs across European countries. It found that Sweden's investment was paying off: its ALMPs had among the quickest response times in setting up interviews and individual action plans for the newly unemployed.[18]

These results all seemed well and good during normal economic times. But would these programs be enough to help protect Sweden from experienc-ing a large rise in suicides during an economic meltdown?

The protective effects of Sweden's ALMPs were put to the test during its recession in the 1990s. In a scenario that resembles the current recession, Sweden's housing market collapsed in 1991 and 1992, bringing nearly all of its 114 banks to near-closure. GDP fell by 12 percent. Ten percent of Swedish workers lost their jobs—a rise on par with unemployment spikes in many countries during the current recession.[19]

Remarkably, despite Sweden's large spike in unemployment, suicide rates actually *fell* steadily during the period between the 1980s and 2000s, when the government invested, on average, about $360 per capita per year in active labor market programs (see Figure 7.3). There was no significant correlation between Sweden's fluctuations in unemployment and its suicide rates.

Like Sweden, Spain experienced large increases in unemployment from its recessions of the 1980s and 1990s. But Spain operated a relatively poorly resourced unemployment program, investing only about $90 capita per year, and focusing this money only on cash benefits. For men in Spain, trends in unemployment correlated strongly with suicide rates, as shown in Figure 7.4.[20]

FIGURE 7.3 Active Labor Market Programs, Unemployment, and Suicide in Swedish Men, 1980–2005[21] (solid line: unemployment; broken line: suicide)

We wanted to be as sure as possible that ALMPs were the determining factor in reducing the risk of suicide during economic recession. So we examined suicide rates and unemployment programs across all of the European countries using over two decades of data, comparing ALMPs to all the other main types of social protection programs, including healthcare services, family support such as childcare support, housing subsidies, old-age pensions, and passive unemployment benefits to see which, if any, could prevent an increase in suicide rates during recessions. Healthcare spending, for example, did not significantly reduce the risk of suicides from unemployment. This made sense: if the main risks of depression came from factors like unemployment, the formal healthcare system would probably not have much power to neutralize these risk factors. We also found that cash benefits didn't reduce the risk. In test after test, we found that the ALMPs had the greatest and most significant preventive effects on suicide when compared to other social protection programs.

We estimated that, if done properly, ALMPs could neutralize the suicide risk of a recession. In our findings, published in the peer-reviewed medical journal *The Lancet*, we estimated that for a $100 investment per capita, on

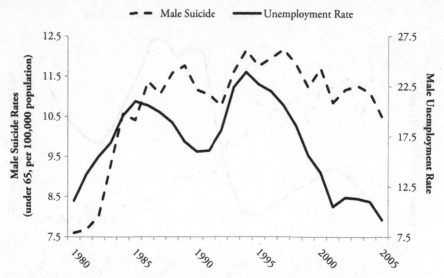

FIGURE 7.4   Active Labor Market Programs, Unemployment, and Suicide in Spanish Men, 1980–2005[22] (solid line: unemployment; broken line: suicide)

average ALMPs appeared to lower the risk of unemployment-related suicide from 1.2 percent to 0.4 percent.

The data provided a striking example of how social protection programs could save lives. When countries invested more than about $200 per capita in ALMPs, the correlation of unemployment with suicides appeared to completely vanish. This was precisely why unemployment spikes had no correlation with increased suicides in Sweden, Finland, and Iceland, but unemployment was strongly correlated to suicide in Spain, the US, Greece, Italy, and Russia.

The lessons we learned from our research on ALMPs provided answers to several puzzles. First, ALMPs statistically explained why becoming unemployed was so much more dangerous for people in Eastern rather than Western Europe. At the time when the Soviet Union disintegrated, Finland, a major trading partner in Western Europe, suddenly lost one-third of its economy as the sales made to Soviet factories evaporated. Finland also had a drinking culture similar to the Soviet Union, and its unemployment had soared during the recession. Yet there was little or no discernible effect of the economic crash on suicides in the country. By contrast, the surge in unemployment in Russia, Kazakhstan, and the Baltic states corresponded to a devastating mortality crisis. This dramatic difference could be explained by the fact that Western European countries like Finland tended to invest considerably more in labor market protections (about $150 per capita) than did Eastern European countries ($37 per capita).[23]

When we presented our findings at research conferences, our colleagues in Russia and Poland suggested that unlike Sweden or Finland, their countries simply couldn't afford to invest in ALMPs. But we found that, if executed well (i.e., in the Swedish style), ALMPs would essentially pay for themselves by boosting employment and reducing the burden on social welfare. A detailed analysis of Danish ALMPs, for example, concluded that the economic benefits of these programs far exceeded their costs, because the programs increased workers' productivity and reduced reliance on welfare support. In Denmark, the programs generated a net savings of 279,000 Danish kroner (about $47,000) per worker over eleven years. Another study in 2010 performed a systematic review of 199 ALMPs studied in 97 research experiments. It found a similar consistent pattern of results as the Danish program: that ALMPs helped people return to work and, by keeping people economically active, reduced pressure on public welfare systems by increasing the economy's labor supply—a main engine of economic growth.

With all of this evidence accumulating in favor of ALMPs, we were eager to translate these data into practice. After we published our research in 2009 about the benefits of ALMPs, we were invited to the British House of Commons and the Swedish Parliament to present our data and recommendations.[24]

The responses were remarkable—that is, remarkably dissimilar—in the two countries. When presented with the data that unemployment led to a rise in suicides, and that ALMPs could help mitigate the risks, the Swedish members of Parliament were unsurprised. One member asked: "Why are you telling us what we already know?" But when we presented the same data in the UK, in July 2009, to the House of Commons, the reaction was that the government was "already doing all it could to reduce unemployment."

When the Conservative government came into power in 2010, the UK response became even worse. In 2012, the *British Medical Journal* published our paper showing that UK suicides had risen by more than 1,000 between 2007 and 2010 above pre-existing trends, corresponding to the continued rise in unemployment. Reporters soon contacted the UK Department of Health for a response. Its spokesman told the *Independent* newspaper: "Losing a loved one [to suicide] can be devastating and we want to make sure that we are doing all we can to prevent suicide by giving people the right support when they need it most. We will shortly be publishing our new suicide prevention strategy, which brings together expertise across healthcare, criminal justice and transport to maintain or even decrease the current rates of suicide." This sounded encouraging. But then the Health Department spokesman continued: "However, suicide rates in England have been at a historical low and remain unchanged since 2005. The department uses three-year rolling averages for monitoring purposes, in order to avoid focusing unnecessarily on fluctuations instead of the underlying trend."[25]

By now, this tactic should sound familiar: averaging-out deaths is the same technique *The Economist* used to cover up death rates in Russia. When using rolling averages, any large jump in death rates can seem like a smooth bump in the road instead of a shocking spike (indeed, the Department appeared to have chosen the three-year period specifically for this end, instead of some other date range like five years). The Department's comments were criticized by several university professors and statisticians, after which the statement quickly disappeared from their Internet webpage.

If it wanted to help its people, the British government could learn much from Sweden's experience. The UK would of course need to invest more in ALMPs and stop job losses from happening. But the Conservative government was doing precisely the opposite: austerity was creating an active labor-*destroying* program. The data revealed that the austerity program cut public-sector jobs in the most deprived regions of the country. Moreover, it was implementing policies that made it easier for the private sector to lay off people during the recession. As one unusually blunt 2010 report commissioned by the government explained, "some people will be dismissed simply because their employer doesn't like them," but argued that this is a "price worth paying" to boost the economy, though the logic of how mass unemployment would drive economic growth was left unexplained.[26]

The consequences of the UK's real-world experiment with austerity soon became tragically apparent in its suicide data. As in the US, the Great Recession in the UK featured an initial spike in unemployment and job losses in 2007. As employment began to recover in 2009, suicides began to fall. But the following year, when the Conservative government came to power, the UK began a massive austerity program, which in 2012 alone cut 270,000

public-sector jobs. The UK then experienced a second wave of "austerity suicides" in 2012.[27]

It is said that those who don't learn from history are doomed to repeat it.
Our models had predicted a repeat of suicide trends in Spain and Sweden,
and we were now seeing their contrasting histories on playback into the present. Sweden and Spain both experienced large recessions, but suicides again
rose substantially in Spain and actually fell in Sweden.

The range of observed suicide trends across the UK, the US, Iceland,
Greece, Italy, Spain, and Sweden revealed that a rise in suicides can be averted
during recessions. More suicides could have been prevented if the right steps
were taken both before and during the recession to help people return to
work.[28] These suicides are only the tip of the iceberg; for each suicide there
are an estimated ten suicide attempts and between 100 and 1,000 new cases
of depression.[29]

As the Swedish and Finnish experiences demonstrate, unemployment
may put people's mental health at risk, but suicides needn't inevitably follow.
Nor should we wait for our healthcare systems to pick up the pieces when
people become depressed or suicidal. Antidepressants may help some people
deal with the consequences of unemployment. But wouldn't it be better to
treat the cause of the problem rather than the symptoms? The Swedish invested proactively in programs that reached out to people who lost jobs and
helped them develop an action plan for returning to work.

The sufferings of the White Widows of Italy and their husbands, "sui-
cided" by austerity, must not be forgotten. The way forward is surprisingly
clear in the data. The question is whether we will now take action.

8

A PLAGUE ON ALL YOUR HOUSES

The crows of Bakersfield started dying in May 2007.

Most Californians knew the town of Bakersfield as a hot little hellhole between San Francisco and Los Angeles—a pit stop for gas and cheap Indian food. It's a town that seemed destined to be ignored.

But when the crows of Bakersfield started dying, people started talking. First came the reports of children finding dead ravens floating in backyard swimming pools. Then other species of birds started falling out of trees. One local news crew filmed a swarm of swallows collapsing like little comets from the sky.[1]

The dying birds were frightening enough, but panic erupted when humans began developing strange symptoms. Some people had tremors. Others experienced a condition that doctors call "myoclonus"—a spasmodic, involuntary contraction of muscles that looked like the shudder of the possessed. Most became confused, and a few were paralyzed.[2]

By the peak of that summer, several people had already presented at the Bakersfield Memorial Hospital with a constellation of these symptoms, which some thought might be polio, and others believed was surely the wrath of an angry God.

"Could it be over-heating?" wondered a doctor, attempting to calm nerves. That year had after all been exceptionally hot, and the winter the driest since

1988. The Kern River, typically rippling downstream from the Sierra Nevada mountains, had baked dry into a cracked muddy road. A truck driver from Arkansas had even collapsed and died of heat stroke at Bruce's truck stop on the eastern edge of town.[3]

But after a few weeks, scientists from the California Encephalitis Project, a state laboratory supported by the Centers for Disease Control and Prevention (CDC), provided the Bakersfield doctors with a more rational explanation. Spinal fluid samples from the affected people tested positive for West Nile Virus.

West Nile Disease had appeared before in New York City and Texas, killing birds at first. Mosquitoes were the main vector for the disease, carrying the virus and transporting it from one victim to the next. Mosquitoes would become infected after biting the dead birds, carry the virus in their salivary glands, then transmit it to living birds, horses, and humans. In some people, West Nile infection led to a day of fever, body aches, and a rash; in others, particularly the elderly or those with weak immune systems, it caused a potentially fatal infection of the brain.

Mosquitoes had rarely caused problems in Bakersfield. Indeed, the last major outbreak of a mosquito-borne disease in Bakersfield was in 1952, when an astonishing 813 people died of Western equine encephalitis transferred by mosquitoes from infected horses. That episode led federal and state health departments to create a Mosquito-Borne Virus Surveillance and Response Plan. The CDC launched the California Encephalitis Project, a specialized lab dedicated to monitoring unexplained symptoms and deaths from around the state.

According to the CDC's data, this particular West Nile outbreak was unusual. The CDC team had found that hot weather usually reduced the chances of a West Nile outbreak, as the pools of water next to the Kern River, where mosquitoes normally bred, had disappeared. Western scrub jays and house finches, two bird species that carried the virus, had also been dying of thirst. The numbers of rural mosquitoes, *Culex tarsalis*, caught in traps by scientists were also below their 5-year averages. Given these conditions, 2007 should have been a very-low risk summer for West Nile.

Yet by the end of August, nearly 140 new human cases of West Nile had been confirmed in and around Bakersfield, a 280 percent increase from the previous year's 50 cases. Twenty-seven people had died. "Once we had one human case, it was almost like popcorn after that," said Dr. Claudia Jonah, the county's interim health officer. "In a year in which we should not have had any cases, we had the most in the nation."[4]

California Governor Arnold Schwarzenegger declared a state of emergency in the county. He was in the midst of busily writing IOUs to cope with California's major budget crisis. But in a desperate attempt to end the epidemic, he started a $6.2 million campaign to reduce the number of mosquitoes around Bakersfield.[5]

Kern County Department of Health officials mass-mailed letters to Bakersfield homes and issued television warnings, urging all residents to stay indoors at dawn and dusk, when mosquitoes are most active. Even in the sweltering heat, Bakersfield's children and the elderly now donned long sleeves and trousers to avoid bites. Then, at 8:30 pm on August 9, planes descended in military-style flyovers across the town, blanketing homes and businesses in thick gray clouds of pyrethrin insecticide, a chemical derived from chrysanthemums.[6]

To discover the causes of the epidemic, the Kern Mosquito and Vector Control team deployed a rapid-response outfit of epidemiologists from the University of California, led by mosquito expert Dr. William Reisen. Many possible explanations were considered. "Perhaps the current drought was crowding birds into smaller watering holes," hypothesized Reisen's team, "where they were more likely to come into contact with mosquitoes?"[7]

First the team requested an aerial scan of Bakersfield to probe for hot spots of dead birds and mosquito-breeding clusters. While airborne cameras provided no sign of dense watering holes where birds might be over-crowding, they did reveal an unexpected clue: clusters of rectangular green fuzz. On closer inspection, about one out of every six swimming pools, bird-baths and Jacuzzis in the town of Bakersfield had turned lime-green.

Quickly, Reisen's team set out to investigate, knocking on doors and ringing bells to find out if the pools and baths were sites of mosquito breeding. At each of the "green-fuzz residences," they found no one home. Instead, they were greeted with "For Sale" and "Bank Owned Foreclosure" signs on nearly every lawn. The researchers had discovered the origins of the West Nile epidemic. Reisen's study found more than 4,000 larvae of mosquitoes infected with West Nile strains in 31 neglected pools.

Bakersfield was not just the epicenter of a West Nile outbreak, but also an epicenter of the nation's foreclosure crisis. Since the collapse of the US housing market in 2006, home foreclosures in the United States had jumped by 225 percent, leading to the repossession of more than 6 million American homes. Bakersfield's situation was even worse; it was at the center of California's mortgage lending bubble, and soon became the center of the foreclosure meltdown that followed. The city had experienced a 300 percent rise in mortgage delinquency as the national foreclosure crisis began, ranking eighth among the worst-affected American cities. Almost two percent of Bakersfield homeowners had filed for foreclosure; the town of about 300,000 people listed more than 5,000 abandoned homes as the recession began. When people's homes were foreclosed and repossessed by bankers, their backyards were abandoned. Weeds overgrew, swimming pool water turned stagnant, and algae bloomed—creating the perfect breeding ground for mosquitoes.[8]

But West Nile Virus was not the worst public health outcome of the foreclosure crisis. The gravest risks to public health came from the rise of homelessness. When people lose their homes and live on the streets or in substandard housing, their health deteriorates. The homeless experience constant stress, and are more likely to skip medications and visits to the doctor. In the worst cases, if they lose all forms of shelter, they face a heightened risk of assault, death from cold exposure, severe mental health problems, substance abuse, and of landing in jail, the hospital, or the morgue.[9]

Public housing and housing benefits are the best medicine for counteracting the health risks of homelessness. But different governments responded in very different ways to the housing crisis brought on by recession, with dramatically different results for the health of their citizens. The United States and the United Kingdom both experienced political regime changes during the Great Recession. These transitions played a critical role in how the American and British governments responded to their foreclosure crises, with subsequently different outcomes for public health. With the American Recovery and Reinvestment Act of 2009, enacted by Congress and signed into law by President Obama, the US government began investing in social protection programs to stop foreclosures from leading to homelessness. Costly hospitalizations, premature deaths, and infectious disease rates related to homelessness were all significantly reduced in the subsequent months. By contrast, the Conservative government that came to power in 2010 in the UK, while not facing as severe a housing crisis as the US, began instituting radical measures, which included cuts to housing support budgets. Homelessness increased following these measures, bringing with it a surge in avoidable hospitalizations and disease outbreaks.

It has long been known that housing is a precondition for good health. Homeless persons are among society's most vulnerable groups. People without homes tend to die forty years earlier than those with a roof over their heads. They often suffer from a raft of health problems and lack adequate access to healthcare. In addition, the homeless are at high risk of contracting infectious diseases like TB, which can then spread to the rest of the population. Poor health and homelessness are so closely linked that it is difficult to ascertain which came first, but the public health outcome is the same: a huge increase in the risk of death and avoidable suffering.[10]

While the relationship between homelessness and disease has long been common knowledge, the foreclosure crisis during the Great Recession taught us something new: the threat of foreclosure can contribute to illness even before anyone loses their home. As people struggled to pay their debts, the accompanying stress increased risks of suicide and depression, and many people were forgoing food and medicines to make their mortgage payments. A study of Americans over age fifty found that between 2006 and 2008, people who fell behind on their mortgage payments were about nine times more likely to develop depressive symptoms, 7.5 times more likely to experience "food insecurity" (meaning a lack of adequate nutrition and skipping meals), and nine times more likely to skip medicines, even after statistically controlling for pre-existing health conditions.[11]

Because so many people couldn't afford medicines, or were sacrificing healthcare to pay their debts, those facing the threat of foreclosure were more likely to experience disease complications that left them in emergency rooms. A large case-control study in Philadelphia compared hospitalization rates among people who had a home foreclosure notice (cases) with those matched for age, gender, sex, residential area, and health insurance status but who didn't face foreclosure (controls). The study found that between 2005 and 2008, people whose homes had a foreclosure notice were at a higher risk of ending up in a local hospital than the control group. Within the six to twenty-four months before the date of foreclosure, people who had a foreclosure notice were 50 percent more likely to visit the emergency room. The two main causes were high blood pressure and kidney failure related to diabetes, conditions that should not result in hospitalizations unless people were forgoing medications.[12]

Once people's homes were actually foreclosed and people forced to leave, their risks of ending up in the ER jumped even higher. As people skipped necessary medicines during the recession in Arizona, California, Florida, and New Jersey, a strong correlation emerged between the rates of home foreclosures in communities and rates of emergency room visits. When we looked across all zip codes between 2005 and 2007, at the peak of the foreclosure crisis, but before unemployment rose, those zip codes with higher foreclosure filings had greater risks of emergency room visits, even after adjusting for housing prices, unemployment, migration, and historical trends in ER visits among those communities. On average, each additional 100 foreclosures were found to correspond to a 7.2 percent rise in emergency room visits and hospitalizations for high blood pressure, as well as an 8.1 percent jump in diabetes-related complications, mostly among people under age 50. Between 2007 and 2009, emergency rooms visits surged by 6 million people over and above the number expected during normal periods.[13]

While it was clear that foreclosure posed a serious threat to Americans ending up in emergency rooms, the real danger to their health was if they had no place to live. Whether more people became homeless during the recession ultimately depended on how governments chose to respond.

When President Obama came into office, the foreclosure crisis was escalating. Since the housing bubble collapsed, the nation's foreclosed population nearly tripled from one in 476 households in 2007 to one in 135 in mid-2009.[14]

This wave of foreclosures put enormous pressure on public housing systems, at a time when they were already overstretched. It's often forgotten that US homelessness rates were already at record highs after Hurricanes Katrina and Rita in 2005, which had displaced thousands of families in New Orleans and on the coast of Texas.

Even before the burst of new foreclosures, public housing services were unable to keep pace with Americans' need for housing assistance. In 2007, a study of 23 large US cities found that half of the cities' public housing programs had to turn people in need of shelter away due to a lack of capacity. While some people experiencing homelessness managed to find temporary housing arrangements—for example, with friends or relatives—others were not so lucky. Before the Great Recession hit, nearly 40 percent of homeless people were living on the street, in a car, or in another place not intended for human habitation. As Neil Donovan, executive director of the National Coalition for the Homeless, explained at the time, for these people, "the U.S. housing safety net isn't just frayed, it's missing."[15]

When foreclosures increased in the United States during the Great Recession, homelessness rose in step. Between 2008 and 2009, more than half a million additional houses were foreclosed. In turn, at least 20,000 additional people became homeless during the same period. In 2009, about 1.6 million people (about one in every 200 persons in the US) used an emergency shelter in at some point. But more than 250,000 homeless people were unsheltered—living in abandoned warehouses, parks, cars, and back alleys among other places not intended for human residence.[16]

Children were among the most tragic victims of the foreclosure crisis. The number of children living without homes increased from 1.2 million in 2007 to about 1.6 million in 2010, or about one in every forty-five American children. Reporters found that in some towns plagued by foreclosure, school buses had to stray from their usual routes to stop in Wal-Mart parking lots, where parents had parked their vans and converted them into make-shift homes. Bedbugs and scabies were but a few of the health problems facing these homeless children.[17]

Homelessness leaves a permanent mark on the health of people who experience it. In the worst of cases, it can be lethal. During the recession in the United States, the homeless were estimated to have been about thirty times more likely than the rest of the population to die from the effects of illegal drugs, 150 times more likely to be fatally assaulted, and thirty-five times more likely to kill themselves. On average, US homeless persons were experiencing a life expectancy on par with that of people in war-torn Sierra Leone and the Congo.[18]

The city of San Francisco's foreclosure crisis put the nation's problems in perspective. Between 2007 and 2008, San Francisco's housing programs couldn't keep up with demand and had to expand wait-lists by 50 percent for families and individuals to access emergency shelters. An analysis of data from California estimated that approximately thirty-seven households entered the shelter system for every 1,000 foreclosure filings, even after adjusting for poverty rates—meaning that those pushed into homelessness by foreclosure weren't simply those who were already likely to need assistance. More people were being turned away, and their health problems were putting a tremendous burden on the healthcare system.[19]

Thomas, a man in his forties, was one such case. He had lost his home and become an alcoholic. Sanjay met Thomas at San Francisco's Housing and Urban Health Clinic, treating his numerous injuries and a seizure problem caused by his drinking. He also landed on the city's list of "high utilizers" of the emergency room, which is to say he cost the city an inordinate amount given the frequent injuries he suffered while drunk from getting into fights, being mugged, and even once falling down the stairs at a subway stop. Repeated attempts to persuade Thomas to stop drinking were unsuccessful.

Sanjay could do little to treat the health consequences of homelessness in patients like Thomas. As another doctor explained, when homeless patients come to the clinic, treating their medical symptoms is "like giving someone aspirin for cancer." Homelessness makes it hard for people to take medicines consistently as required for high blood pressure and diabetes, as co-payments for those medicines are expensive. Homeless persons also face extreme depression and anxiety, so they often self-medicate with drugs and alcohol. To treat all of these conditions, a homeless person would need up to ten different medications, and even then it is unlikely that they would work as intended without the security of stable housing.

The best medicine for people without homes is simple and obvious: put a roof over their heads. It is an approach known as "Housing First," because it first seeks to address people's immediate need for shelter, before dealing with their other concerns. Of course, this costs money up front, but the evidence shows that it saves money (and lives) in the long run if done correctly.

That is precisely what the US government began to do soon after President Obama took office. On May 20, 2009, Obama implemented a massive stimulus package to help people like Thomas and boost the economy. The Congress passed a $1.5 billion Homelessness Prevention and Rapid Re-Housing Program bill, creating a program designed to prevent victims of foreclosure from becoming homeless and to help those already homeless regain housing. As part of the program, local governments identified these people and helped them to find and pay for new places to live. The US Department of Housing and Urban Development (HUD) also used the funds to increase the number of emergency shelters and units for long-term housing.[20]

Homelessness prevention programs, like those supported by the stimulus, helped Thomas get his life back on track. At the clinic, nurses and doctors had tried everything they could to help Thomas, but it was only when the city of San Francisco found him an apartment through its longstanding, but oversubscribed, Direct Access to Housing program that his underlying depression substantially improved. Thomas joined Alcoholics Anonymous and eventually recovered from his drinking problem. He now works as a chef's assistant at a local restaurant, paying his rent and taxes, as well as avoiding the emergency room at the hospital.

Over the long run, San Francisco saved money by putting a stable roof over Thomas's head. It turned out to be cheaper for the city to provide Thomas a modest apartment than to pay for his stays in hospitals and jails. A statistical analysis of programs like San Francisco's Direct Access to Housing found that they often saved money for cities and states by reducing healthcare (and often jail) expenditures.[21]

With support from Obama's stimulus package, mayors in New York City, Denver, San Diego, Chicago, and Philadelphia soon began expanding Housing First programs similar to San Francisco's. In Philadelphia, each group of 100 people housed saved the city $421,893 per year, over and above the costs of running the program and covering housing bills.[22]

Across the United States, despite an historic housing and economic downturn, homelessness actually decreased between 2009 and 2011 in tandem with the rollout of HUD's homelessness prevention program. Even as another 1.9 million homes were foreclosed in 2010, the homeless population actually fell. In 2010, the stimulus-financed program helped 700,000 at-risk and homeless people find shelter, and by 2012 it had averted homelessness for 1.3 million Americans.[23]

The United Kingdom presented a stark contrast to the US example during the Great Recession. In the UK, housing had long been recognized as a public health issue. Government housing programs were considered so integral to health that the UK Housing Department was under the control of the Department of Health until 1951 (when the Tories defeated Labour, at which point housing was separated, seen partly as a move to weaken the power of the National Health Service). Before the Great Recession, the British Department for Communities and Local Government operated a successful social housing program analogous to the Housing First programs in the United States. Britons who qualified could receive housing subsidies of up to several hundred pounds per month—not a huge sum, but enough to help people keep a roof over their heads. British housing support had managed to keep homelessness at about two-fifths of US prevalence rates (about 1 homeless person per 500 people in the UK versus about 1 per 200 in the US) and had helped bring about a roughly 50 percent reduction in homelessness rates between 2000 and 2007.[24]

As in the US, the British government faced the decision of how to respond to a foreclosure crisis after its own housing bubble burst. Under the Labour Party's government, between 2007 and 2009, the number of foreclosed homes in the United Kingdom taken into possession nearly doubled, from 25,900 to 48,000. At first, the British social housing programs not only prevented a rise in homelessness but helped more people find homes, as the total number of homeless families fell from 63,170 in 2007 to 40,020 families in 2009.

Those rosy statistics changed dramatically starting in 2010, when the Tory Coalition government came into power and began cutting the safety nets that had kept people from homelessness. In 2010, Chancellor of the Exchequer George Osborne announced an austerity package comprised of £83 billion ($113 billion) in cuts, of which £8 billion ($13 billion) was cut from the government's affordable housing budget. This plan was what the Tories called Big Society, which shrank the role of the state in the hope that local communities would fill the gap. As their pamphlet explained, the plan was "underpinned by radical reform of public services to build the Big Society where everyone plays their part, shifting power away from central government to the local level as well as getting the best possible value for taxpayers' money." The rationale was that many people simply didn't need these housing supports, and were cheating the system at a time when government spending should be cut to spur economic recovery. This would turn out to be false reasoning that actually prolonged the recession while simultaneously worsening the housing crisis and its associated health problems. Previously, the Labour government had built over 22,000 new "affordable" homes in 2009, helping the 1.8 million households on the waiting list for support. But Labour's program to expand public housing came to a halt across the UK when the Tory government chopped the housing budget.[25]

For a great many families who were barely managing to make ends meet, the cut to housing benefits threw them into financial chaos. During the recession, 93 percent of those signing up for housing benefits had jobs but could not earn enough money to keep pace with rising rents.

The Tory government's austerity measures tipped about 10,000 UK families into homelessness. Homelessness did not rise in the UK immediately after the foreclosure crisis, as it had in the US. But 2010 was a turning point, precisely when the government began cutting its housing support budgets. In those years, homelessness increased by 30 percent, just as homelessness rates began falling in the US with the introduction of its stimulus-financed Homelessness Prevention Program.[26]

These outcomes were not a surprise to the Tory government. In 2010, the British government's Social Security Advisory Committee (SSAC) reported that cuts to the Local Housing Authority "are expected to result in financial hardship, household disruption and displacement, and pressures on non-HB [Housing Benefit] budgets." They even went on to question, given these outcomes, "whether they [the housing cuts] fulfil the Government's own criteria for effective, principled reform of the benefits system."[27]

The Tory government also understood the health impact of austerity. A 2010 report by the Department of Health stated that the average homeless person could expect to live 45 years, compared to over 80 years for the rest of the population. Within five years of losing a home, it was estimated that persons who became homeless—even temporarily—were 4.4 times more likely to die prematurely than people of the same sex and age who kept their homes. And the government was made aware that over time, the costs of homelessness would outstrip any savings achieved through austerity. Shelter, the UK's housing and homelessness charity, published a report finding that the fiscal multiplier for housing was 3.5—so that for each pound in cuts, the economy would slow by a further £3.5. Already in 2011, the housing budget cuts were estimated to have cost 200,000 jobs in construction and housing maintenance.[28]

So if the government knew the immediate human and economic costs of austerity, there were only a few possible reasons to explain why they went ahead with the program. One was ideology—the belief that it is always better to have less government involvement in the economy and housing market.

Another was the mistaken belief that cutting debt would eventually boost the economy, and that homelessness and its trappings were a "price worth paying" for recovery—that short-term pain would lead to long-term gain.

The impacts of austerity were quick to manifest in infectious disease statistics. As more people were living on the streets in London, tuberculosis rates jumped. In total, there were 279 new cases in 2011—an 8 percent rise over the previous year. Homelessness was one of the major factors driving London's TB outbreak; other risk factors included drug use and jail history (which are themselves correlated with homelessness). One TB expert from the Health Protection Agency explained, "The risk of contracting TB is largely confined to a number of specific groups within London. These include the homeless, problem drug and alcohol users, prisoners." This high-risk cluster of people spread the airborne epidemic across the city. As the director of the Health Protection Agency noted in 2012, "TB is one of the biggest public health problems we have."[29]

Tuberculosis wasn't the only dire consequence of cuts to housing safety nets. Other public health problems associated with homelessness have also been on the rise after austerity. As the number of young people sleeping on the streets of London rose by 32 percent between 2010 and 2011, an increasing number have reported assaults and rapes, as well as a descent into substance abuse. To add insult to injury, the austerity didn't even boost the economy to improve the working prospects of the young. Instead, it coincided with a further slowing of the economy, such that the number of unemployed youth (aged sixteen to twenty-four) hit 1 million, a new high.[30]

The contrast between the American and British policy approaches—and the rates of homelessness that ensued—is stark. When the US invested in effective housing programs, it protected many people from the ravages of homelessness, even during a massive recession and housing crisis. But when the UK cut its housing budgets midway through the crisis, its homelessness rates—having held steady during the wave of foreclosures at the start of the crisis—began to rise.

Across Europe, the divergent experiences of the US and UK were recapitulated as different governments chose to pursue either stimulus or austerity in response to recession. We found that those governments pursuing the greatest austerity under pressure from the European Central Bank and International Monetary Fund experienced the most damaging health effects of the housing crisis. And the burden of austerity tended to fall on society's most vulnerable groups: the homeless and disabled.

An illustrative example is Greece, where IMF austerity programs triggered the largest cuts to housing safety nets in all of Europe. Homelessness rose by a quarter, creating the conditions of crowding and drug abuse in downtown Athens that contributed to the spread of HIV. Greece also suffered an epidemic of West Nile Virus in July and August 2010—the first large outbreak of West Nile among humans in Europe since the Romanian outbreak in 1996 and 1997.[31]

While the differences in national data collection practices make it difficult to compare the number of homeless persons across European countries in an absolute sense, it's striking that homelessness rose in virtually all countries cutting their housing support budgets. Ireland suffered the second largest cuts to housing programs after Greece and experienced a 68 percent increase in homelessness, though its rates had previously been falling. Spain and Portugal also implemented deep cuts in housing budgets during their recessions, driving large increases in homelessness. The number of homeless in Barcelona rose 31 percent between 2008 and 2011, from an estimated 2,013 to 2,791. Portugal, similarly, experienced a 25 percent increase in homelessness between 2007 and 2011.[32]

By contrast, in 2008, Finland launched a new program to provide 1,250 dwellings for homeless people, with the ultimate goal of eliminating homelessness by 2015. The Finnish program focused on providing immediate access to housing—similar to San Francisco's Housing First approach—but went a step further by providing social workers to help homeless persons reintegrate into society. Rather than cut housing budgets during its recession, Finland's policy decisions led to a decrease in homelessness between 2009 and 2011, just as homelessness was on the rise in the UK, Ireland, Greece, Spain, and Portugal.[33]

While the US initially stood out as a success story, implementing a highly effective program to curb the health risks of foreclosure, there is now a danger that these gains will be reversed. The US housing stimulus will end prematurely. In 2011, the US Congress cut Housing and Urban Development programs by $3.8 billion, a 10 percent cut to a budget that was—prior to the stimulus package—already at its lowest level in a decade after the Bush presidency had slashed social support programs, following the same ideological reasoning as the British Tories.[34]

These policy decisions resulted in too few homes for too many homeless people across the country. In Dallas, for example, 21,000 people applied for just 5,000 subsidized apartments in May 2011, prompting a stampede in the waiting line for housing applications, which itself led to at least eight injuries. In Oakland, 100,000 people signed up for only 10,000 public housing spots. New York City's homeless shelters burst at the seams after its austerity measures eliminated a rent-subsidy program. The city hit a record of 41,000 homeless people requesting shelter each night. As people were turned away from overcrowded shelters, homelessness was projected to rise again in the US by 5 percent in 2013.[35]

Meanwhile, the foreclosure crisis continues in the US, and California and Florida remain two of the worst-affected states. In Florida in 2011, the state suffered more than 25,000 foreclosures (about one in every 350 homes); at the time of this writing, foreclosures continue at a high rate. Duval County, one of the epicenters of the foreclosure crisis, is experiencing foreclosures at a rate of one in 254 houses, with an accompanying 10 percent rise in homeless people in 2011, the latest year of available data at the time of this writing.[36]

In concert with the rise in homelessness, Florida experienced the worst TB outbreak in the US in two decades. Ninety-nine cases were detected in Jacksonville, and TB has caused at least thirteen deaths. The CDC was called in to investigate, and concluded that the TB spike arose from Duval County's 20 percent rise in homelessness during the recession and the airborne transmission of TB in overcrowded homeless shelters—just as in London.[37]

While the CDC officials monitored the situation in Florida, news of yet another outbreak arrived from across the country—again, in Bakersfield. Things had not gone well since 2007. The California state government had decided to take the path of austerity, cutting the phone lines in some of the state universities that had helped detect the previous West Nile outbreak. About 15 percent of the public health workforce was cut. Following the large austerity measures, the California Department of Public Health's website announced in 2011: "Unfortunately, the California Encephalitis Project (CEP) has discontinued its services due to funding constraints." The program's past triumph in Bakersfield wasn't enough to keep its doors open.[38]

But in June 2012, the crows started dying again, and a seventy-year-old woman turned up at the hospital with confusion and multiple mosquito bites on her arm. West Nile Virus had returned.

This time, Bakersfield was on its own.

CONCLUSION

Healing the Body Economic

What do we mean by our term "the body economic"? It is, of course, a response to the term "the body politic."

Here is a standard dictionary definition of body politic: "a group of persons organized under a single governmental authority; a people considered as a collective unit."[1]

We adapt that format for body economic: "a group of persons organized under a common set of economic policies; a people whose lives are collectively affected by these policies."

The body economic signifies not just the financial systems of which we are all a part, but the health effects of economic policies. As epidemiologists, we study the patterns, causes, and effects of disease. When we think of the body economic, we seek to understand how governmental budgets and economic choices affect life and death, resilience and risk, for entire populations around the world.

Of course, economic policies are not the pathogens or viruses *per se* that directly induce illness. Rather, they are the "causes of the causes" of ill health—the underlying factors that powerfully determine who will be exposed to the greatest health risks. Economic forces determine who is more likely to binge on alcohol, catch tuberculosis in a homeless shelter, or spiral into depression. They can affect not just risk but also protection, determining

139

who is more likely to get social support, maintain a roof over their head, or recover from a bad spell in life. That is why even a small change in government budgets can have large—and possibly unintended—effects on the body economic, for better and for worse.

What are the health effects of the choice between austerity and stimulus? Today there is a vast natural experiment being conducted on the body economic. It is similar to the policy experiments that occurred in the Great Depression, the post-communist crisis in eastern Europe, and the East Asian Financial Crisis. As in those prior trials, health statistics from the Great Recession reveal the deadly price of austerity—a price that can be calculated not just in the ticks to economic growth rates, but in the number of years of life lost and avoidable deaths.

Had the austerity experiments been governed by the same rigorous standards as clinical trials, they would have been discontinued long ago by a board of medical ethics. The side effects of the austerity treatment have been severe and often deadly. The benefits of the treatment have failed to materialize. Instead of austerity, we should enact evidence-based policies to protect health during hard times. Social protection saves lives. If administered correctly, these programs don't bust the budget, but—as we have shown throughout this book—they boost economic growth and improve public health.

Austerity's advocates have ignored evidence of the health and economic consequences of their recommendations. They ignore it even though—as with the International Monetary Fund—the evidence often comes from their own data. Austerity's proponents, such as British Prime Minister David Cameron, continue to write prescriptions of austerity for the body economic, in spite of evidence that it has failed.

Ultimately austerity has failed because it is unsupported by sound logic or data. It is an economic ideology. It stems from the belief that small government and free markets are always better than state intervention. It is a socially constructed myth—a convenient belief among politicians taken advantage of by those who have a vested interest in shrinking the role of the state, in privatizing social welfare systems for personal gain. It does great harm—punishing the most vulnerable, rather than those who caused this recession.[2]

Instead of spouting ideology, we give you facts, explanations, and hard evidence. Figure C.1 demonstrates how austerity has choked off economic growth—deepening recessions. By contrast, governments that have increased

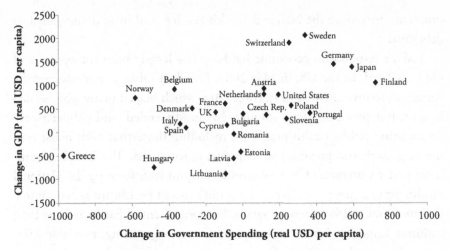

FIGURE C.I Greater Public Spending, Faster Economic Recovery,
2009–2010[3]

public-sector spending have seen faster economic recoveries, which in turn
helps them to grow out of debt.

The greatest tragedy of austerity is not that it has hurt our economies. The
greatest tragedy is the unnecessary human suffering that austerity has caused.
Olivia, Dimitris, Brian, Vladimir, Diane, and Kanya, are a few of the billions
of people harmed by austerity. There is no economic recovery powerful enough
to reverse the damage done to their bodies and their minds. The proponents
of austerity promise that short-term pain leads to long-term gain. That promise
has been repeatedly proven false in recessions both past and present.

Austerity is a choice. And we don't have to choose it.

In previous crises, during times of greater hardship than today, people
chose to respond to recessions with programs like FDR's New Deal. The
New Deal not only prevented public health disasters at a vulnerable time. It
also generated some of the most vital social protection programs that continue today, such as Food Stamps and Social Security. After World War II,
Britain's debt was over 400 percent of its GDP. Yet the UK did not cut its
budget to reduce its deficits. It instead attacked what the economist and social reformer Sir William Beveridge called the "Five Giants": Want, Disease,
Ignorance, Squalor, and Idleness. In 1948, though the British economy was
in shambles, the Labour Party launched hugely successful social protection

programs, including the National Health Service, and in so doing ended its debt crisis.

Today's response to economic hardship has largely been the opposite of the New Deal. In the US, in May 2009, President Obama implemented the American Reinvestment and Recovery Act, which helped many who needed it most. But that US federal stimulus has mostly ended, and politicians are now cutting public health programs, including those that both boost economic growth and prevent hardship during recessions. The British government under Cameron's Conservatives has begun transforming the National Health Service, once considered the world's model healthcare system, into a dysfunctional, market-based program. European Central Banks and the IMF continue imposing brutal austerity on Greece—spawning avoidable HIV and malaria epidemics.[4]

There is an alternative—the democratic option. Iceland suffered the worst banking crisis in its history and came under pressure to follow the dictates of austerity. But after people went into the streets to protest, Iceland's politicians took a radical step. They let the people decide—democratically—whether they would swallow the bitter pill of austerity to pay for their bankers' greed. The loud "No" heard round the world from Iceland was controversial, but history has vindicated the people's choice. Iceland's economy is stronger than before, and in spite of a massive recession, public health actually improved during the recession. Similarly, protesters at the Ford Hunger March during the Great Depression and the Malaysian food riots during the East Asian Financial Crisis also called on their governments to act against austerity. What started as the efforts of a few citizens developed into a social movement, ultimately enabling people to regain control over their body economic from independent bankers and the International Monetary Fund. They were able to transform their countries' futures. Never doubt the ability of organized citizens to make a difference.

If we take the truly democratic option, the first step is to identify those policies that are supported by evidence, and those that are not. With stakes so high, we cannot entrust our decisions to ideologies and beliefs. As the mathematician W. Deming said: "In God we trust; all others must bring data." Often politicians on both the left and the right peddle ideas based on preconceived social theories and economic ideologies, not facts, figures, and hard evidence. Only when citizens have access to, and can engage with, the data can politicians truly be held accountable for their budget decisions, and for the effects of those decisions on life and death. This book, we hope, is a first step to democratizing the health choices of the body economic.

To break the cycle of radical austerity programs, we need a New New Deal. The data show that it worked the first time and the other times it has been tried under different names. Economies bounced back, and people's health improved. Inherent in a New New Deal is a path away from austerity and toward a healthier body economic. To work, it must follow three key principles.

"FIRST, DO NO HARM"

"First, do no harm" is the ancient higher law of the healing professions. Because social and economic policies have collateral effects on health and sickness, the doctors' mantra should become a requirement for all such policies. For democracies to work, we need to know the full consequences of our policy choices. We need to evaluate public policies with the same rigor that we use to evaluate new drug treatments and medical devices. Then we can make informed decisions about the trade-offs: would you prefer a 0.3 percent lower short-term budget deficit or 2,000 more dead Americans? If, during the Great Recession, our policy makers and politicians had done their austerity math in this brutally honest way, they would have likely chosen different priorities.

To ensure that health is considered in all policies that affect it, we should establish public health review mechanisms. At the federal level, we could call it the Office of Health Responsibility. There should be similar offices in government at almost every level. They would be similar to government agencies that protect the public from dangerous products and unsafe medications. The Office of Health Responsibility would analyze government programs and disclose to the public how various policies affect public health.[5]

SECOND, HELP PEOPLE RETURN TO WORK

In hard times, having a stable job is often the best medicine. Unemployment and the fear of unemployment are among the most significant drivers of poor health that people face in an economic crisis. The stock market may be bullish again, but unemployment is still too high to constitute a truly democratic recovery—that is, recovery for all, not just a few. Innovative programs like the active labor market programs (ALMPs) help the unemployed stay active during recessions. ALMPs prevent depression and suicide among not just the unemployed but also the employed who may be worried about losing their job. But ALMPs can also get people back to work, thus saving the government money in unemployment compensation and also increasing the labor supply, an engine of economic growth and recovery.

Jobs can be hard to find in times of recession, so economic stimulus is also needed to help create work. As Keynes argued, perhaps a bit tongue in cheek, it would be better to employ half the unemployed to bury fifty pound notes and the other half to dig them up again than to have people remain idle and on unemployment checks. If we wish to do more to activate workers and boost the economy, however, we have to enact the right kind of stimulus. Health, education, and social protection programs have among the highest fiscal multipliers. In the case of the health sector, public investment boosts the economy by more than three dollars for every dollar spent. Meanwhile, the fiscal multiplier for bank bailouts and defense spending is often negative. With this type of government spending, the economy shrinks, because the money tends to flow out of productive new business ventures that employ people, and to private bank accounts and offshore tax havens.[6]

THIRD, INVEST IN PUBLIC HEALTH

If any family member is sick and suffering, we do all we can to help. The same logic applies to the body economic. At a time when people are hurting from recession, politicians should act to protect people from the dangers of unemployment and poverty. They should enact laws that provide care based on people's health needs, rather than their ability to pay. This approach would eliminate many costly hospitalizations caused by care provided too late—as with Diane. A recession may hurt people's pocketbooks, but no one should lose their access to healthcare because of an economic downturn. As citizens we should call on our government to make decisions that safeguard public health. In the UK the opposite is being done, with the dismantling of the National Health Service.

It is easy to lose sight of how important disease prevention programs are until it is too late. The US Centers for Disease Control and Prevention, and its counterparts in Europe, protect our communities from epidemics as varied as food-borne illnesses and tuberculosis, usually without any fanfare. The California Encephalitis Project helped Bakersfield curb its West Nile epidemic, but when a second outbreak happened in 2012, budget cuts left Bakersfield without critical assistance. This strong public-sector presence in health and healthcare is necessary to improve disease surveillance, speed up our response to epidemics, and prevent us from experiencing more tragedies. In the US, we have seen what happens when we cede health to the private sector. Public health departments are left to pick up the pieces when private companies fail to protect people during hard times. Public health programs need to be supported, not slashed, in times of great distress.

To achieve a real, lasting human recovery, we must fundamentally change the way we think about what's important. Economic growth is a means to an end, not the end in itself. This was Robert Kennedy's fundamental insight in his 1968 presidential campaign speech. What good is an increased growth rate, he asked, if it is hazardous to our health?

When we tell our children about the Great Recession, they will judge us not by growth rates or by deficit reductions. They will judge us by how well we took care of society's most vulnerable, and whether we chose to address our community's most basic health needs: healthcare, housing, and jobs.

The ultimate source of any society's wealth is its people. Investing in their health is a wise choice in the best of times, and an urgent necessity in the worst of times.

NOTES

PREFACE

1. See Robert Wood Johnson Foundation. 2009. *Breaking Through on the Social Determinants of Health and Health Disparities: An Approach To Message Translation*. RWJF Issue brief 7. Of course, everyone must die of something, but decades of public health research have shown that over half of all deaths are premature, from diseases that could have been prevented. One study concluded that "in the United States, perhaps 10–15 percent [of preventable mortality], could be avoided by better availability or quality of medical care." The other 85–90 percent are attributable to sociological factors such as the environment and smoking. See J. McGinnis, P. Williams-Russo, J. R. Knickman. 2002. "The Case for More Active Policy Attention to Health Promotion," *Health Affairs* v21(2): 78–93.

World Health Organization. 2013. *The Determinants of Health*. Available at: http://www.who.int/hia/evidence/doh/en/

2. Source for Figure P.1: EuroStat 2013 Statistics. Gross domestic product is seasonally adjusted and adjusted by working days. Baseline is 2nd quarter of 2008.

3. Source for Figure P.2: Adapted from: D. Stuckler, S. Basu, M. McKee. 2010. "Budget Crises, Health, and Social Welfare Programmes," *British Medical Journal* v340:c3311. Social welfare in purchasing-power-parity adjusted, constant 2005 US dollars per head of population. Life expectancy is at birth.

4. In the US, road traffic deaths fell to 60-year lows when people drove less for reasons such as having less money to pay for gasoline.

5. *The Gospel According to RFK: Why It Matters Now*, edited with commentary by Norman MacAfee (New York, 2008), p. 45.

INTRODUCTION

1. Olivia was a patient seen by Sanjay's colleagues in the pediatrics department at a hospital in California. Her name and any potential details of her story that might identify her have been changed to protect her identity.

2. About 770,000 additional Americans during the recession would binge on alcohol, as we found in Bor, et al. 2013. "Alcohol Use During the Great Recession of 2008–2009," *Alcohol and Alcoholism.* Available at:
http://alcalc.oxfordjournals.org/content/early/2013/01/28/alcalc.agt002.short

3. Niki Kitsantonis, "Pensioner's Suicide Continues to Shake Greece," *New York Times*, April 5, 2012. Available at: http://www.nytimes.com/2012/04/06/world/europe/pensioners-suicide-continues-to-shake-greece.html?_r=1&

4. Makis Papasimakopoulos, "Note Found on Syntagma Suicide Victim," *Athens News*, April 5, 2012. http://www.athensnews.gr/portal/1/54580

5. A. Kentikelenis, M. Karanikolos, I. Papanicolas, S. Basu, M. McKee, D. Stuckler. 2011. "Health Effects of Financial Crisis: Omens of a Greek Tragedy," *The Lancet* 378(9801): 1457–58.

6. M. Suhrcke and D. Stuckler. 2012. "Will the Recession Be Bad for Our Health? It Depends," *Social Science & Medicine* v74(5): 647–53; C. Ruhm. 2008. "A Healthy Economy Can Break Your Heart," *Demography* v44(4): 829–48; D. Stuckler, C. Meissner, P. Fishback, S. Basu, M. McKee. 2012. "Was the Great Depression a Cause or Correlate of Significant Mortality Declines? An Epidemiological Response to Granados," *Journal of Epidemiology & Community Health*; K. Smolina, et al. 2012. "Determinants of the Decline in Mortality from Acute Myocardial Infarction in England Between 2002 and 2010: Linked National Database Study," *British Medical Journal* v344:d8059.

7. International Monetary Fund. Oct 2012. "World Economic Outlook, Coping with High Debt and Sluggish Growth." Available at: http://www.imf.org/external/pubs/ft/weo/2012/02/pdf/text.pdf

PART I: HISTORY

Chapter 1: Tempering the Great Depression

1. J. Burns, "Atos Benefit Bullies Killed My Sick Dad, Says Devastated Kieran, 13," *Daily Record*, Nov 1, 2012. Available at: http://www.dailyrecord.co.uk/news/scottish-news/atos-killed-my-dad-says-boy-1411100

2. "Public Sector, Welfare Faces Budget Axe—Cameron," Reuters UK, June 18, 2010. Available at: http://uk.reuters.com/article/2010/06/18/uk-britain-budget-cameron-idUKTRE65H5TC20100618; "Conservative Conference: Cameron in Benefit Cuts Warning," BBC, Oct 7, 2012. Available at: http://www.bbc.co.uk/news/uk-politics-19864056. See Table 2: "Estimates for Fraud and Error by Client Group and Error Type and Error Reason—Overpayments (2011/2012)." Less than 0.1 percent of total fraud, totaling £2 million, were estimated to have arisen from fraud surrounding conditions of entitlement. In Department for Work & Pensions. Fraud and Error in the Benefit System. Available at: http://statistics.dwp.gov.uk/asd/asd2/index.php?page=fraud_error;

M. D'Arcy, "Protests Against Paralympics Partner Get Senior Support," 2012, *Public Service UK*. Available at: http://www.publicservice.co.uk/news_story.asp?id=20757

3. Atos newsroom website: "The Department for Work and Pensions Awards Two of the PIP Assessment Contracts to Atos." Available at: http://atos.net/en-us/Newsroom /en-us/Press_Releases/2012/2012_08_02_01.htm and http://uk.atos.net/en-uk/careers /career_directions/systems_integration/default.htm; R. Ramesh, "Atos Wins £400m Deals to Carry Out Disability Benefit Tests," *The Guardian*, Aug 2, 2012. Available at: http://www.guardian.co.uk/society/2012/aug/02/atos-disability-benefit-tests

4. "Work Test Centres 'Lack Disabled Access'," BBC, Nov 21, 2012. Available at: http://www.bbc.co.uk/news/uk-politics-20423701; Burns, "Atos Benefit Bullies."

5. See also J. Ball, "Welfare Fraud Is a Drop in the Ocean Compared to Tax Avoidance," *The Guardian*, Feb 3, 2013. Available at: http://www.guardian.co.uk/commentisfree /2013/feb/01/welfare-fraud-tax-avoidance; Atos's official response was that "We do not make decisions on people's benefit entitlement or on welfare policy but we will continue to make sure that service that we provide is as highly professional and compassionate as it can be." Cited in M. D'Arcy, "Protests Against Paralympics Partner Get Senior Support," *Public Service UK*, 2012. Available at: http://www.publicservice.co.uk/news_story .asp?id=20757

6. Just as the writings of John Maynard Keynes and John Kenneth Galbraith came back into popularity, so too did other histories of the Depression—such as that of Milton Friedman, a conservative free-market economist. Whereas Keynes had been a proponent of government spending to stimulate demand in the economy, Friedman emphasized the role of monetary policy—to lower interest rates and increase the money supply, so that people would resume borrowing and the market would start moving again. Friedman's school of thought emphasized the importance of the market. For the market to work, it would be necessary for those who made bad decisions to suffer the consequences.

7. M. Thoma, "Too Much Too Big to Fail," *Economist's View*, Sept 2, 2010. Available at: http://economistsview.typepad.com/economistsview/2010/09/too-much-too-big-to -fail.html

8. S. Fleming, "UK Hit Hardest by Banking Bailout, with £1 Trillion Spent to Save the City," *Daily Mail*, Dec 17, 2009. Available at: http://www.dailymail.co.uk/news /article-1236800/UK-hit-hardest-banking-bailout-1trillion-spent-save-City.html; see also http://www.pbs.org/wnet/need-to-know/economy/the-true-cost-of-the-bank-bailout /3309/. Government bailouts saved many corporations, and by 2013, many had paid back the loans, with interest. L. Vo and J. Goldstein, "Where the Bailouts Stand, in 1 Graphic," *NPR Planet Money*, Oct 9, 2010. Available at: http://www.npr.org/blogs /money/2012/09/10/160886823/where-the-bailouts-stand-in-1-graphic; "AIG Subsidiary Parties in Style in OC, Two Weeks after Bailout," *Orange County Register*, Oct 2, 2008. Available at: http://taxdollars.ocregister.com/2008/10/02/after-federal-bailout -aig-fetes-in-style-in-oc/; M. Wolfe, "Keynes Offers Us the Best Way to Think About

the Financial Crisis," *Financial Times,* Dec 23, 2008. Available at: http://www.ft.com /intl/cms/s/0/be2dbf2c-d113-11dd-8cc3-000077b07658.html#axzz2IArd1Y5r

9. P. Krugman, "Inflation Lessons," *New York Times*, Aug 25, 2012. Available at: http://krugman.blogs.nytimes.com/2012/08/25/inflation-lessons/

10. P. Krugman, "Soup Kitchens Caused the Great Depression," *New York Times*, Nov 3, 2012. Available at: http://krugman.blogs.nytimes.com/2012/11/03/soup-kitchens -caused-the-great-depression/

11. D. Stuckler, S. Basu, M. McKee, M. Suhrcke. 2010. "Responding to the Economic Crisis: A Primer for Public Health Professionals," *Journal of Public Health* v32(3): 298–306. Available at: http://jpubhealth.oxfordjournals.org/content/32/3/298.short; T. Pettinger, "UK National Debt," *Economics: UK Economy Statistics*, Jan 23, 2013. Available at: http://www.economicshelp.org/blog/334/uk-economy/uk-national-debt/

12. J. Hardman, "The Great Depression and the New Deal. Poverty & Prejudice: Social Security at the Crossroads." Available at: http://www.stanford.edu/class/e297c /poverty_prejudice/soc_sec/hgreat.htm; D. Stuckler, S. Basu, C. Meissner, P. Fishback, M. McKee. 2012. "Banking Crises and Mortality During the Great Depression: Evidence from US Urban Populations, 1927–1939," *Journal of Epidemiology and Community Health* v66:410–19.

13. Increasing investments, typically by the wealthiest, caused the average stock to quadruple in price between 1921 and 1929. The super-rich, including the Rockefellers, Fords, Carnegies, and Vanderbilts, helped drive a real estate bubble. Sellers would reap small profits quickly by turning over properties to the next buyer in a high-demand marketplace; John Kenneth Galbraith, *The Great Crash: 1929* (Boston, 1988); see also E. N. White, "Lessons from the Great American Real Estate Boom and Bust," National Bureau of Economic Research, 2009, Working Paper 15573. Available at: http://www .clevelandfed.org/research/seminars/2010/white.pdf. Most people who bought land never set foot in the state they were buying in. Instead, real estate speculators hired young, attractive men and women to advertise the land and accept down payments on an ad hoc basis.

14. Hardman, "The Great Depression and the New Deal. Poverty & Prejudice"; T. H. Watkins, *The Great Depression: America in the 1930s* (Boston, 1993).

15. Racial tensions also escalated: in 1933 alone, twenty-four lynchings of black Americans were officially reported—likely to be an underestimate as few lynchings were ever addressed by the police at the time. Centers for Disease Control, "CDC Study Finds Suicide Rates Rise and Fall with Economy," April 14, 2011. Available at: http:// www.cdc.gov/media/releases/2011/p0414_suiciderates.html. See also "Did Investors Really Jump out of Windows?" Available at: http://news.kontentkonsult.com/2008 /10/did-investors-really-jump-out-of.html; George H. Douglas, *Skyscrapers: A Social History of the Very Tall Building in America* (London, 2004).

16. "Death Rate Drops in North America: Mortality Figures for This Year Show Lowest Level for the United States and Canada," *New York Times*, Oct 26, 1930. As the

New York Times further reported that year, "the country was in the grip of the most serious industrial depression in a generation. No large area was exempt from its effects. Town and country, farmer and mechanic, East and West, North and South all were affected. Everywhere poverty was accentuated. Family budgets had to be sharply reduced. Men and women skimped their own rations to provide for their children. The demands on charitable organizations were without parallel, coming often from families who never before knew the meaning of want. By all the signs and all the precedents, hard times so seriously prolonged should have brought in their train disease and death. Actually, 1931 was one of the healthiest years in the history of the country. The evidence is overwhelming." Cited in "No Slump in Health," *New York Times*, Jan 5, 1932. For further contemporary analysis see "Sees Public Health Unhurt by Slump," *New York Times*, Oct 30, 1931.

17. "It is indubitable evidence," Sydenstricker concluded, "that up to this time unemployment, diminished purchasing power, altered standards of living, even privation, have not killed very many of the population. Just what caused this gratifying showing is difficult to say." See E. Sydenstricker. 1933. "Health and the Depression," *Milbank Mem Q* v11:273–80.

18. Another physician agreed, speculating that the "the weather may have been a contributing factor," preventing outbreaks of pneumonias. Yet another doctor suggested that "the medical profession is becoming more and more skilled in the diagnosis and treatment of disease." Another group of thinkers held that it was perhaps the Depression itself, leading to "a more normal mode of living than in boom times" and lower stress levels. All of these explanations, however, seemed unlikely. Most of the changes in death rates didn't correspond to winter-time diseases, and the winter was not actually particularly mild—especially for those living in shantytowns. There had not been any new discoveries of drugs or new techniques in surgery. Sulfonamide antibiotics would not be invented until the late 1930s, and penicillin until the 1940s. It was also unclear how the Depression might improve health through less stress. All of the historical evidence suggests that people faced enormous stress during the Depression—much more so than in the boom years of the roaring 20s. Cited in D. Stuckler, S. Basu, et al., "Banking Crises and Mortality During the Great Depression"; see also US Climate at a Glance, *National Climatic Data Center*. Available at: http://www.ncdc.noaa.gov/oa/climate/research/cag3/cag3.html; R. Pearl, *The Rate of Living* (New York, 1928).

19. For more details about our study see Stuckler, et al., "Banking Crises and Mortality During the Great Depression." We are grateful to our colleague Professor Price Fishback for making these data available. Mortality data came from the Center for Disease Control, US Historical Mortality Database, 1929–1937 (Atlanta, 1929). Banking crisis data were taken from Federal Deposit Insurance Corporation Bank Data and Statistics, 2010.

20. Source for Figure 1.1: Adapted from Stuckler, et al. "Banking Crises and Mortality During the Great Depression."

21. Source for Figure 1.2: Ibid.

22. A. R. Omran. 1971. "The Epidemiologic Transition: A Theory of the Epidemiology of Population Change," *Milbank Mem Fund Q* v49:509–38. Available at: http://www.jstor.org/stable/10.2307/3349375

23. Other commentators have suggested that the Great Depression was the direct cause of very large health improvements. See, for example, J. Tapia-Granados and A. Diez-Roux. 2009. "Life and Death During the Great Depression," *Proceedings of the National Academy of Sciences* v106(41): 17290–95. Their analysis used 20 data points from aggregated US data. One sign of a lack of validity in their analysis is in attributing the Great Depression as a cause of short-term improvements in cancer. Yet, at the time, no effective cancer treatments existed, and changes in cancer would require decades to occur. When we revisited their analysis using state-level data, and disentangled short- and long-term trends, we demonstrated how such implausible findings were spurious. See D. Stuckler, S. Basu, et al. 2012. "Was the Great Depression a Cause or Correlate of Significant Mortality Declines? An Epidemiological Response to Granados," *Journal of Epidemiology and Community Health.*

24. For methodological details see Stuckler, et al. "Banking Crises and Mortality During the Great Depression." Briefly, we used a Hodrick-Prescott filter to differentiate short- and long-term trends. This is a technique, which decomposes movements in time-series data into short-term and trend components in two steps. First, the HP filter finds a smoothed time trend in the log level of the mortality for each state. Then, short-run deviations of the original time series from the estimated long-run trend can be used for subsequent statistical analysis. We performed a sensitivity analysis using different smoothing parameters for estimating long-term trends (the standard is 6.25, although Granados and colleagues use 100), finding that our results did not differ qualitatively. We also replicated our analysis using short-term changes in the mortalities (using annual levels of the percentage change in mortalities). We also controlled for relatively fixed differences between states, such as geographic location, by means of state dummy variables. Overall, we found bank suspensions were significantly associated with increased suicide rates but reduced transport-related death rates. No effect was observed on cardiovascular death rates, homicide rates, pneumonia, cirrhosis, or cancer death rates. Because the population risk of deaths attributable to road traffic accidents (RTA) was 50 percent higher than suicides, the reductions due to RTA outweighed the rises in suicides, yielding a negative net effect of bank suspensions on all-cause mortality.

25. Source for Figure 1.3: Adapted from Stuckler, et al. "Banking Crises and Mortality During the Great Depression."

26. Indeed, so many people died in accidents that car ownership had to be disclosed to life insurance companies. "Vital Statistics." 1932. Report of the *American Journal of Public Health*. Available at: http://ajph.aphapublications.org/doi/pdf/10.2105/AJPH.22.4.413. See Associated Press, "Traffic Deaths Drop in 1932; First Decline in Auto His-

tory," *New York Times*, Nov 28, 1932; M. Kafka, "An Appalling Waste of Life Marks the Automobile," *New York Times*, Aug 28, 1932.

27. A. Reeves, D. Stuckler, M. McKee, D. Gunnell, S. S. Chang, S. Basu. 2012. "Increase in State Suicide Rates in the USA During Economic Recession," *The Lancet* v380:1813–14.

B. Barr, D. Taylor-Robinson, A. Scott-Samuel, M. McKee, D. Stuckler. 2012. "Suicides Associated with the 2008–10 Economic Recession in England: A Time-Trend Analysis," *British Medical Journal* v345:e5142. Available at: http://www.bmj.com/content /345/bmj.e5142

28. See for example, "U.S Highway Deaths at Lowest Level in 60 Years," *Washington Post*, Sept 9, 2010. According to the Governors Highway Safety Association, "We attribute the progress to a host of factors, including increased seat belt use, stronger enforcement of drunk driving laws, better roads, safer vehicles and an increasingly well-coordinated approach to safety among state stakeholders and the federal government. [Transportation] Secretary [Ray] LaHood's focus on distracted driving has brought an unprecedented focus to behavioral highway safety, and as a result, lives are being saved." The more likely explanation for this favorable turn is the Great Recession itself. See also M. Cooper, "Happy Motoring: Traffic Deaths at 61-Year Low," *New York Times*, April 1, 2011. Available at: http://www.nytimes.com/2011/04/01/us/01driving.html?_r=0

NIDirect Government Services, "Lowest Number of Road Deaths on Record," Jan 3, 2013. Available at: http://www.nidirect.gov.uk/news-jan13-lowest-number-of-road -deaths-on-record; for Ireland see Ireland's National Police Service. Garda National Traffic Bureau. Fatalities and Other Traffic Statistics. Available at: http://www.garda .ie/Controller.aspx?Page=138. The consequences have had knock-on effects elsewhere. Across the globe in India, more and more farmers are selling kidneys to pay debts, as the black market for organs has increased.

29. Edward Behr, *Prohibition: Thirteen Years That Changed America* (Boston, 1996), pp. 78–79. For additional time-trend estimates based on aggregate, rather than state-level data comparing "wet" and "dry" states, see J. A. Miron and J. Zwiebel. 1991. "Alcohol Consumption During Prohibition," *American Economic Review* v81(2): 242–47.

30. M. Davis, *Jews and Booze: Becoming American in the Age of Prohibition* (New York, 2012), p. 191.

31. Source for Figure 1.4: Adapted from Stuckler, et al. "Banking Crises and Mortality During the Great Depression."

32. Total government debt also increased from $16.2 billion in 1930 to $19.4 billion in 1932.

33. Charles R. Geisst, *Wall Street: A History* (New York, 2012).

34. Maurice Sugar, *The Ford Hunger March* (Berkeley, 1980), p. 108.

35. Irving Bernstein, *A History of the American Worker 1933–1941: The Turbulent Years* (Boston, 1970), pp. 499–571. The Socialist Party of America's membership doubled between 1928 and 1932.

36. William E. Leuchtenburg, *Franklin D. Roosevelt and the New Deal 1932–1940* (New York, 1963), pp. 1–17. It is perhaps ironic that the New Deal, which in part arose from Socialist agitation, made the Socialist Party much less relevant.

37. C. E. Horn and H. S. Schaffner, *Work in America: An Encyclopedia of History, Policy, and Society* (Santa Barbara, 2003). We are grateful to Price Fishback and his team for the insight about marked variations in state's implementation of the New Deal.

38. As part of election politics, more relief funds were distributed to cities with Democratic presidential candidates, those with more representation on the House Labor committee during the New Deal, and those with Democratic governors.

39. E. Amenta, K. Dunleavy, M. Bernstein. 1994. "Stolen Thunder? Huey Long's 'Share Our Wealth,' Political Mediation, and the Second New Deal," *American Sociological Review* v59(5): 678–702. Available at: http://www.jstor.org/discover/10.2307 /2096443?uid=3739560&uid=2&uid=4&uid=3739256&sid=21101670536097; W. I. Hair, *The Kingfish and His Realm: The Life and Times of Huey P. Long* (Baton Rouge, 1991).

40. See also P. Fishback, M. R. Haines, S. Kantor. 2007. "Births, Deaths and New Deal Relief During the Great Depression," *The Review of Economics and Statistics* v89(1): 1–14.

41. Cited in G. Perrott and S. D. Collins. 1934. "Sickness and the Depression: A Preliminary Report upon a Survey of Wage-earning Families in Ten Cities," *The Milbank Memorial Fund Quarterly* v12(3): 218–24. Available at: http://www.jstor.org /discover/10.2307/3347891?uid=3739560&uid=2&uid=4&uid=3739256& sid=21101670536097

42. Our colleague Dr. Price Fishback, an economist at University of Arizona, looked at the data and drew similar conclusions: "Even though relief programs were targeted at a broad range of social and economic problems, they display similar costs per life saved as modern programs that are targeted more specifically at reducing mortality, such as Medicaid." See Fishback, et al., "Births, Deaths and New Deal Relief."

43. The First New Deal totaled about 10–20 percent of GDP. In the six years after it was implemented, government spending doubled. Yet it was not until World War II and a large rise in government stimulus in the 1940s that the Depression ended. Price Fishback and colleagues estimate that the personal income multiplier for public works and relief was around 1.67. This is similar in magnitude to our estimates for total government spending and social protection, cited in chapter 4. P. Fishback and V. Kachanovskaya, "In Search of the Multiplier for Federal Spending in the States During the New Deal." Working Paper. 2010. Available at: http://econ.arizona.edu/docs/Working_Papers /2010/WP-10-09.pdf

44. And the New Deal put in place reforms to prevent another recession from occurring. The 1933 Banking Act, the Glass-Steagall Act, as it is commonly known, separated commercial and investment banking and prohibited banks from dealing in debt and derivative securities, the types of investments that had precipitated the Stock Market

Crash of 1929. Because of Glass-Steagall, more than six decades passed without another Crash or Depression. But, sadly, in 1999, after intense lobbying by the banks, a Republican Congress and a Democratic president, Bill Clinton, repealed Glass-Steagall. The floodgates reopened for risky investment to create another real estate bubble and a Great Recession. In 1939 Roosevelt also passed an additional "undistributed profits tax," establishing the principle that corporate earnings could be taxed to pay for the negative effects of corporations' actions on the rest of the economy. But it was watered down by Congress and soon expired. "The Wall Street Fix: Mr. Weill Goes to Washington: The Long Demise of Glass-Steagall," *Frontline*, PBS, May 5, 2003.

45. M. Harhay, J., Bor, S. Basu, M. McKee, J. Mindell, N. Shelton, D. Stuckler, "Differential Impact of Economic Recession on Alcohol Use Among White British Adults, 2006–2009," unpublished analysis; J. Bor, S. Basu, A. Coutts, M. McKee, D. Stuckler. In press. "Alcohol Use During the Great Depression of 2008–2009," *Alcohol and Alcoholism*.

Chapter 2: The Post-Communist Mortality Crisis

1. United Nations Development Program. *The Human Cost of Transition: Human Security in South East Europe* (New York: UNDP). Available at: http://hdr.undp.org/en /reports/regional/europethecis/name,2799,en.html. Technically Russia was not a state until 1992. World Bank World Development Indicators 2013 edition. Available at: http://data.worldbank.org/indicator. See also J. DaVanzo and G. Farnsworth, "Russia's Demographic 'Crisis'," RAND, 1996. The Russian census had projected that the population would grow during this period, while the official US estimates also forecast continued growth. However, astute demographers, including Nicholas Eberstadt, who had been studying Russia's mortality data since the early 1980s were quick to recognize that mortality had been on a long-term adverse path and that the early-1990s reflected a short-term shock superimposed upon this long-term deterioration.

2. USSR Census 1989. Published by the State Committee on Statistics. *Natsional'ny Sostav Naseleniia Chast' II*. Informatsionno-izdatel'ski Tsentr (Moscow, 1989). See also "Abandoned Cool Mining Town in Siberia: Kadychan, Russia, *Sometimes Interesting*, July 24, 2011. Available at: http://sometimes-interesting.com/2011/07/24/abandoned -coal-mining-town-in-siberia-kadykchan-russia/. See population statistics from Russian Census 2002: Всероссийская перепись населения 2002 гóда.

3. E. Tragakes and S. Lessof, *Healthcare Systems in Transition: Russian Federation* (Copenhagen: European Observatory on Health Systems and Policies, 2003).

There had always been a low level of unemployment of about 1.4 percent in 1990. S. Rosefielde. 2000. "The Civilian Labour Force and Unemployment in the Russian Federation," *Europe-Asia Studies* v52(8): 1433–47. Available at: http://www.tandfonline .com/doi/pdf/10.1080/713663146. Estimates of poverty rates based on analysis using the Russian Longitudinal Monitoring Survey; see P. Mosley and A. Mussurov, "Poverty and Economic Growth in Russia's Regions," Sheffield Department of Economics, 2009. Available at: http://eprints.whiterose.ac.uk/10002/1/SERPS2009006.pdf; London School of Hygiene & Tropical Medicine, "Living Conditions, Lifestyles, and Health Survey 2001." Details available at: http://www.lshtm.ac.uk/centres/ecohost/research _projects/hitt.html

4. See also G. Kitching. 1998. "The Revenge of the Peasant? The Collapse of Large-Scale Russian Agriculture and the Role of the Peasant 'Private Plot' in That Collapse, 1991–97," *The Journal of Peasant Studies* v26(1): 43–81; R. J. Struyk and K. Angelici. 1996. "The Russian Dacha Phenomenon," *Housing Studies* v11(2). Available at: http://www.tandfonline.com/doi/abs/10.1080/02673039608720854

5. These projections were done by the US Bureau of the Census, led by Stephen Rapawy. See S. Rosefielde. 2000. "The Civilian Labour Force and Unemployment in the Russian Federation," *Europe-Asia Studies* v52(8): 1433–47. Available at: http://www .tandfonline.com/doi/pdf/10.1080/713663146. The massive loss of people was in part driven by declining fertility (as documented by G. Cornia and R. Paniccia in their seminal book, *The Mortality Crisis in Transitional Economies* [New York, 2000]), but in terms of workforce losses the break that began in 1990 would not have affected working-ages as youth would not have become adults within the eight year timeframe.

6. United Nations Development Programme, "The Human Cost of Transition: Human Security in South East Europe." Available at: http://hdr.undp.org/en/reports /regional/europethecis/name,2799,en.html

7. S. Rosefielde. 2001. "Premature Deaths; Russia's Radical Economic Transition in Soviet Perspective," *Europe-Asia Studies* v53(8): 1159–76.

8. Source for Figure 2.1: Authors. Data from the World Bank World Development Indicators 2013 Edition.

9. M. Field. 1999. "Reflections on a Painful Transition: From Socialized to Insurance Medicine in Russia," *Croatian Medical Journal* v40(2). Available at: http://neuron .mefst.hr/docs/CMJ/issues/1999/40/2/10234063.pdf; cited from S. Sachs, "Crumbled Empire, Shattered Health," *Newsday*, Oct 26, 1997, p. A4. In 1937, the head of the census was executed for getting the "wrong" data.

10. Another sign that the former Soviet mortality data were reliable was that as all-cause death rates had increased greatly between 1991 and 1994, but breast and lung cancers rates among all age groups over the whole decade were steady. This stability is an indication of internal validity, as cancer deaths should not fluctuate rapidly and aren't directly impacted by the economy. See V. Shkolnikov, M. McKee, D. Leon, L. Chenet. 1999. "Why Is the Death Rate from Lung Cancer Falling in the Russian Federation?" *Eur J Epidemiology* 15:203–6.

11. M. McKee. 1999. "Alcohol in Russia," *Alcohol and Alcoholism* 34:824–29; M. McKee, A. Britton. 1998. "The Positive Relationship Between Alcohol and Heart Disease in Eastern Europe: Potential Physiological Mechanisms," *Journal of the Royal Society of Medicine* v91; O. Nilssen, et al. 2005. "Alcohol Consumption and Its Relation

to Risk Factors for Cardiovascular Disease in the North-west of Russia: The Arkhangelsk Study," *International Journal of Epidemiology* v34(4): 781–88. Available at: http://ije.oxfordjournals.org/content/34/4/781.full

12. D. Lester. 1994. "The Association Between Alcohol Consumption and Suicide and Homicide Rates: A Study of 13 Nations," *Alcohol and Alcoholism* v30(4): 465–68. Available at: http://alcalc.oxfordjournals.org/content/30/4/465.short; M. McKee, A. Britton. 1998. "The Positive Relationship Between Alcohol and Heart Disease in Eastern Europe: Potential Physiological Mechanisms," *Journal of the Royal Society of Medicine* v91; C. S. Fusch, et al. "Alcohol Consumption and Mortality Among Women," *New England Journal of Medicine* a332(10): 1245–50. Available at: http://www.ncbi.nlm.nih.gov/pubmed/7708067; R. Doll, et al. 1994. "Mortality in Relation to Consumption of Alcohol: 13 Years' Observations on Male British Doctors," *BMJ* v309(6959). Available at: http://www.ncbi.nlm.nih.gov/pmc/articles/PMC2541157/; A. L. Klastky, M. A. Armstrong, G. D. Friedman. 1992. "Alcohol and Mortality," *Ann Intern Med* v117(8): 646–54. Available at: http://www.ncbi.nlm.nih.gov/pubmed/1530196

13. World Health Organization. European Health for All Database 2012 edition. See also V. M. Shkolnikov and A. Nemtsov, "The Anti-Alcohol Campaign and Variations in Russian Mortality," Ch. 8 in *Premature Death in the New Independent States* (Washington, DC, 1997). Available at: http://www.nap.edu/openbook.php?record_id=5530&page=239; V. Shkolnikov, G. Cornia, D. Leon, F. Mesle. 1998. "Causes of the Russian Mortality Crisis: Evidence and Interpretations," *World Development* v25:1995–2011.

Some economists have contended Russia's mortality crisis in the 1990s was simply a rebound effect from ending the anti-alcohol campaign. The Russians who lived through Gorbachev's anti-alcohol campaign were, they argued, effectively "dead-men walking"—as soon as the campaign ended, they would simply drink themselves to death (e.g., Jay Bhattacharya, Christina Gathmann, and Grant Miller, "The Gorbachev Anti-Alcohol Campaign and Russia's Mortality Crisis," March 2011. Available at: https://iriss.stanford.edu/sites/all/files/iriss/Russia_mortality_crisis.pdf). But when we looked closely at the data, we found that the people who were saved by Gorbachev's campaign weren't dying after the campaign ended. If they were, the dip in death rates in persons ages 20 to 24 in 1985 would correspond to an equal rise in deaths in persons 25 to 29 in 1990. But it did not. Instead, the rise in deaths in the early 1990s vastly outweighed the falls between 1985 and 1987 by more than 2 million deaths. In other words, the end of the anti-alcohol campaign was not the major cause of the rise in drinking-related deaths among Russian men.

Shkolnikov and colleagues investigated the possibility of a rebound effect in a detailed set of epidemiological studies in the mid-1990s, arriving at similar conclusions as we did. Shkolnikov et al. 1998 report evidence that the age-distribution of the mortality drops between 1985 and 1987 and increases between 1988 and 1992 were similar. However, they also find that the excess deaths were beyond the deaths avoided during the 1985–1987 improvements. Further, the probabilities of death in 1995 had become much higher than the initial levels of 1984 (see p. 1999). An examination of mortality fluctuations between 1985 and 1987 and those occurring between 1992 and 1994 show that the magnitude of the mortality drop under Gorbachev's anti-alcohol campaign is far outweighed by the rise in between 1992 and 1994. Among others, see Shkolnikov and Nemtsov, "The Anti-Alcohol Campaign and Variations in Russian Mortality"; and V. M. Shkolnikov, D. A. Leon, S. Adamets, E. Andreev, and A. Deev. 1998. "Educational Level and Adult Mortality in Russia: An Analysis of Routine Data 1979 to 1994," *Soc Sci Med* 47:357–69; Cornia and Paniccia, in their book, *The Mortality Crisis in Transition Economies*, conclude that, "Contrary to widespread opinion, the mortality changes of the 1990s are not a continuation of past trends" (Ch. 1, p. 4), which they subsequently prove (Ch. 1, section 5, pp. 20–21), noting that "In the case of Russia, Ukraine and Bulgaria (for males) the pre-transition trend is unable to capture the recent evolution of life expectancy. In addition, in the case of Russia, the negative divergences from the life expectancy trend observed during the transition outpace by far the positive ones estimated for the years of the anti-alcohol campaign." Cornia and Paniccia further indicate that "even if causality between the initial falls and the subsequent rises in mortality could be unambiguously established, the former would explain only between 25 and 35 percent of the latter." For a more detailed discussion see Appendix 1.1 and 5.5 in D. Stuckler, "Social Causes of Post-communist Mortality," doctoral dissertation, University of Cambridge, 2009.

14. Alcohol became such a contributing factor to illness that people were much more likely to die over weekends in the 1990s, when they were free from work and went on weekend-long benders—leaving the country in a hangover that lasted from Saturday morning to Monday. M. McKee, et al. 2006. "The Composition of Surrogate Alcohols Consumed in Russia," *Alcoholism: Clinical and Experimental Research*. Available at: http://onlinelibrary.wiley.com/doi/10.1097/01.alc.0000183012.93303.90/abstract. See D. Leon, et al. 2007. "Hazardous Alcohol Drinking and Premature Mortality in Russia: A Population Based Case-Control Study," *The Lancet* 369:2001–9.

15. In the countryside, people were drinking homebrewed liquors, *samogon*. M. Wines, "An Ailing Russia Lives a Tough Life That's Getting Shorter," *New York Times*, Dec 30, 2000. Available at: http://faculty.usfsp.edu/jsokolov/ageruss1.htm

16. S. Tomkins, et al. 2007. "Prevalence and Socio-economic Distribution of Hazardous Patterns of Alcohol Drinking: Study of Alcohol Consumption in Men Aged 25–54 Years in Izhevsk, Russia," *Addiction* v102(4): 544–53.

17. A. Bessudnov, M. McKee, D. Stuckler. 2012. "Inequalities in Male Mortality by Occupational Class, Perceived Status and Education in Russia, 1994–2006," *European Journal of Public Health* v22(3): 332–37. Available at: http://eurpub.oxfordjournals.org/content/22/3/332.short; Perlman and Bobak. 2009. "Assessing the Contribution of Unstable Employment to Mortality in Posttransition Russia: Prospective Individual-Level Analyses from the Russian Longitudinal Monitoring Survey," *American Journal of Public Health* v99(10): 1818–25.

18. For this reason, not only was unemployment itself but the fear of unemployment led to an increased risk of dying in Russia. See F. Perlman, and M. Bobak, "Assessing the Contribution." These social benefit programs contributed to a very high health/ GDP ratio in Soviet countries.

In general Soviet economies tended to have much higher life expectancies than capitalist economies at similar levels of GDP per capita (such as Chile, Turkey, Botswana, South Africa, etc.). On average, Soviet men had 4.8 years greater health and Soviet women had 7.7 years greater health for their country's level of income compared with capitalist economy averages.

19. D. Stuckler, L. King, M. McKee. 2000. "Mass Privatization and the Postcommunist Mortality Crisis," *The Lancet* v373(9661): 399–407. Available at: http://www .thelancet.com/journals/lancet/article/PIIS0140-6736%2809%2960005-2/abstract; see also Perlman and Bobak, "Assessing the Contribution."

20. L. Balcerowicz and A. Gelb. 1995. "Macropolicies in Transition to a Market Economy: A Three-Year Perspective," *Proceedings of the World Bank Annual Conference on Development Economics 1994*. The International Bank for Reconstruction and Development. Available at: http://www-wds.worldbank.org/servlet/WDSContentServer/IW3P /IB/1995/03/01/000009265_3970716143745/Rendered/PDF/multi0page.pdf

21. "The need to accelerate privatization is the paramount economic policy issue facing Eastern Europe," wrote Jeffrey Sachs. "If there is no breakthrough in the privatization of large enterprises in the near future, the entire process could be stalled for years to come. Privatization is urgent and politically vulnerable." J. Sachs, "What Is to Be Done?" *The Economist*, Jan 13, 1990. Available at: http://www.economist.com/node /13002085; J. Sachs, "Shock Therapy in Poland: Perspectives of Five Years," 1995. Available at: http://tannerlectures.utah.edu/lectures/documents/sachs95.pdf

22. A third major element of Shock Therapy was stabilization: a combination of austerity and tight monetary policy to keep inflation low. Lawrence Summers summarized the support for these three central policies of Shock Therapy: "The legions of economists who have descended on the formerly Communist economies have provided advice very similar. The three "-ations"— privatization, stabilization, and liberalization—must all be completed as soon as possible." Cited in R. Stevens. 2004. "The Evolution of Privatisation as an Electoral Policy, c. 1970–90," *Contemporary British History* v18(2): 47–75.

23. M. Friedman, "Economic Freedom Behind the Scenes," Preface to *Economic Freedom of the World: 2002 Annual Report*, by James Gwartney and Robert Lawson, with Chris Edwards, Walter Park, Veronique de Rugy, and Smitha Wagh (Vancouver, BC, 2002). Summers cited in T. Anderson, *The Concise Encyclopedia of Economics*. Available at: http://www.econlib.org/library/Enc/EnvironmentalQuality.html

24. Stevens, "The Evolution of Privatisation as an Electoral Policy." There was no shortage of advice about which approach to take. *The Economist* magazine's editors argued in support of Shock Therapy, writing that the growing acceptance of gradualism

is "the greatest peril now facing the countries of Eastern Europe." The editors of *Foreign Affairs* agreed: "The radiance of Western justice and success is the power that caused the east European nations and the Soviet Union to abandon what they were and attempt to become what we, the democracies, have made of ourselves. It is a moment to seize." O. J. Blanchard, K. A. Froot, J. D. Sachs, *The Transition in Eastern Europe* (Chicago, 1994).

25. B. Naughton, *Growing out of the Plan: Chinese Economic Reform, 1978–1993* (Cambridge, 1996).

26. Richard A. Melanson, *American Foreign Policy Since the Vietnam War: The Search for Consensus from Richard Nixon to George W. Bush* (New York, 2005). Graham Allison and Robert Blackwill, "On with the Grand Bargain," *Washington Post*, Aug 27, 1991. L. Berry. "How Boris Yeltsin Defeated the 1991 Communist Coup," *The Guardian*, Aug 18 2011. Available at: http://www.guardian.co.uk/world/feedarticle/9803554

27. Source for Figure 2.2: Authors, adapted from P. Hamm, L. King, D. Stuckler. 2012. "Mass Privatization, State Capacity, and Economic Growth in Post-Communist Countries," *American Sociological Review* v77(2): 295–324. Central and Eastern European countries (CEE) include the Czech Republic, Hungary, Poland, Slovakia, and Slovenia. Former Soviet countries (FSU) for which data are available since 1990 include Armenia, Azerbaijan, Belarus, Estonia, Georgia, Latvia, Lithuania, Kazakhstan, Kyrgyzstan, Moldova, Russia, Tajikistan, Ukraine, and Uzbekistan. Percentage changes are scaled to GDP per capita in 1990 using constant 2000 international dollars as reported in the April 2008 edition of the UNICEF TransMonEE database.

28. World Bank World Development Indicators (Washington, DC, 2013 edition); Penn World Tables. Center for International Comparisons of Production, Income and Prices. University of Pennsylvania. Available at: https://pwt.sas.upenn.edu/

29. Stuckler, "Social Causes of Post-communist Mortality." See P. Klebnikov, *Godfather of the Kremlin: Boris Berezovsky and the Looting of Russia* (Boston, 2000). See M. Ellman. 1994. "The Increase in Death and Disease Under 'Katastroika'," *Cambridge Journal of Economics* v18:329–55; C. Bohlen, "Yeltsin Deputy Calls Reforms 'Economic Genocide'," *New York Times*, Feb 9, 1992. Available at: http://www.nytimes.com/1992/02/09/world/yeltsin-deputy-calls-reforms-economic-genocide.html

30. For a discussion see T. Meszmann, "Poland, Trade Unions and Protest, 1988–1993," *International Encyclopedia of Revolution and Protest*, 2009. Available at: http://www.blackwellreference.com/public/tocnode?id=g9781405184649_yr2012_chunk_g97814051846491199

Also, see Stuckler, "Social Causes of Post-Communist Mortality." See Klebnikov, *Godfather of the Kremlin*. See Ellman, "The Increase in Death and Disease Under 'Katastroika'." Polish government. Official promotional website of the Republic of Poland, Foreign Investment. Available at: http://en.poland.gov.pl/Foreign,investment,468.html

As the Polish government's foreign investment website notes, "The foreign capital coming into the Polish economy has fulfilled a very important role in the process of privatisation and restructuring. The majority of foreign investment to Poland has taken the most desirable form—direct investment (FDI). Such investments have meant new companies starting from scratch or enterprises already existing on the Polish market being taken over."

31. P. Hamm, L. King, D. Stuckler. 2012. "Mass Privatization, State Capacity, and Economic Growth in Post-Communist Countries," *American Sociological Review* v77(2): 295–324.

32. As Noreena Herz, who then worked for the World Bank explained, she was sent to Russia to oversee the implementation of privatization, living in the factories and feeding information back to headquarters. "I spent months in the factories. In one, I slept in an empty ward in the sanatorium. I realized very quickly that the master plan of privatizing Russian industry overnight was going to impose huge costs on hundreds of thousands of people. These factories were producing goods that once they were launched, no one would want in a too competitive market. They would have to slash tens of thousands of jobs. But also, these factories provided schools, hospitals, health care and retirement—cradle to grave. I raised these concerns in Washington, to say there weren't any safety nets in place. It became clear to me that it was really a political play, that they wanted to take assets out of the state's hands, so the Communist Party wouldn't come back."

33. O. Adeyi, et al. 1997. "Health Status During the Transition in Central and Eastern Europe: Development in Reverse?" *Health Policy and Planning* v12(2): 132–45.

34. Sachs, "Shock Therapy in Poland."

35. Hamm, et al., "Mass Privatization, State Capacity, and Economic Growth in Post-Communist Countries." The consequences would prove most severe for the employees of large-scale heavy industry and manufacturing enterprises. Of all the privatized firms, these large enterprises were the least equipped successfully to suddenly compete under real market conditions. Their greater inefficiency and technological backwardness meant they would suffer the greatest job losses while their employees, whose skills with Soviet technologies would become redundant, would have a hard time finding new jobs. L. King, P. Hamm, D. Stuckler. 2009. "Rapid Large-Scale Privatization and Death Rates in Ex-Communist Countries: An Analysis of Stress-Related and Health System Mechanisms," *International Journal of Health Services* v39(3): 461–89; we estimated this loss was about fifteen doctors per 10,000 population.

36. A. Åslund, *Building Capitalism: The Transformation of the Former Soviet Bloc* (Cambridge, 2002); see also Anders Åslund, "Is the Belarusian Economic Model Viable?" in A. Lewis, ed., *The EU and Belarus: Between Moscow and Brussels* (London, 2002), p. 182.

37. Stuckler, King, McKee, "Mass Privatization and the Postcommunist Mortality Crisis."

38. Source for Figure 2.3: Adapted from Ibid.

39. See also P. Grigoriev, V. Shkolnikov, E. Andreev, et al. 2010. "Mortality in Belarus, Lithuania, and Russia: Divergence in Recent Trends and Possible Explanations,"

European Journal of Population v26(3): 245–74. The paper's conclusion is consistent with ours: "differences in the speed and the extent of the move to a market economy resulted in quite different effects on mortality trends. Russia experienced the sharpest mortality growth in the beginning of the 1990s, caused by painful market reforms that were not accompanied by the creation of strong market institutions or by a commitment of the state to fulfill its social obligations. By contrast, Belarus, which followed the slowest transition path, suffered the lowest increase in mortality."

40. To put this effect in perspective, we found that military conflict in the region had caused a 20 percent rise in mortality. In other words, the choice to mass privatize had an impact almost as damaging as violent military conflicts in eastern Europe. Stuckler, King, McKee, "Mass Privatization and the Postcommunist Mortality Crisis." L. King, P. Hamm, D. Stuckler. 2009. "Rapid Large-Scale Privatization and Death Rates in Ex-Communist Countries: An Analysis of Stress-Related and Health System Mechanisms," *International Journal of Health Services* v39(3): 461–89.

41. L. Pritchett and L. Summers. 1996. "Wealthier Is Healthier," *The Journal of Human Resources* v31(4): 841–68. Available at: http://www.jstor.org/discover/10.2307 /146149?uid=3739560&uid=2129&uid=2&uid=70&uid=4&uid=3739256& sid=21101670942437. At a population level, wealthier is also found to be healthier because governments have greater resources to invest in social protections. When statistical models are used to adjust for the benefits of greater social protection that accompanies increasing GDP, the association of GDP with better health drops by three-quarters. For more details see D. Stuckler, S. Basu, M. McKee. 2010. "Budget Crises, Health, and Social Welfare Programmes," *British Medical Journal* v340:c3311.

42. When people's income doubled, on average their life expectancy improved by two years. Yet on average it takes two decades for economic growth to double, when the economy is growing at a rate of 4 percent. So it can safely be said that, by reducing life expectancy by two years, mass privatization amounted to setting back human development in Russia for at least 20 years. See Hamm, King, Stuckler, "Mass Privatization, State Capacity, and Economic Growth in Post-Communist Countries."

43. Economist Elizabeth Brainerd, who had collaborated with other economists from the Harvard Shock Therapy team, replicated our results and drew the same conclusion as we had: "One indicator of the disruption in the working person's life is the extent of privatization of state-owned enterprises. While undoubtedly a beneficial development for the economy as a whole and a clear indicator of reform progress, privatization may also create additional stress and uncertainty for individual workers. This interpretation of privatization may explain the positive and significant correlation between the increase in private sector share and rising cardiovascular death rates." E. Brainerd. 1998. "Market Reform and Mortality in Transition Economies," *World Development* v26(11): 2013–27. Cited in E. Brainerd. 1998. "Market Reform and Mortality in Transition Economies," *World Development* v26(11): 2013–27. Available at: http:// people.brandeis.edu/~ebrainer/worlddev198.pdf. Stanley Fischer, another Shock Ther-

apy advocate, was by the late 1990s struggling to grapple with the fact that "countries that undertook the greatest degree of reform in this period (by this measure) appear to have experienced the highest increases in death rates. This is puzzling." Cited in Brainerd, "Market Reform and Mortality in Transition Economies." Friedman cited in M. Hirsh, *Capital Offense: How Washington's Wise Men Turned America's Future over to Wall Street* (New Jersey, 2010), p. 134.

44. Source for Figure 2.4: Authors. World Bank World Development Indicators 2012 edition.

45. J. Sachs, " 'Shock Therapy' Had No Adverse Effect on Life Expectancy in Eastern Europe," *Financial Times*, Jan 19, 2009. Available at: http://www.ft.com/cms/s/0 /0b474e44-e5c9-11dd-afe4-0000779fd2ac.html; C. J. Gerry, T. M. Mickiewicz, Z. Nikoloski. 2010. "Did Mass Privatization Really Increase Mortality?" *The Lancet* v375: 371. See also our response: Authors' reply. 2010. *The Lancet* v375:372–73.

46. "Mass Murder and the Market," *The Economist*, Jan 22, 2009. Available at: http://www.economist.com/node/12972677. See D. Huff, *How to Lie with Statistics* (New York, 1993). This classic book contains excellent textbook examples of data torture such as these, as a way to teach statistics student of what not to do with data and how to spot foul play.

47. Our studies had also looked at countries implementing rapid privatization to understand why some fared worse than others. Russia, for example, had a steeper rise in deaths than Ukraine. While one driver of their differences was how rapidly they had privatized (Russia faster than Ukraine), another aspect was that Ukraine had better upheld its social support programs. It also had a higher degree of what social scientists call "social capital." We had found that when people were members of social organizations such as churches, unions, or sports clubs, their risk of dying during rapid privatization was much lower than that of lonely, single people. Similarly, in the Czech Republic, where more than half of the population belonged to such community groups, privatization carried virtually no risks of stress-related deaths. In Romania, however, where fewer than 10 percent of people were part of a community organization of one kind or another, there was about a 15 percent increase in deaths from rapid privatization. As described by Bob Putnam in his book *Bowling Alone*, the benefits of social capital are strong: during hard times, it helps to have something or someone you can count on, whether a church pew to sleep on or a friend's shoulder to cry on, rather than drinking by yourself.

48. Source for Figure 2.5: "Mass Murder and the Market."

As one of the founders of sociology, Émile Durkheim, wrote in *Le Suicide* in 1897, "Whenever serious readjustments take place in the social order, whether or not due to a sudden growth or to an unexpected catastrophe, men are more inclined to self-destruction." Rapid privatization was a case in point. While some short-term pain was predicted, the Shock Therapists never anticipated that their methods would cause quite so much harm. Economies may have been able to restructure, yes—but people were not able to adjust so rapidly. The Russian transition showed us how dangerous it can be when policymakers make economic choices without regard to their potential effects on health.

49. World Bank World Development Indicators 2013 edition. Available at: http://data.worldbank.org/indicator/SP.DYN.LE00.IN

50. However, there are some who question whether the transition fully occurred, as the social and political backlash against rapid reform has created pressure for the state to regain control over the economy. For details about TB spread in eastern Europe, see World Health Organization, *Global Tuberculosis Report* (Geneva, 2012). Available at: http://www.who.int/tb/publications/global_report/en/; D. Stuckler, S. Basu, L. King. 2008. "International Monetary Fund Programs and Tuberculosis Outcomes in Post-communist Countries," *Public Library of Science Medicine* v5(7):e143.

51. National Bureau of Statistics of China. 2013. Available at: http://www.stats.gov.cn/english/statisticaldata/; World Bank World Development Indicators 2013 edition.

Chapter 3: From Miracle to Mirage

1. W. Bello, S. Cunningham, K. Poh Li, *A Siamese Tragedy: Development and Disintegration in Modern Thailand* (Oakland, 1999).

2. World Bank. May 1996. *Managing Capital Flows in East Asia*. Available at: http://elibrary.worldbank.org/content/book/9780821335291; World Bank, GDP Growth annual %. Available at: http://data.worldbank.org/indicator/NY.GDP.MKTP.KD.ZG?page=3

3. World Bank. 1993. *The East Asian Miracle: Economic Growth and Public Policy*. World Bank Policy Research Reports.

4. M. Brauchli, "Speak No Evil: Why the World Bank Failed to Anticipate Indonesia's Deep Crisis," *Wall Street Journal*, July 14, 1998. Available at: http://www.library.ohiou.edu/indopubs/1998/07/14/0013.html. In September 1997, just a few months before the crash, the World Bank showed a remarkable lack of foresight. Their report praised Indonesia: "Indonesia has achieved a remarkable economic development success over the past decade and is considered to be among the best performing East Asian economies. Indonesia has made great strides in diversifying its economy and promoting a competitive private sector through sound macro-economic management, increased deregulation and deeper investment in infrastructure services." N. Bullard, W. Bello, K. Malhotra, "Taming the Tigers: The IMF and the Asian Crisis," *Third World Quarterly* 19:505–55. Available at: http://focusweb.org/node/358

5. Paul Krugman. 1994. "The Myth of Asia's Miracle," *Foreign Affairs* v73(6): 62–78. Available at: http://www.ft.com/intl/cms/b8268ffe-7572-11db-aea1-0000779e2340.pdf; Pietro Masina, *Rethinking Development in East Asia: From Illusory Miracle to Economic Crisis* (London, 2001).

6. Brauchli, "Speak No Evil." See also T. Ito, "Asian Currency Crisis and the International Monetary Fund, 10 Years Later: Overview." Available at: http://www.researchgate.net/publication/4720855_Asian_Currency_Crisis_and_the_International_Monetary_Fund_10_Years_Later_Overview. Currency exchange data available at Index Mundi:

http://www.indexmundi.com/xrates/graph.aspx?c1=IDR&c2=USD&days=5650; Stephen Radelet and Jeffrey Sachs, "The Onset of the East Asian Financial Crisis," NBER, August 1998. Available at: http://online.sfsu.edu/jgmoss/PDF/635_pdf/No_29_Radelet _Sachs.pdf; Iskandar Simorangkir, "Determinants of Bank Runs in Indonesia," *Bulletin of Monetary, Economics and Banking*, July 2011. Available at: http://www.bi.go.id/NR /rdonlyres/59B51C7D-140E-405E-A67C-5ADBD2108CAE/25291/IskandarSimorangkir.pdf; Stanley Fischer, "Lessons from East Asia and the Pacific Rim," *Brookings Papers on Economic Activity* 2:1999. Available at: http://www.brookings.edu/~/media/Projects/ BPEA/1996%202/1996b_bpea_fischer.PDF; Bello, et al., *A Siamese Tragedy*; Brauchli, "Speak No Evil."

7. I. Fisher, "The Debt-Deflation Theory of Great Depressions." Available at: http:// fraser.stlouisfed.org/docs/meltzer/fisdeb33.pdf. Economist Irving Fisher described debt-deflation spirals in the Great Depression: "Unless some counteracting cause comes along to prevent the fall in the price level, such a depression as that of 1929–33 (namely when the more the debtors pay the more they owe) tends to continue, going deeper, in a vicious spiral, for many years. There is then no tendency of the boat to stop tipping until it has capsized. Ultimately, of course, but only after almost universal bankruptcy, the indebtedness must cease to grow greater and begin to grow less. Then comes recovery and a tendency for a new boom-depression sequence. This is the so-called 'natural' way out of a depression, via needless and cruel bankruptcy, unemployment, and starvation." International Labour Organization, "ILO Meeting Highlights Asia Jobs Challenge," 1999. Available at: http://www.ilo.org/asia/info/public/pr/WCMS_BK_PR_1_EN/lang–en /index.htm. See also Milken Institute, "Indonesia: Current Economic Conditions," Asia and the Pacific Rim, March 10, 1999. C. Peter Timmer, "Food Security in Indonesia: Current Challenges and the Long-Run Outlook," Center for Global Development, Nov 2004. Available at: http://www.cgdev.org/files/2740_file_WP_48_Food_security _in_Indonesia.pdf; Report from CARE. 1998. El Niño in 1997–1998: Impacts and CARE's Response. Available at: http://reliefweb.int/report/world/el-ni%C3%B1o -1997–1998-impacts-and-cares-response. This rise corresponded to about 33 million people being pushed into poverty. See D. Suryadarma and S. Sumarto. 2011. "Survey of Recent Developments." *Bulletin of Indonesian Economic Studies* v47(2): 155–81. Available at: http://www.danielsuryadarma.com/pdf/bies11.pdf

8. Jemma Purdey, *Anti-Chinese Violence in Indonesia, 1996–1999* (Honolulu, 2006). Volunteers for Humanity documented 168 rapes in Jakarta, Solo, Medan, Palembang, and Surabaya. Of those raped, at least twenty died during or after the trauma. Cited in G. Wandita, "The Tears Have Not Stopped, the Violence Has Not Ended: Political Upheaval, Ethnicity and Violence Against Women in Indonesia," *Gender & Development* v6(3): 34–41. The US government estimates there were sixty-six confirmed rapes. See US Department of State Report: Indonesia Country Report on Human Rights Practices for 1998. Available at: http://www.state.gov/www/global/human_rights/1998 _hrp_report/indonesi.html. For further discussion, see J. Purdey, "Problematizing the

Place of Victims in Reformasi Indonesia: A Contested Truth About the May 1998 Violence," *Asian Survey* v42(4): 605–22; Purdey, *Anti-Chinese Violence in Indonesia*.

9. The economist Robert Wade summarized the situation this way: "Explanations are about the only thing not in short supply in the Asian crisis." See also IMF, Articles of Agreement of the International Monetary Fund, 1944. Available at: http://www.imf.org/external/pubs/ft/aa/index.htm

10. John Williamson, "What Washington Means by Policy Reform," in John Williamson (ed.), *Latin American Readjustment: How Much Has Happened* (Washington, DC, 1989). Available at: http://www.iie.com/publications/papers/paper.cfm?researchid=486. The IMF recommended these actions to the East Asian countries, but went further to put even more stringent conditions on its loans, calling for the immediate closure of banks to stem capital flowing out of the country, and setting up standards for how much money banks should keep in order to limit risk-taking, reduce credit, and prevent borrowing.

11. As the deputy managing director of the IMF, Stanley Fischer, explained in July 1998, "The real issue is how rapidly the underlying structural problems in the financial and corporate sectors are dealt with. The faster that is done, the shorter the period of pain, and the sooner the return to growth." Stiglitz noted that this one-size-fits-all policy was so commonly applied that some economists forgot that the 'find and replace' feature in Microsoft Word sometimes missed country names. He said: "I heard stories of one unfortunate incident when team members copied large parts of the text for one country's report and transferred them wholesale to another. They might have gotten away with it, except the 'search and replace' function on the word processor didn't work properly, leaving the original country's name in a few places. Oops." "For Sensitive and Sensible Economics," in V. Anantha-Nageswaran (ed.), *Global Financial Markets: Issues and Perspectives* (India: ICFAI Press, 2002), p. 11.

Ha-Joon Chang argues the opposite: that the Tigers got rich by doing the opposite of what was advised; protecting markets so that infant industries in technology could grow up and compete on global markets before liberalizing.

12. Critics also raised concerns about precisely whom the IMF was helping. "It was the rich who benefited from the boom," said Khun Bunjan, a community leader from the slums of Khon Kaen in northeast Thailand. "But we, the poor, pay the price of the crisis. Even our limited access to schools and health is now beginning to disappear. We fear for our children's future." See C. M. Robb, "Can the Poor Influence Policy? Participatory Poverty Assessments in the Developing World," World Bank, 1999.

But why should governments make deep structural reforms and cut budgets when the causes of the crisis were short-term and temporary? The region didn't need massive budget cuts or tight monetary policy, but more government investment and increasing the money supply to offset the fall in foreign loans. After all, these East Asian countries did not have significant debt problems before the crisis, and had previously run budget surpluses. Several economists argued that since excessive government spending was not the cause of the crisis, it didn't make sense to focus on cutting spending to fix the problem; in fact, since panicky and speculative transactions in the markets had caused the crisis in the first place, deregulating such transactions didn't seem likely to produce stability. "The problem was not imprudent government, as in Latin America," said Joseph Stiglitz, "the problem was an imprudent private sector—all those bankers and borrowers, for instance, who'd gambled on the real estate bubble."

13. With most of the IMF loans going to the foreign bankers who had created the financial mess, criticism abounded. The East Asian countries had few options, however, but to agree with the IMF stipulations. Without the injection of IMF funds, it would have been difficult for any of them to get enough money to cope with the immediate crisis. To make its plan enticing, the IMF mobilized its largest-ever loan—$110 billion from the US and other rich country members of the Fund. R. P. Buckley, S. M. Fitzgerald. 2004. "An Assessment of Malaysia's Response to the IMF During the Asian Economic Crisis," *Singapore Journal of Legal Studies*, pp. 96–116. Available at: http://papers .ssrn.com/sol3/papers.cfm?abstract_id=1020508

Other reasons for Malaysia's "No" to the IMF were related to its history, in the 1980s, of banking crisis when regulations were put in place to limit foreign borrowing. The result was that Malaysia was less exposed to a rise in the value of foreign debt when its currency, the ringgit, dropped in value. J. K. Sundaram. 2006. "Pathways Through Financial Crisis: Malaysia," *Global Governance* v12:489–505. Available at: http://www .globaleconomicgovernance.org/wp-content/uploads/sundaram-pathways_malayisa .pdf

It has also been argued that in Indonesia, President Suharto's family network played a role in the decision to accept help from the IMF, as much of the money was kept in the country and not solely in Swiss bank accounts, unlike the political leadership of Malaysia at the time which reportedly held financing abroad. N. Jones and H. Marsden, "Assessing the Impacts of and Responses to the 1997–98 Asian Financial Crisis Through a Child Rights Lens," UNICEF Social and Economic Policy Working Paper, 2010. Available at: http://www2.unicef.org/socialpolicy/files/Assessing_the_Impacts _of_the_97_98_Asian_Crisis.pdf

14. Based on current GDP per capita in USD. World Bank World Development Indicators 2013 edition. Sundaram, "Pathways Through Financial Crisis."

15. G. P. Corning, "Managing the Asian Meltdown: The IMF and South Korea. Institute for the Study of Diplomacy." Available at: http://graduateinstitute.ch/webdav /site/political_science/shared/political_science/1849/southkorea&imf.pdf; S. S. Chang, D. Gunnell, J. A. C. Sterne, et al. 2009. "Was the Economic Crisis 1997–1998 Responsible for Rising Suicide Rates in East/Southeast Asia? A Time-Trend Analysis for Japan, Hong Kong, South Korea, Taiwan, Singapore, and Thailand," *Social Science & Medicine* v68:1322–31. Available at: http://www.ncbi.nlm.nih.gov/pubmed/19200631; rates had

been rising in South Korea prior to the crisis, but began to accelerate coinciding with the market crash.

Ministry of Public Health Thailand. Thailand Health profile 1999–2000. Accessed Jan 29, 2004. Available at: www.moph.go.th/ops/thealth 44/index eng.htm. Cited in S. Hopkins. 2006. "Economic Stability and Health Status: Evidence from East Asia Before and After the 1990s Economic Crisis," *Health Policy* v75:347–57.

16. AusAID, "Impact of the Asian Financial Crisis on Health: Indonesia, Thailand, the Philippines, Vietnam, Lao PDR, 2000." Accessed Feb 12, 2004. Available at: http:// www. ausaid.gov.au/publications/pubout.cfm?Id=4105 1515 1662 2276 2647&Type=

J. Knowles, E. Pernia, M. Racelis, *Social Consequences of the Financial Crisis in East Asia* (Manila: Asian Development Bank, 1999); P. Gottret, et al., "Protecting Pro-Poor Health Services During Financial Crises: Lessons from Experience," World Bank, 2009. Health and Nutrition Program. Available at: http://www.google.com/url?sa=t &rct=j&q=&esrc=s&source=web&cd=3&cad=rja&ved=0CEcQFjAC&url=http%3A %2F%2Fsiteresources.worldbank.org%2FINTHSD%2FResources%2F376278 -1202320704235%2FProtProPoorHealthServFin.doc&ei=MHX4UNHhDaWVi AK7hYCICw&usg=AFQjCNFWm3rlVyeIDnoEVERsAfb1CMEvAg& sig2=rPmVK71IY3Z_Yi1o7s8MWw&bvm=bv.41248874,d.cGE; Child Rights International Network, *Harnessing Globalisation for Children: A Report to UNICEF*, 2002. Available at: http://www.crin.org/resources/infoDetail.asp?ID=2918

17. "Indonesia Unrest Growing Despite IMF Bailout." *Albion Monitor News*, Jakarta, Indonesia. Available at: http://www.monitor.net/monitor/9801a/jakartaunrest.html

18. S. Fischer, "A Year of Upheaval: The IMF Was Right on High Interest Rates and Immediate Restructuring," *AsiaWeek Magazine*. Available at: http://www-cgi.cnn.com /ASIANOW/asiaweek/98/0717/cs_12_fischer.html

19. P. Krugman explains: "Since the East Asian crisis, the IMF's stance has changed on the use of capital controls. "The International Monetary Fund has cemented a substantial ideological shift by accepting the use of direct controls to calm volatile cross-border capital flows, as employed by emerging market countries in recent years." In Alan Beattie, "IMF Drops Opposition to Capital Controls," *Financial Times*, Dec 3, 2012.

Hopkins, "Economic Stability and Health Status."

20. Cited in H. Waters, F. Saadah, M. Pradhan. 2003. "The Impact of the 1997–1998 East Asian Economic Crisis on Health and Health Care in Indonesia," *Health Policy and Planning* v18(2): 179.

21. Table 9 in V. Tangcharoensathien, et al. 2000. "Health Impacts of Rapid Economic Changes in Thailand," *Social Science & Medicine* v51:789–807. Available at: http://www.ncbi.nlm.nih.gov/pubmed/10972425

Cited in Waters, Saadah, Pradhan, "The Impact of the 1997–1998 East Asian Economic Crisis on Health and Health Care in Indonesia," p. 174.

C. Simms and M. Rowson. 2003. "Reassessment of Health Effects of the Indonesian Economic Crisis: Donors Versus the Data," *The Lancet* v361:1382–85. Available at:

http://mvw.medact.org/content/health/documents/poverty/Simms%20and%20Rowson%20-%20Reassessment%20of%20health%20effects%20Indonesia.pdf

22. Cited as: "The use of any health care by children aged 10 to 19 years was particularly affected, declining by 26.8% overall and by 33.0% for public providers between the 1997 and 1998 SUSENAS surveys," in Waters, Saadah, Pradhan, "The Impact of the 1997–1998 East Asian Economic Crisis on Health and Health Care in Indonesia."

The clinics also feared that patients would sue doctors for providing substandard care as necessary medicines became unavailable and as people were removed from healthcare subsidy programs.

Asian Development Bank, *Assessing the Social Impact of the Financial Crisis in Asia.* Report RETA 5799. (Manila: Asian Development Bank, 1999); and RAND Corporation, "Effects of the Indonesian Crisis—Evidence from the Indonesian Family Life Survey," Rand Labor and Population Program Research Brief (Santa Monica, CA: RAND, 1999).

23. UNAIDS. Country profile: Thailand. Available at: http://www.unaids.org/en/regionscountries/countries/thailand/

"Thailand's New Condom Crusade." 2010. *Bulletin of the World Health Organization* v88(6):404–5. Available at: http://www.who.int/bulletin/volumes/88/6/10-010610/en/index.html

24. http://www.thelancet.com/journals/lancet/article/PIIS0140-6736%2808%2960091-4/fulltext

25. "Thailand's New Condom Crusade."

26. Ibid.

27. AusAid, *Impact of the Asian Financial Crisis on Health: Indonesia, Thailand, The Philippines, Vietnam, Lao PDR,* (AusAid, 2000). See also S. Hopkins, "Economic Stability and Health Status," in *The Impact of the Asian Financial Crisis on the Health Sector in Thailand* (AusAid, 2000), p. 6.

UN Office for the Coordination of Humanitarian Affairs, "Thailand: Activists Want Rights of HIV-Positive People Protected," Aug 10, 2006. Available at: http://www.irinnews.org/printreport.aspx?reportid=60176

28. Source for Figure 3.1: Adapted from ibid.

29. V. Tangcharoensathien, et al. 2000. "Health Impacts of Rapid Economic Changes in Thailand," *Social Science & Medicine* v51:789–807.

In 2001, the Thai Working Group on HIV/AIDS estimated that 4,000 children were born infected with HIV, with the disease transmitted to them from their mothers. With the effective use of drugs, nevirapine, this transmission is avoidable. Hopkins, "Economic Stability and Health Status."

March 2001 projection of the Thai working group on HIV/AIDS; cited in UNICEF. Chapter 1. Introduction and Summary. Long Term Socio-Economic Impact of HIV/AIDS on Children and Policy Response in Thailand.

In Indonesia, after a similar IMF-imposed 50 percent cut to HIV/AIDS prevention in 1999, there was a 10 percent rise in untreated STDs and HIV in the female population.

"Figures on new admissions of abandoned children (under five and older) from the Social Welfare Department showed an increasing trend during the crisis," cited in Tangcharoensathien, et al. "Health Impacts of Rapid Economic Changes in Thailand."

30. S. Aungkulanon, M. McCarron, J. Lertiendumrong, S. J. Olsen, K. Bundhamcharoen. 2012. "Infectious Disease Mortality Rates, Thailand, 1958–2009," *Emerg Infectious Diseases* v18(11). Available at: http://wwwnc.cdc.gov/eid/article/18/11/12-0637 _article.htm

31. Hopkins, "Economic Stability and Health Status"; "Thailand's New Condom Crusade."

32. Y. J. Han, S. W. Lee, Y. S. Jang, D. J. Kim, S. W. Lee, *Infant and Perinatal Mortality Rates of Korea in 1999 and 2000* (Seoul: Korea Institute for Health and Social Welfare, 2002).

C. Simms and M. Rowson. 2003. "Reassessment of Health Effects if the Indonesian Economic Crisis: Donors Versus the Data," *The Lancet* v361:1382–85. Available at: http://mvw.medact.org/content/health/documents/poverty/Simms%20and%20Rowson%20-%20Reassessment%20of%20health%20effects%20Indonesia.pdf; UNDP. Human Development Report 2001 (New York: UNDP). Available at: http://hdr.undp.org/en/reports/global/hdr2001/. Note that Indonesia has since added eight more provinces for a total of thirty-six.

33. Mahani Zainal-Abidin, "Malaysian Economic Recovery Measures: A Response to Crisis Management and for Long-term Economic Sustainability." Available at http://www.siue.edu/EASTASIA/Mahani_020400.htm

34. Joseph Stiglitz, "What I Learned at the World Economic Crisis," *The New Republic*, April 17, 2000.

35. Based on real economic terms, adjusting for currency devaluation. Waters, Saadah, Pradhan, "The Impact of the 1997–1998 East Asian Economic Crisis on Health and Health Care in Indonesia."

36. D. E. Sanger, "IMF Now Admits Tactics in Indonesia Deepened the Crisis," *New York Times*, Jan 14 1998. Available at: http://www.nytimes.com/1998/01/14/business/international-business-imf-now-admits-tactics-in-indonesia-deepened-the-crisis.html

37. S. Kittiprapas, N. Sanderatne, G. Abeysekera, "Financial Instability and Child Well-Being: A Comparative Analysis of the Impact of the Asian Crisis and Social Policy Response in Indonesia, Malaysia, Thailand, and South Korea," UNICEF Office for Thailand; Ch. 9 in G. A. Cornia (ed.), *Harnessing Globalisation for Children*; Hopkins, "Economic Stability and Health Status."

Waters, Saadah, Pradhan, "The Impact of the 1997–1998 East Asian Economic Crisis on Health and Health Care in Indonesia."

38. F. Ardiansyah, "Bearing the Consequences of Indonesia's Fuel Subsidy," East Asia Forum, May 4, 2012. Available at: http://www.eastasiaforum.org/2012/05/04/26135/

39. E. Kaiser, S. Knight, "Analysis: Aid Recipients Welcome IMF's Shift on Austerity," Reuter's, Oct 14, 2012. Available at: http://www.reuters.com/article/2012/10/14/us-imf-aid-admission-idUSBRE89D0GQ20121014

PART II: THE GREAT RECESSION

Chapter 4: God Bless Iceland

1. Financial crisis; full statement by Iceland's prime minister Geir Haarde. *The Telegraph.* Available at: http://www.telegraph.co.uk/news/worldnews/europe/iceland/3147806/Financial-crisis-Full-statement-by-Icelands-prime-minister-Geir-Haarde.html

2. Cited in H. Felixson, *God Bless Iceland (Guðblessilsland),* 2009.

3. "Iceland: Cracks in the Crust," *The Economist,* Dec 11, 2008. Available at: http://www.economist.com/node/12762027?story_id=12762027; IMF Country Report, Iceland, April 2012. Available at: http://www.imf.org/external/pubs/ft/scr/2012/cr1291.pdf; H. Stewart, et al., "Five Countries That Crashed and Burned in the Credit Crunch Face a Hard Road to Recovery," *The Guardian,* Jan 3, 2010. Available at: http://www.guardian.co.uk/business/2010/jan/03/credit-crunch-iceland-ireland-greece-dubai-spain; "Fighting Recession the Icelandic Way," Bloomberg, Sept 26, 2012. Available at: http://www.bloomberg.com/news/2012-09-26/is-remedy-for-next-crisis-buried-in-iceland-view-correct-.html

4. Even during World War II the Germans seemed to take little notice of the small island, which had declared itself neutral, until the British invaded the island to prevent it being used as a German base.

5. J. Carlin, "No Wonder Iceland Has the Happiest People on Earth," *The Guardian,* May 18, 2008. Available at: http://www.guardian.co.uk/world/2008/may/18/iceland; Jaime Díez Medrano, "Map of Happiness," Banco de datos. Available at: http://www.jdsurvey.net/jds/jdsurveyMaps.jsp?Idioma=I&SeccionTexto=0404&NOID=103

6. G. Karlsson, *Iceland's 1100 Years: History of a Marginal Society* (London, 2000).

7. Silla Sigurgeirsdóttir and Robert H. Wade, "Iceland's Loud No," *Le Monde Diplomatique,* Aug 8, 2011. Available at http://mondediplo.com/2011/08/02iceland

8. BBC. 2006. Foreign banks offer best buys. Radio 4, Money Box. Available at: http://news.bbc.co.uk/2/hi/programmes/moneybox/6051276.stm; "Customers Face Anxious Wait Over Fate of Icesave Accounts," *The Guardian,* Oct 8, 2008. Available at http://www.guardian.co.uk/money/2008/oct/08/banks.savings; Sigurgeirsdóttir and Wade, "Iceland's Loud No."

9. World Bank World Development Indicators.

"From Capital Flow Bonanza to Financial Crash," *Vox,* Oct 23, 2008. Available at http://www.voxeu.org/article/capital-inflow-bonanza-financial-crash-danger-ahead-emerging-markets

"Better Life Index," OECD. Available at http://www.oecdbetterlifeindex.org/countries /iceland/

10. H. H. Gissurarson, "Miracle on Iceland," *Wall Street Journal,* Jan 29, 2004. Available at: http://online.wsj.com/article/0,,SB107533182153814498,00.html. Cited in R. H. Wade, and S. Sigurgeirsdottir. 2011. "Iceland's Meltdown: The Rise and Fall of International Banking in the North Atlantic." *Revista de EconomiaPolitica* v31(5). Available at: http://www.scielo.br/scielo.php?pid=S0101-31572011000500001&script=sci_arttext; see also Arthur Laffer, "Overheating Is Not Dangerous," *Morgunblaðið,* Reykjavik, Nov 17, 2007.

11. Danske Bank, "Iceland: Geyser Crisis," 2006; Robert Wade. 2009. "Iceland as Icarus," *Challenge* v52(3): 5–33; R. Boyes, *Meltdown Iceland: Lessons on the World Financial Crisis from a Small Bankrupt Island* (New York, 2009); Speech by Geir Haarde to the 2008 annual meeting of the Central Bank of Iceland. Cited in Robert H. Wade and Silla Sigurgeirsdóttir. 2010. "Lessons from Iceland," *New Left Review* v65:5–29. Available at: http://newleftreview.org/II/65/robert-wade-silla-sigurgeirsdottir-lessons-from -iceland

12. See Felixson, *God Bless Iceland.*

13. EuroStat 2012 edition. Brussels, European Commission. "Hundreds in Iceland Protest Foreclosures," *Agence France Presse,* Oct 1, 2010. Available at: http://www.google .com/hostednews/afp/article/ALeqM5ikamLDTVrWkyqkkLOHx8a89nNPQA ?docId=CNG.c41a43301a2a0ba462c063759615c08e.ad1

14. "Iceland: Britain's Unlikely New Enemy," BBC News, Oct 15, 2008. Available at: http://news.bbc.co.uk/1/hi/magazine/7667920.stm

15. Nordic countries did supply Iceland with aid funding to spur recovery. For an analysis of Iceland's stark rise in inequality, in which 1 percent of the population accrued an additional 10 percentage points of the population's total income between 2004 and 2007, see S. Olafsson and A. S. Kristjansson. 2011. "Income Inequality in a Bubble Economy—The Case of Iceland 1992–2008." LIS—Luxembourg Income Study Conference, Inequality and the Status of the Middle Class, Luxembourg June 28–30, 2010. Available at: http://www.lisproject.org/conference/papers/olafsson-kristjansson.pdf; "Iceland Faces Immigrant Exodus," BBC, Oct 21, 2008. Available at: http://news.bbc .co.uk/2/hi/europe/7680087.stm; L. Veal, "Iceland: Recovering Dubiously from the Crash," *Al Jazeera,* Jan 31 2012. Available at: http://www.aljazeera.com/indepth/features /2012/01/2012131144757624586.html

16. T. Gylfason, et al., "From Boom to Bust: The Iceland Story." Ch. 7 in *Nordic Countries in Global Crisis: Vulnerability and Resilience* (2010), p. 157. Available at: http:// www.etla.fi/wp-content/uploads/2012/09/B242.pdf

17. Ibid. Iceland's inequality rose markedly before the crash. The debt burdens were also disproportionately held. Additionally, 440 families have debts in excess of their assets of USD $400,000 or more. Of Iceland's 182,000 families, 81,000 have assets below $40,000, whereas 1,400 families have assets of $1.2 million or more.

18. This conclusion was largely based on studies that found national healthcare spending tended to rise as economies grew (J. P. Newhouse. 1977. "Medical-care Expenditure: A Cross-National Survey," *Journal of Human Resources*. As a more recent paper explains, "The General Finding Has Been That Income Elasticity Estimates Exceed Unity, Implying That Health Care Is a Luxury Good." Cited in J. Costa-Font, et al., "Re-visiting the Healthcare Luxury Good Hypothesis: Aggregation, Precision, and Publication Biases?" HEDG Working Paper 09/02, 2009. Available at: http://www.york .ac.uk/media/economics/documents/herc/wp/09_02.pdf. The health minister was publicly outspoken about the need to bolster health systems. In his resignation, he noted that he could not follow the government stance to continue the negotiation process to repay IceSave and the large fiscal consolidation that would result.

19. Personal communication with D. Stuckler, European Health Forum at Gastein, Austria, 2009.

20. In Europe we estimated the defense multiplier was negative. See A. Reeves, S. Basu, M. McKee, C. Meissner, D. Stuckler. In press. "Does Investment in the Health Sector Promote or Inhibit Economic Growth?" *Health Policy*.

21. The last time a referendum had been called in Iceland was in 1944, when Iceland voted independence from Denmark.

22. Iris Erlingsdottir, "Iceland Is Burning," *Huffington Post,* Jan 20, 2009. Available at: http://www.huffingtonpost.com/iris-lee/iceland-is-burning_b_159552.html

23. Ibid.

24. This vote should not be taken to indicate that all Icelanders agreed, particularly since not all voters turned out to the referendum. There had previously been a divisive debate about whether to repay IceSave's loans and shoulder the debt and austerity that would result. In this process, IMF economists issued conflicting messages to the Icelandic media: at times arguing not to socialize private debt, but also advising on its repayment and associated fiscal consolidation.

25. Friedman led the push for Central Bank Independence, to divorce economic decision-making about interest rates and the money supply from democratic accountability.

26. Wade and Sigurgeirsdóttir, "Lessons from Iceland."

27. Sigurgeirsdóttir and Wade, "Iceland's Loud No."

28. See D. Stuckler, C. Meissner, L. King. 2008. "Can a Bank Crisis Break Your Heart?" *Globalization & Health* v4(1). Available at: http://www.globalizationandhealth .com/content/4/1/1. See G. R. Gudjonsdottir, et al. 2012. "Immediate Surge in Female Visits to the Cardiac Emergency Department Following the Economic Collapse in Iceland: An Observational Study," *Emerg Med J* v29:694–98.

29. S. Sigurkarlsson, et al. 2011. "Prevalence of Respiratory Symptoms and Use of Asthma Drugs Are Increasing Among Young Adult Icelanders," *Laeknabladid* v97(9): 463–67. H. K. Carlsen, et al. 2012. "A Survey of Early Health Effects of the Eyjafjallajokull 2010 Eruption in Iceland: A Population-based Study," *BMJ Open* v2:e000343.

30. A. Kleinman, *The Illness Narratives: Suffering, Healing, and the Human Condition* (New York, 1988).

31. C. McClure, et al. 2013. "Increase in Female Depressive Symptoms Following the 2008 Financial Crisis in Iceland: A Prospective Cohort Study." Forthcoming.

32. J. Helliwell, R. Layard, J. Sachs. *World Happiness Report* (New York, 2012). See Figure 2.11, average positive affect by country, based on the GWP 05–11. One explanation that has been proposed is that during the crisis Iceland experienced a rising degree of political openness. Discussion and debate, previously suppressed during the boom years, emerged, increasing people's happiness and life satisfaction.

33. T. L. Asgeirsdottir, et al. "Are Recessions Good for Your Health Behaviors? Impacts of the Economic Crisis in Iceland." Working Paper 18233. National Bureau of Economic Research, Cambridge, MA, 2012.

34. D. Batty, "McDonald's to Quit Iceland as Big Mac Costs Rise," *The Guardian*, Oct 27 1999. Available at: http://www.guardian.co.uk/world/2009/oct/27/mcdonalds-to-quit-iceland; C. Forelle, "Fishing Industry Aids Iceland's Recovery," *Wall Street Journal*, May 18, 2012. Available at: http://live.wsj.com/video/fishing-industry-aids-iceland-recovery/E1ED2AC5-D98B-4760-844E-67F8BA64A136.html

35. A member of Parliament from the Independence party has also proposed the plan to privatize the state-alcohol monopoly in early 2009.

36. EuroStat. Statistics. Available at: http://epp.eurostat.ec.europa.eu/portal/page/portal/statistics/search_database; P. Gobry, "No, the United States Will Not Go into a Debt Crisis, Not Now, Not Ever," *Forbes*, Oct 19, 2012. Available at: http://www.forbes.com/sites/pascalemmanuelgobry/2012/10/19/no-the-united-states-will-not-go-into-a-debt-crisis-not-now-not-ever/. Iceland's rise in social spending was significant even after adjusting for the fall in GDP, as a result of maintaining the automatic stabilizers built into its social protection system.

37. OECD. Economic Survey of Iceland, 2011. Available at: https://community.oecd.org/docs/DOC-27221/diff?secondVersionNumber=2

38. EuroStat. Statistics. Available at: http://epp.eurostat.ec.europa.eu/portal/page/portal/statistics/search_database; "Fighting Recession the Icelandic Way," Bloomberg. This corresponded to a series of suicides that garnered headlines in Spain. See, for example, M. Bennett-Smith, "4th Eviction-Motivated Suicide Rocks Indebted Spain; Protesters Shout Eviction Is 'Murder'," *Huffington Post*, Feb 15, 2013. Available at: http://www.huffingtonpost.com/2013/02/15/4th-eviction-suicide-spain_n_2697192.html; IMF Country Report No. 12/89, April 2012, 2012 Article IV Consultation and First Post-Program Monitoring Discussion. See p. 6, Box 1: Safeguarding Iceland's social welfare system. Available at: http://www.imf.org/external/pubs/ft/scr/2012/cr1289.pdf. The social democratic party government had raised the minimum income guarantee in 2007/2008 to protect the most vulnerable group of retired persons, which came into effect in 2008/2009. Such programs were planned prior to the crisis and upheld during it. See Welfare Watch, *The Welfare Watch Report to the Althingi*. [English trans-

lation]. Ministry of Social Affairs and Social Security, Iceland, Jan 2010. Available at: http://eng.velferdarraduneyti.is/media/velferdarvakt09/29042010The-Welfare-Watch _Report-to-the-Althingi.pdf

39. For an analysis of how Iceland's social capital helped promote resilience, see K. Growiecz, "Social Capital During the Financial Crisis. The Case of Iceland." 2011. Available at: https://renewal.hi.is/wp-content/uploads/2011/05/KatarzynaSocial-Capi tal-during-Financial-Crisis-Growiec.pdf; OECD, Society at a Glance 2011: OECD Social Indicators. Available at: http://www.oecd-ilibrary.org/sites/soc_glance-2011-en /06/01/index.html?contentType=&itemId=/content/chapter/soc_glance-2011-16-en& containerItemId=/content/serial/19991290&accessItemIds=/content/book/soc_glance -2011-en&mimeType=text/html

40. EDA, Oct 12, 2009. Film review. Available at: http://www.economicdisasterarea .com/index.php/features/eda-film-review-god-bless-iceland-not-enough-mustard/

41. S. Lyall, "A Bruised Iceland Heals amid Europe's Malaise," *New York Times,* July 8, 2012. Available at: http://www.nytimes.com/2012/07/08/world/europe /icelands-economy-is-mending-amid-europes-malaise.html?pagewanted=all&_r=0; "Fighting Recession the Icelandic Way," Bloomberg. Fitch upgraded Iceland's sovereign rating from BBB- to BB+. See also BBC, "Iceland Debt 'Safe to Invest' After Ratings Upgrade," Feb 2012. Available at: http://www.bbc.co.uk/news/business -17075011

42. As the IMF further explained, rather than through austerity, fiscal adjustment was achieved by introducing greater taxes on the wealthy and focusing cuts outside of social welfare programs: "A key post crisis objective of the Icelandic authorities was to preserve the social welfare system in the face of the fiscal consolidation needed to put public finances on a sustainable path. With unemployment rising fast and real wages plummeting, it was recognized early on that the social impact of the crisis would be significant. Thus, in designing the fiscal consolidation, the authorities sought to protect vulnerable groups, notably by introducing a more progressive income tax, increasing only the upper VAT rate, and focusing expenditure cuts on areas where efficiency gains could be made—thereby creating space to preserve social benefits." IMF, "Iceland: Ex Post Evaluation of Exceptional Access Under the 2008 Stand-By Arrangement," IMF Country Report No 12/91, 2012. Available at: http://www.imf.org/external/pubs/ft/scr /2012/cr1291.pdf; the IMF further explained that "the *social impact* can be eased in the face of fiscal consolidation following a severe crisis by cutting expenditures without compromising welfare benefits."

43. Sigurgeirsdóttir and Wade, "Iceland's Loud No"; R. Milne and J. Cumbo, "Ex-Iceland Bank Chief Convicted of Fraud," *Financial Times,* Dec 30, 2012. Available at: http://www.ft.com/intl/cms/s/0/76ff5a36-525e-11e2-aff0-00144feab49a.html#axzz2I T1E9eU8. They went even further by hiring bounty-hunters (called "neo-vikings" by the Icelanders) to track down bankers who fled from imprisonment. See Charlotte Chabas, "Comment l'Islande traque ses 'néo-vikings' de la finance, responsables de la

crise," *Le Monde*, July 11, 2012. Available at: abonnes.lemonde.fr/europe/article/2012/07/11/l-islande-traque-ses-neo-vikings-de-la-finance-responsables-de-la-crise_1728783_3214.html?xtmc=islande&xtcr=2#reactions

44. R. Robertsson, "Voters in Iceland Back New Constitution, More Resource Control," Reuters, Oct 21, 2012. Available at: http://www.reuters.com/article/2012/10/21/us-iceland-referendum-idUSBRE89K09C20121021. For details about the innovative crowdsourcing model used to draft the constitution, see Philippa Warr, "Iceland Vites for Crowdsourced Constitution," *Wired*, Oct 23, 2012. Available at: http://www.wired.co.uk/news/archive/2012–10/23/iceland-crowdsourced-constitution

45. Source for Figure 4.1: EuroStat 2013 Statistics. Gross domestic product is seasonally adjusted and adjusted by working day, compared with the previous year. Note: Greece data are the latest available at the time of this writing.

46. Felixson, *God Bless Iceland*.

Chapter 5: Greek Tragedy

1. Law 4075/11.04.2012 amended article 13 of Presidential Decree 114/2010 on the "establishment of a single procedure for granting the status of refugee or of beneficiary of subsidiary protection to aliens or to stateless persons in conformity with Council Directive 2005/85/EC on minimum standards on procedures in Member States for granting and withdrawing refugee status (Law 326/13.12.2005)." Cited in Human Rights Watch, Joint letter to UN Special Rapporteur on Health, May 2012. Available at: http://www.hrw.org/news/2012/05/09/joint-letter-un-special-rapporteur-health

A. Kentikelenis, M. Karanikolos, I. Papanicolas, S. Basu, M. McKee, D. Stuckler. 2011. "Health Effects of Financial Crisis: Omens of a Greek Tragedy," *The Lancet* v378(9801): 1457–58; D. Paraskevis and A. Hatzakis, "An Ongoing HIV Outbreak Among Intravenous Drug Users in Greece: Preliminary Summary of Surveillance and Molecular Epidemiology Data," EMCDDA Early Warning System, 2011.

See also "Shocking Rise in HIV Infections, Health Ministry Reports," *Athens News*, Nov 21, 2011. Available at: http://www.athensnews.gr/portal/9/50680

2. Following riots in 2008 Greece was labeled as "the sick man of Europe." See EurActive, 2008. Available at: http://www.euractiv.com/socialeurope/greece-appear-sick-man-eu-summit-news-220919; A. Carassava, "Euro Crisis: Why Greece Is the Sick Man of Europe," *BBC News Europe*, 2011. Available at: http://www.bbc.co.uk/news/world-europe-16256235

3. On the morning of May 1, Loverdos and his team went from brothel to brothel, 315 in all, detaining 275 prostitutes (and a few stray immigrants). He then subjected them to public humiliation. Their photographs and identities were published, and blood samples were taken from them. When twenty-nine of these women tested positive for HIV, Loverdos had them prosecuted for "intended injuries" to the public.

Charlotte McDonald-Gibson, "The Women Greece Blames for Its HIV Crisis," *The Independent*, July 25, 2012. Available at: http://www.independent.co.uk/news/world/europe

/the-women-greece-blames-for-its-hiv-crisis-7973313.html; Rights Equality & Diversity European Network, 2012. Minister of Health speaks of "sanitary bombs" in Athens center due to foreign prostituted women. Photos published by the police in Fileleftheros, 04.05.2012, Στη δημοσιότητα τα στοιχεία άλλων πέντε ιερόδουλων, αντιδράσεις για το μέτρο (Published details of five other prostitutes, reactions to the measure). Available at: http://www.philenews.com/el-gr/Eidiseis-Ellada/23/103185/sti-dimosiotita-ta-stoicheia-allon-pente-ierodoulon-antidraseis-gia-to-metro. Accessed April 5, 2012; D. Gatopoulos, "Greece Arrests 17 HIV-Positive Women in Brothels," *The Guardian*, May 2, 2012. Available at: http://www.guardian.co.uk/world/feedarticle/10224544. In total the number of positive cases reached twenty-nine. See "Five of First 100 Men Checked After Unprotected Sex with HIV+ Prostitutes Test Positive," Athens New Agency, May 9, 2012. Available at http://www.accessmylibrary.com/article-1G1-289305377/five-first-100-men.html; McDonald-Gibson, "The Women Greece Blames for Its HIV Crisis."

4. Embassy Athens, 2006. "2006 Investment Climate Statement Greece." Available at: http://www.cablegatesearch.net/cable.php?id=06ATHENS131; A. Carassava, "In Athens, Museum Is an Olympian Feat," *New York Times*, June 20, 2009. Available at: http://www.nytimes.com/2009/06/20/arts/design/20acropolis.html?_r=0. The marbles were stolen from the Athens Acropolis by Lord Elgin in the early 19th century and put on display in the British Museum in London. Greek diplomats and historians have wanted them back ever since.

5. D. Decloet, "As Greece Has Found, Foreign Investors Are No Cure," *Global and Mail*, Sept 6, 2012. Available at: http://m.theglobeandmail.com/report-on-business/rob-commentary/as-greece-has-found-foreign-investors-are-no-cure/article4318255/?service=mobile

6. On May 2, 2008, the Athens Stock Exchange was at 4,214, falling to 1,507 on March 3, 2009. Bloomberg. Athens Stock Exchange General Index. Available at: http://www.bloomberg.com/quote/ASE:IND/chart/

7. See B. Rauch, et al. 2011. "Fact and Fiction in EU-Governmental Economic Data," *German Economic Review* v12(3): 243–55.

8. In January 2013, Greek prosecutors launched an investigation into whether the Greek deficit numbers were artificially inflated by vested interests in order to provoke austerity measures. N. Kitsantonis, "Prosecutors Call for Investigation on Greek Deficit," *New York Times*, Jan 22, 2013. Available at: http://www.nytimes.com/2013/01/23/world/europe/greek-prosecutors-seek-inquiry-over-deficit-claims.html?src=recg

9. "Greek Bonds Rated 'Junk' by Standard & Poor's," BBC, April 27, 2010. Available at: http://news.bbc.co.uk/1/hi/business/8647441.stm.

10. M. Boesler, "The Controversial 'Lagarde List' Has Leaked, and It's Bad News for the Greek Prime Minister," *Business Insider*, Oct 27, 2012. Available at: http://www.businessinsider.com/lagarde-list-of-swiss-bank-accounts-leaked-2012-10

11. Proposals were made to forgive Greece's debt, since it accounted for only 4 percent percent of all debt held in Europe, as well as to create a "Eurobond" to help finance

Greece's obligations. But these compassionate solutions were outside of the Greek government's control; the country's destiny was in the hand of Europe and the international financial community, which were not sympathetic to Greece's plight.

12. H. Smith, "Greece's George Papandreou Announced €140bn Bailout Deal," *The Guardian*, May 2, 2010. Available at: http://www.guardian.co.uk/world/2010/may/02 /greece-economy-bailout-euro-eu-imf

13. G. Thesing and F. Krause-Jackson, "Greece Gets $146 Billion Rescue in EU, IMF Package," Bloomberg, 2010. Available at: http://www.bloomberg.com/apps /news?pid=2065100&sid=aqUKEXajkSzk. Amnesty International filed reports about police brutality, citing the alleged use of cancer-causing chemicals and excessive tear gas. See N. Kosmatopoulos, "Europe's Last Sick Man. Greek Austerity Measures Result in Cuts of Public Sectors Services with One Exception—The Police Force," *Al Jazeera*, 2011. Available at: http://www.aljazeera.com/indepth/opinion/2011/09 /20119269954438617.html. Interviewed on PBS News Hour in December 2012, an American poet, Alicia Stallings, living in her adopted country of Greece, read from a poem: "Weep, Pericles, or maybe just get drunk. / We will hawk the Parthenon to buy our bread. / If you believe the headlines, then we're sunk, / Greece downgraded deeper into junk."

At the Venice Biennale, the Greek artist Diohandi showed an exhibit entitled "The Ephemeral Is Eternal: Beyond Reform." Visitors to the Greek Pavilion found themselves confused by walking into a room that was empty except for pools of water on the floor. The art critic Maria Marangou wrote of the work for the Greek Ministry of Tourism and Culture: "The installation at the Greek pavilion in a way reflects, with Diohandi's specific work, the current political state of Europe and of the world at large. It is at the same time, obviously, a comment on the contemporary Greek experience of economic recession and IMF tutelage: a place of light thrown into darkness and decline, holding on, almost willy-nilly it seems, to hopes of spiritual and socio-political reconstruction; in other words, to a vision of light that should bring along clarity of mind, as if the ultimate catharsis." "Greek Pavilion at the Venice Biennale," Greek Ministry of Tourism and Culture, June 2, 2011. http://www.e-flux.com/announcements/greek-pavilion-at -the-54th-venice-biennale/

14. L. Alderman, "Greek Unemployed Cut Off from Medical Treatment," *New York Times*, Oct 24, 2012. Available at: http://www.nytimes.com/2012/10/25/world/europe /greek-unemployed-cut-off-from-medical-treatment.html?pagewanted=all&_r=0

15. E. Mossialos. 1997. "Citizens' Views on Health Care Systems in the 15 Member States of the European Union," *Health Econ* v6:109–16.

16. C. Boyle, "What's the Solution to Chronic Greek Corruption?" CNBC, June 16, 2012. Available at: http://www.cnbc.com/id/47830137/Whatrsquos_the_Solution_to _Chronic_Greek_Corruption

17. "Insulin Giant Pulls Medicine from Greece Over Price Cut," BBC, May 29, 2010. Available at: http://www.bbc.co.uk/news/10189367. Watching these frightening

trends develop, we pleaded with the National School of Public Health in Greece to carry out a rapid assessment and to propose a strategy to avoid medical disasters. We hoped to identify vulnerable groups and direct healthcare funds to those most at-risk. The School initially expressed interest, even developing a list of data from surveys we would analyze together, but after our exchange with the Greek Department of Health in the *Lancet,* our international team's emails went unanswered. It became clear that they would never deliver. We then asked the Nobel Peace Prize–winning organization Doctors Without Borders, to look into the issue. Their response in 2010 was that Greece had the capacity, if not the willpower, to deal with its own health problems. Pharmaceutical companies have withdrawn more than 200 medical products because of falling prices and payments. "Over 200 Medicines Taken Off Greek Market Because of Low Prices," *Ekathimerini,* March 8, 2013. Available at: http://ekathimerini.com/4dcgi/_w _articles_wsite1_1_07/03/2013_486155

18. Surveys of over 10,000 Greeks were taken in 2007 and 2009: EU Statistics on Income and Living Conditions.

19. In 2010 Greece had one of the highest shares of out-of-pocket payments for healthcare (38 percent): OECD Health at a Glance in Europe 2012, OECD. Available at: http://ec.europa.eu/health/reports/docs/health_glance_2012_en.pdf. As reports from Russia had taught us, "a hungry doctor can be bad for your health."

20. World Health Organization, European Health for All Database, Copenhagen, Denmark, 2012.

21. S. Bonovas and G. Nikolopoulos. 2012. "High-Burden Epidemics in Greece in the Era of Economic Crisis. Early Signs of a Public Health Tragedy," *J Prev Med Hyg* v53:169–71.

P. Andriopoulos, A. Economopoulou, G. Spanakos, G. Assimakopoulos. 2012. "A Local Outbreak of Autochthonous Plasmodium Vivax Malaria in Laconia, Greece—A Re-Emerging Infection in the Southern Borders of Europe?" *Int J Infect Dis* v17(2): e125–28.

22. Romania was the only other European country found to suffer a rise in HIV. The increase was attributed to injection drug use and withdrawal of HIV treatment.

23. Two epidemiologists called for "urgent public health action." D. Paraskevis and A. Hatzakis, "An Ongoing HIV Outbreak Among Intravenous Drug Users in Greece: Preliminary Summary of Surveillance and Molecular Epidemiology Data." EMCDDA Early Warning System, 2011. See also D. Paraskevis, G. Nikolopoulos, C. Tsiara, et al. 2011. "HIV-1 Outbreak Among Injecting Drug Users in Greece, 2011: A Preliminary Report," *EuroSurveillance* 16:19962; A. Fotiou, et al., *HIV Outbreak Among Injecting Drug Users in Greece: An Updated Report for the EMCDDA on the Recent Outbreak of HIV Infections Among Drug Injectors in Greece* (Athens: European Monitoring Centre for Drugs and Drug Addiction, 2012).

24. CDC Fact Sheets. 2005. *Syringe Exchange Programs.* Available at: http://www .cdc.gov/idu/facts/aed_idu_syr.pdf; UCSF Fact Sheet. 1998. "Does HIV Needle Exchange

Work?" Available at: http://caps.ucsf.edu/factsheets/needle-exchange-programs-nep/ EKTEPN. Annual Report on the State of the Drugs and Alcohol Problem. Athens: Greek Documentation and Monitoring Centre for Drugs, 2010.

25. Kentikelenis, et al., "Health Effects of Financial Crisis: Omens of a Greek Tragedy."

26. Amidst all these signs of suffering, Greece's economy continued to sink. GDP fell further 6.9 percent in 2011, as youth unemployment broke the 50 percent mark. Commentators have pointed out, however, that Papandreou's popularity had been falling in Greece and that, irrespective of the proposed austerity referendum, he may have been likely to have been forced out of office under escalating public protests.

27. See full report in N. Polyzos. 2012. "Health and the Financial Crisis in Greece," *The Lancet* v379(9820): 1000. A group of independent Greek psychiatrists and social scientists at the University of Athens conducted a nationwide survey and screening examination for mental health. They had been performing ongoing surveys of 2,820 people representative of the Greek population and were able to compare before and after the recession. They found that the prevalence of major depression rose from 3 percent before the recession to 8 percent in 2011. Those who suffered the most were, predictably, those facing the greatest economic hardship, and having the least access to social support.

28. L. Liaropoulos. 2012. "Greek Economic Crisis: Not a Tragedy for Health," *British Medical Journal* v345:e7988.

29. K. Kelland, "Basic Hygiene at Risk in Debt-Stricken Greek Hospitals," Reuters, Dec 4, 2012. Available at: http://newsle.com/article/0/48972507/; K. Kelland, "Health Officials Tell Greece to Act Fast to Control HIV," Reuters, Nov 29, 2012. Available at: http://www.reuters.com/article/2012/11/29/greece-health-hiv-idUSL5E8 MT71H20121129

30. Polyzos, "Health and the Financial Crisis in Greece."

31. "Health Scourge Hits Greece: Malaria, Once Mostly Eradicated, Returns as Crisis Erodes Government Safety Net," *Wall Street Journal*, Nov 14, 2012. Available at: http://online.wsj.com/article/SB10001424052970204789304578089463387817162 .html

32. Ibid. This was consistent with expert Greek epidemiologists' indication: "An additional factor the committee believed worth considering is the well-founded suspicion that some problem users are intentionally infected with HIV, because of the benefit they are entitled to (approximately €1,400 every two months), and also because they are granted "exceptional admission" to the Substitution Programme. It is well-known that the Substitution Programme has a long waiting list and that the waiting time can be over 3–4 years." I. Gregoriadi, et al. Report of the ad hoc expert group of the Greek focal point on the outbreak of HIV/AIDS in 2011. University Mental Health Research Institute. Available at: http://ewsd.wiv-isp.be/Rapid%20communications%20%20extra

%20information/Report%20of%20the%20Greek%20FP%20expert%20group%20
-%20AIDS.pdf

The BBC World Service reported in January 2012: "One morning a few weeks before Christmas a kindergarten teacher in Athens found a note about one of her four-year-old pupils." It read: "I will not be coming to pick up Anna today because I cannot afford to look after her. Please take good care of her. Sorry. Her mother." C. Hadjimatheou, "The Greek Parents Too Poor to Care for Their Children," BBC, Jan 10, 2012.

"Shocking Rise in HIV Infections, Health Ministry Reports," *Athens News*, Nov 21, 2011. Available at: http://www.athensnews.gr/portal/9/50680

33. "Shocking Rise in HIV Infections."

IMF, *IMF Staff Country Report. Greece: Fourth Review Under the Stand-by Arrangement and Request for Modification and Waiver of Applicability of Performance Criteria* (Washington, DC, July 2011). Available at: http://www.imf.org/external/pubs/ft/scr /2011/cr11175.pdf; Andrew Jack and Kerin Hope, "Greek Crisis Gets Under Skin of Vulnerable," *Financial Times*, May 12, 2012. Available at: http://www.ft.com/intl/cms/s /0/d1cc3256-78c3-11e1-9f49-00144feab49a.html#axzz2KBJ3FFxp

34. H. Smith, "IMF Official Admits Austerity Is Harming Greece," *The Guardian*, Feb 1, 2012. Available at: http://www.guardian.co.uk/business/2012/feb/01/imf-austerity -harming-greeve

O. Blanchard, and D. Leigh, "Growth Forecast Errors and Fiscal Multipliers." Available at: http://www.imf.org/external/pubs/cat/longres.aspx?sk=40200.0. See also B. Scoble, "The IMF Admits That Austerity Was a Miscalculation," *L'Humanité*, Jan 11, 2013. Available at: http://www.humaniteinenglish.com/spip.php?article2212

35. This was puzzling logic; the "let them fail" argument was one that Iceland had applied to its bankers, not its people. BBC. "Eurozone Approves Massive Greece Bailout," 2010. Available at: http://news.bbc.co.uk/2/hi/europe/8656649.stm

36. "Iceland: Cracks in the Crust," *The Economist*, Dec 11, 2008.

K. Connolly, "Germany Approves 50 Billion Euro Stimulus Package," *The Guardian*, Jan 27, 2009. Available at: http://www.guardian.co.uk/world/2009/jan/27/germany-europe

At the World Health Summit 2012, Daniel Bahr explained, "without our social security system, Germans economic growth would never have been possible." UHC Forward. Nov 11, 2012. Available at: http://uhcforward.org/headline/german-federal-minister -health-daniel-bahrs-opening-remarks-world-health-summit-focus-stron

37. Cited in D. Stuckler and M. McKee, "There Is an Alternative: Public Health Professionals Must Not Remain Silent at a Time of Financial Crisis," *European Journal of Public Health* v22(1): 2–3. Krugman also referred to austerity as "collective punishment." Cited in D. Aitkenhead and Paul Krugman, "I'm Sick of Being Cassandra. I'd Like to Win for Once," *The Guardian*, June 3, 2012. Available at: http://www.guardian .co.uk/business/2012/jun/03/paul-krugman-cassandra-economist-crisis

38. One former Labour MP in the UK went so far as to argue, "Just as Germany destroyed Europe once in World War II, it is now bent on doing so for a second time." See "Athens Police Fire Tear Gas in Crackdown Clashes at Anti-Merkel Protest," RT, Oct 8, 2012. Available at: http://rt.com/news/greece-protests-germany-merkel-946/

PART III: RESILIENCE

Chapter 6: To Care or Not to Care

1. Name changed for confidentiality.

2. J. Steinhauer, "California Budget Deal Closes $26 Billion Gap," *New York Times*, July 25, 2009. Available at: http://www.nytimes.com/2009/07/25/us/25calif.html?hp IRS, Administrative, Procedural and Miscellaneous. http://www.irs.gov/pub/irs-drop /rp-09–29.pdf

Routine care was often covered, but not all Americans were aware of what was covered and what was not. See C. Fleming. "New Health Affairs: High-Deductible Health Plan Enrollees Avoid Preventive Care Unnecessarily." Health Affairs Blog, Dec 3, 2012. Available at: http://healthaffairs.org/blog/2012/12/03/new-health-affairs-high-deduct ible-health-plan-enrollees-avoid-preventive-care-unnecessarily/

3. A. Wilper, et al. 2009. "Health Insurance and Mortality in US Adults," *American Journal of Public Health* v99(12): 2289–95.

4. Ibid. People who are uninsured are just one emergency room visit away from bankruptcy. During the recession about one-quarter of uninsured persons used their entire savings to pay medical bills. About three out of every four Americans are now struggling to cope with medical bills or healthcare-related debt, which is more than those with mortgage-payment difficulties. New Hampshire Medicaid Enrollment Forecast, SFY 2011–2013 Update. Available at: http://www.dhhs.nh.gov/ombp/documents /forecast.pdf. K. Carollo, 2010. American Medical Association condemns insurance "purging." Available at: http://abcnews.go.com/Health/HealthCare/american-medical -association-condemns-insurance-purging/story?id=10920504

5. Prior to the Affordable Care Act in order to qualify for Medicaid the applicant had to be poor *and* a) a family with children who met certain eligibility requirements (e.g. disabled), b) elderly, disabled or blind, c) with child less than six years old or pregnant mother, d) with school-age children ages six to eighteen.

6. Kaiser Commission of Medicaid and the Uninsured, State Fiscal Conditions and Medicaid Program Changes, FY 2012–2013, Nov 28, 2012. Available at: http://www .kff.org/medicaid/7580.cfm; Erica Williams, Michael Leachman, and Nicholas Johnson, "State Budget Cuts in the New Fiscal Year Are Unnecessarily Harmful—Cuts Are Hitting Hard at Education, Health Care, and State Economies," Center for Budget and Policy Priorities, updated July 28, 2011. Available at: http://www.cbpp.org/cms/index .cfm?fa=view&id=3550

7. A. Haviland, et al. "High-Deductible Health Plans Cut Spending but Also Reduce Preventive Care." RAND Health Fact Sheet, 2011. Available at: http://www.rand.org/pubs/research_briefs/RB9588.html; M. Buntin, et al. 2011. "Healthcare Spending and Preventive Care in High-Deductible and Consumer-Directed Health Plans," *The American Journal of Managed Care* v17(3): 222–30.

8. The Commonwealth Fund, "Help on the Horizon," March 2011. Available at: http://www.commonwealthfund.org/~/media/Files/Publications/Fund%20Report/2011/Mar/1486_Collins_help_on_the_horizon_2010_biennial_survey_report_FINAL_v2.pdf; S. Dorn, et al. 2012. "Impact of the 2008–2009 Economic Recession on Screening Colonoscopy Utilization Among the Insured," *Clinical Gastroenterology and Hepatology* v10(3): 278–84. Available at: http://www.sciencedirect.com/science/article/pii/S154235651101278X; J. D. Piette, et al. 2011. "Medication Cost Problems Among Chronically Ill Adults in the US: Did the Financial Crisis Make a Bad Situation Even Worse?" *Patient Preference and Adherence* v5:187.

9. Since 2008, more than 49,000 state and local public health department jobs have been cut. "Kaiser Commission on Medicaid and the Uninsured. Emergency Departments Under Growing Pressures," 2009. Available at: http://www.kff.org/uninsured/upload/7960.pdf

10. Emily Walker, "Health Insurers Post Record Profits," ABC News, Feb 12, 2010. Available at: http://abcnews.go.com/Health/HealthCare/health-insurers-post-record-profits/story?id=9818699

See, for example, Emily Berry, "Health Plans Say They'll Risk Losing Members to Protect Profit Margins," *American Medical News*, May 19, 2008. Available at: http://www.ama-assn.org/amednews/2008/05/19/bil10519.htm

Company	2010 Profits (first nine months)	2009 Profits (first nine months)	Change in Profits (first nine months)	Percent Change in Profits
UnitedHealthcare	$3.59 billion	$2.88 billion	+$713 million	+24.8%
WellPoint	$2.34 billion	$2.00 billion	+334 million	+16.7%
Aetna	$1.55 billion	$1.11 billion	+441 million	+39.7%
Humana	$992 million	$789 million	+203 million	+25.7%
Coventry	$288 million	$133 million	+155 million	+116.4%
AmeriGroup	$194 million	$109 million	+84.6 million	+77.5%
HealthSpring	$143 million	$94.8 million	+48.6 million	+51.3%
HealthNet	$124 million	−$3.8 million	+127.6 million	—
Centene	$69.4 million	$60.0 million	+9.4 million	+15.7%
Molina	$37.3 million	$35.3 million	+2.0 million	+5.7%

FIGURE 6.1   For-Profit Insurers—Profits for the First Nine Months of 2010
Source: Third quarter earnings reports compiled by the Office of Congressman Pete Stark

11. Kenneth J. Arrow, "Uncertainty and the Welfare Economics of Medical Care," *The American Economic Review,* Dec 1963; P. Krugman, "Why Markets Can't Cure Healthcare," *New York Times,* 2009. Available at: http://krugman.blogs.nytimes.com /2009/07/25/why-markets-cant-cure-healthcare/

12. J. Hart. 1971. "The Inverse Care Law," *The Lancet* v297(7696): 405–12. As the paper notes, "this inverse care law operates more completely where medical care is most exposed to market forces, and less so where such exposure is reduced."

13. Contrary to conventional wisdom, Americans don't visit the doctor as much, or use more expensive technologies, either—for example, they get fewer MRIs per person than Japan and fewer expensive hip surgeries than much of Europe, but are simply being charged more for the same MRI. The nursing home population is also smaller, proportionally. Institute of Medicine. "U.S. Health in International Perspective: Shorter Lives, Poorer Health," 2013. Available at: http://www.iom.edu/Reports/2013/US -Health-in-International-Perspective-Shorter-Lives-Poorer-Health.aspx. The reasons for high US healthcare spending are reviewed in a report by the Commonwealth Fund, available at: http://www.commonwealthfund.org/Publications/Issue-Briefs/2012/May /High-Health-Care-Spending.aspx. For the data on drug research and development spending, see Families USA. "Profiting from Pain: Where Prescription Drug Dollars Go," 2009. Available at: http://www.policyarchive.org/handle/10207/6305

14. Institute of Medicine, "U.S. Health In International Perspective: Shorter Lives, Poorer Health," 2013. Available at: "http://www.iom.edu/Reports/2013/US-Health-in -International-Perspective-Shorter-Lives-Poorer-Health.aspx. The United States now ranks last in male life expectancy among developed countries (even after taking into account its exceptionally high death rate from firearms).

15. A. Lusardi, D. Schneider, P. Tufano, "The Economic Crisis and Medical Care Usage," Dartmouth College. Available at: http://www.dartmouth.edu/~alusardi/Papers /healthcare_031610.pdf

16. Many factors contributed to the rise in the NHS. It was implemented as part of a suite of major reforms that launched the British welfare state in the postwar period. See D. Stuckler, A. Feigl, S. Basu, M. McKee, "The Political Economy of Universal Health Coverage. First Global Symposium on Health Systems Research," Nov 2009. Available at: http://www.pacifichealthsummit.org/downloads/UHC/the%20political %20economy%20of%20uhc.PDF

17. Jeremy Laurance, "NHS Watchdog Is Winning the Price War with Drug Companies," *The Independent,* Dec 21, 2009. Available at: http://www.independent.co.uk/life -style/health-and-families/health-news/nhs-watchdog-is-winning-the-price-war-with -drug-companies-1846352.html. See NHS core principles, 2013. Available at: http:// www.nhs.uk/NHSEngland/thenhs/about/Pages/nhscoreprinciples.aspx

18. The Commonwealth Fund and the OECD had previously labeled the NHS the most efficient, effective, and responsive system in the world; the Tory government is now turning it into an unresponsive market-based healthcare system like that in the US.

19. Sunny Hundal, "Revealed: The Pamphlet Underpinning Tory Plans to Privatise the NHS," *Liberal Conspiracy*, June 3, 2011. Available at: http://liberalconspiracy .org/2011/06/03/revealed-the-pamphlet-underpinning-tory-plans-to-privatise-the -nhs/

Andy McSmith, "Letwin: 'NHS Will Not Exist Under Tories'," *The Independent*, June 6, 2004. Available at: http://www.independent.co.uk/life-style/health-and-families /health-news/letwin-nhs-will-not-exist-under-tories-6168295.html. Austerity went a step further: "For unto every one that hath shall be given, and he shall have abundance: but from him that hath not shall be taken away even that which he hath."

20. The big difference in costs were coming from private healthcare, which added 1.6 percent in the UK, 2.6 percent in France, 2.7 percent in Germany, and 9.1 percent in the US. The Commonwealth Fund 2010 International Health Policy Survey. See also Rita O'Brien, "Kent, Keep Our NHS Public." Available at: http://www.keepournhspublic .com/pdf/howdoestheNHScompare.pdf

21. The British Medical Association held its first emergency meeting in two decades, calling on the government to withdraw the bill.

Helen Duffett, "Nick Clegg's Speech on NHS Reform," *Liberal Democratic Voice*, May 26, 2011. Available at: http://www.libdemvoice.org/nick-cleggs-speech-on-nhs -reform-24260.html

22. Tom Jennings, "Action to Turn Round Health Centre Wins Praise," *Oxford Times*, Jan 16, 2013. Available at: http://www.oxfordtimes.co.uk/news/yourtown/witney /10162757.print/

23. "Further Privatisation Is Inevitable Under the Proposed NHS Reforms," *British Medical Journal*, May 17, 12012. Available at: http://www.bmj.com/content/342/bmj.d2996

24. Randeep Ramsh, "Public Satisfaction with NHS Slumped During Reforms Debate, Thinktank Finds," *The Guardian*, June 11, 2012. Available at: http://www .guardian.co.uk/society/2012/jun/12/public-satisfaction-nhs-thinktank. These patterns were consistent with research of a natural experiment in Italy's National Health Service, which found that those regions undergoing greater privatization of healthcare delivery had worse healthcare performance. C. Quercioli, G. Messina, S. Basu, M. McKee, N. Nante, D. Stuckler. 2013. "The Effect of Health Care Delivery Privatization on Avoidable Mortality: Longitudinal Cross-Regional Results from Italy, 1993–2003," *Journal of Epidemiology & Community Health* v67(2): 132–38.

25. "A&E Waits Highest for a Decade," BBC News, Feb 13, 2012. Available at: http://www.bbc.co.uk/news/health-21444444

26. "NHS Shakeup Spells 'Unprecedented Chaos,' Warns Lancet Editor," *The Guardian*, March 24, 2012. Available at: http://www.guardian.co.uk/society/2012/mar /24/nhs-shakeup-chaos-lancet

27. Under current EU competition law, the NHS would be fully opened up to compulsory competitive markets, and private corporations are to be eligible to receive the same government subsidies as publicly funded services.

28. F. Ponsar, K. Tayler-Smith, M. Philips, S. Gerard, M. Van Herp, T. Reid, R. Zachariah, "No Cash, No Care: How User Fees Endanger Health—Lessons Learnt Regarding Financial Barriers to Healthcare Services in Burundi, Sierra Leone, Democratic Republic of Congo, Chad, Haiti and Mali," *International Health,* 2011. Available at: http://fieldresearch.msf.org/msf/bitstream/10144/203642/1/Ponsar%20No%20cash, %20No%20care.pdf

29. D. Stuckler, A. Feigl, S. Basu, M. McKee. "The Political Economy of Universal Health Coverage." First Global Symposium on Heath Systems Research, 2009. Available at: http://www.pacifichealthsummit.org/downloads/UHC/the%20political%20economy %20of%20uhc.PDF

Chapter 7: Returning to Work

1. B. Wedeman, "Death and Taxes in Italy," CNN, Sept 9, 2010. Available at: http:// edition.cnn.com/2012/09/10/business/italy-economy-suicide/index.html; A. Vogt, "Widows of Italian Suicide Victims Make Protest March Against Economic Strife." *The Guardian*, 2012. Available at: http://www.guardian.co.uk/world/2012/may/04/widows-italian -businessmen-march

2. "May Day: Italy's 'White Widows' Give Private Pain a Public Face." Available at: http://thefreelancedesk.com/?p=543; A. Vogt, "Italian Women Whose Husbands Killed Themselves in Recession Stage March," *The Guardian*, April 30, 2012. Available at: http:// www.guardian.co.uk/world/2012/apr/30/italian-women-husbands-recession-march

3. K. N. Fountoulakis, et al., "Economic Crisis-Related Increased Suicidality in Greece and Italy: A Premature Overinterpretation,"*Journal of Epidemiology and Community Health*, March 12, 2012. Available at: http://jech.bmj.com/content/early/2012/12/03/jech -2012-201902.full.pdf+html; to which we responded in R. De Vogli, M. Marmot, D. Stuckler. 2012. "Strong Evidence That the Economic Crisis Caused a Rise in Suicides in Europe: The Need for Social Protection." *Journal of Epidemiology and Community Health*. Available at: http://jech.bmj.com/content/early/2013/01/14/jech-2012-202112

4. "In Debt or Jobless, Many Italians Choose Suicide," NBC News, May 9, 2012. Available at: http://worldblog.nbcnews.com/_news/2012/05/09/11621840-in-debt-or -jobless-many-italians-choose-suicide?lite

5. Looking at data disaggregated by state from the US Centers for Disease Control and Prevention, we found that increases in state suicide rates corresponded in timing and size to the changes in each state's unemployment rate.

6. Source for Figure 7.1: Authors'. Adapted from R. De Vogli, M. Marmot, D. Stuckler. 2012. "Excess Suicides and Attempted Suicides in Italy Attributable to the Great Recession," *Journal of Epidemiology & Community Health*. doi: 10.1136/jech-2012-201607.

7. G. Lewis and A. Sloggett. 1998. "Suicide, Deprivation, and Unemployment; Record Linkage Study," *British Medical Journal* v317:1283. Available at: http://www.bmj .com/content/317/7168/1283

8. Source for Figure 7.2: Adapted from A. Reeves, D. Stuckler, M. McKee, D. Gunnell, S. Chang, S. Basu. November 2012. "Increase in State Suicide Rates in the USA During Economic Recession," *The Lancet* v380(9856): 1813–14.

9. The leading advocate of this theory was Professor Hugh Gravelle, who argued that people were not sick because they were unemployed, but unemployed because they were sick. Professor Mel Bartley, a social epidemiologist, criticized Gravelle's logic in the *BMJ*: Where, Bartley asked, was the sudden massive epidemic that preceded the rise in unemployment by 3 million people? He noted, "we really cannot plausibly argue that an increase in the incidence of mental ill health or alcoholism could cause an increase in unemployment at the level of a national population."

K. Moser, P. Goldblatt, A. Fox, et al. 1987. "Unemployment and Mortality: Comparison of the 1971 and 1981 Longitudinal Study Census Samples," *British Medical Journal* v294:86–90.

For suicide risk, see Lewis and Sloggett, "Suicide, Deprivation, and Unemployment; Record Linkage Study"; T. Blakely, S. C. D. Collings, J. Atkinson, "Unemployment and Suicide: Evidence for a Causal Association?" *Journal of Epidemiology & Community Health* v57(8): 594–600.

Montgomery and colleagues found that unemployment predated symptoms of depression and anxiety. See S. Montgomery, D. Cook, M. Bartley, et al. 1999. "Unemployment Pre-dates Symptoms of Depression and Anxiety Resulting in Medical Consultation in Young Men," *Int J Epidemiol* v28:95–100.

10. In 1994 Professor Mel Bartley later explained in the *Journal of Epidemiology and Community Health*: "It is no longer seriously argued that there is no such relationship [between unemployment and illness]. Lower levels of psychological well-being are found in all studies which compared unemployed people, at all ages and in both sexes. More persuasively, these differences in mental health have been shown to emerge after entry into the labor market in young people showing no such differences while still at school. Mental health improves when young people find jobs." Available at: http://jech .bmj.com/content/48/4/333.full.pdf. Women report higher rates of depression, but men are about three times as likely as women to experience suicide. The reasons are multiple, but are in part because women are more likely to seek help.

R. Davis, "Antidepressant Use Rises as Recession Feeds Wave of Worry," *The Guardian*, June 11, 2010. Available at: http://www.guardian.co.uk/society/2010/jun/11/antide pressant-prescriptions-rise-nhs-recession

11. "Workers Turn to Antidepressants as Recession Takes Its Toll," *Mind*, May 17, 2010. Available at: http://www.mind.org.uk/news/3372_workers_turn_to_antidepressants _as_recession_takes_its_toll

The *Telegraph* reported an even larger rise of 7 million prescriptions during the recession. See Martin Evans, "Recession Linked to Huge Rise in Use of Antidepressants," *Telegraph*, April 7, 2011. Available at: http://www.telegraph.co.uk/health/8434106 /Recession-linked-to-huge-rise-in-use-of-antidepressants.html

12. Unemployment was also correlated with rising prescriptions for pain medicines and stomach ulcers. F. Jespersen and M. Tirrell, "Stress-Medication Sales Hold Up as Economy Gives Heartburn to U.S. Jobless," *Bloomberg*, Dec 27, 2011. Available at: http://www.bloomberg.com/news/2011-12-27/stress-medications-holding-up-through -economic-doldrums-study-suggests.html

13. Consistent with existing research, our further evidence found that fear of unemployment—economic insecurity—could be as harmful to mental health as actual job loss.

14. We found this applied not only to the individual but also whether any member of the family had recently lost work. M. Gili, M. Roca, S. Basu, M. McKee, D. Stuckler. 2012. "The Mental Health Risks of Economic Crisis in Spain: Evidence from Primary Care Centres, 2006 and 2010," *European Journal of Public Health* v23(1): 103–8. Available at: http://eurpub.oxfordjournals.org/content/23/1/103. We also found eviction was a major risk factor for mental health diagnoses.

15. The OECD defines ALMPs as follows: "First, they make receipt of benefits conditional on the benefit recipient demonstrating active job search and/or a willingness to take steps to improve employability. Second, they provide a range of pre-employment services and advice to help the individuals in question find work or get ready for work." For a distribution of passive versus active labor market policies, see J. P. Martin, "What Works Among Active Labour Market Policies: Evidence from OECD Countries' Experiences." Available at: http://www.rba.gov.au/publications/confs/1998/martin.pdf

16. J. Vuori and J. Silvonen, et al. 2002. "The Tyohon Job Search Program in Finland: Benefits for the Unemployed with Risk of Depression or Discouragement," *J Occup Health Psychol* v7(1): 5–19; J. Vuori and J Silvonen. 2005. "The Benefits of a Preventive Job Search Program on Re-employment and Mental Health at 2-year Follow-up," *Journal of Occupational and Organizational Psychology* v78(1): 43–52. The specific Työhön program included the following components: The program paired a job-search trainer with newly unemployed people. The trainer worked five half-day sessions to help place unemployed people into the job search databases, and improve their skills—interviewing techniques, how to find jobs through social networks, how to assemble resumes and job applications—to overcome common setbacks and prevent the slump of chronic unemployment. The ALMPs also featured encouragement to take even part-time work or help gain job-training to switch to other types of work. Financial support was also a component of ALMP programs, but funds were provided only to those who participated in the part of the program that also helped them get back to work. Those participating in the program also found better-quality jobs, with the greatest benefits observed among those who had lost jobs within the past few years. Similar evidence that ALMPs helped prevent depression came from studies in the United States.

A. Vinokur, R. Price, and Y. Schul. 1995. "Impact of the JOBS Intervention on Unemployed Workers Varying in Risk for Depression," *American Journal of Community Psychology* v23(1): 39–74; A. Vinokur, et al. 2000. "Two Years After a Job Loss: Long-term Impact of the JOBS Program on Reemployment and Mental Health," *J Occup*

Health Psychol v5(1): 32–47. ALMP strategies were tested at Michigan's Prevention Research Center. The Michigan researchers introduced a JOBS workshop program in which 1,801 participants were randomly assigned to a job-search intervention or to a control group. This was the equivalent of a laboratory study, but done in the real world. It found that within two years, those who received job-search support were more likely to be working again, had higher monthly earnings, and lower risks of depression. Further research found that these persons were not simply jumping the queue to find jobs; ALMPs were helping to increase overall employment rates across countries.

17. Another way was that ALMPs help promote full employment. Some ALMPs had a component to work with firms to help them retain workers instead of making them redundant. This would help prevent a recession from leading firms to shed more jobs, so that fewer people were put in the risky situation of unemployment in the first place. As the World Bank defines them, "ALMPs have two basic objectives: (i) economic, by increasing the probability of the unemployed finding jobs, productivity and earnings; and (ii) social, by improving inclusion and participation associated with productive employment. As a consequence, they can contribute to increased employment opportunities and address the social problems that often accompany high unemployment."

18. OECD Database on Social Expenditure. Available at: http://www.google.co
.uk/url?sa=t&rct=j&q=&esrc=s&source=web&cd=2&cad=rja&ved=0CDoQFjAB&
url=http%3A%2F%2Fstats.oecd.org%2Ffileview2.aspx%3FIDFile%3D91c26892-ed
0b-41f6-bf61-fd46e39a40e8&ei=gZMOUc2JJqnD0QX75oCgDA&usg=AFQjCNG–
faugVqOyViluaA1OX_9ZlYwMQ&sig2=qOCNRgH_F7x2unphGfzd8w&bvm=bv.4
1867550,d.d2k; http://www.oecd.org/els/employmentpoliciesanddata/36780874.pdf

19. L. Jonung and T. Hagberg, "How Costly Was the Crisis of the 1990s? A Comparative Analysis of the Deepest Crises in Finland and Sweden over the Last 130 Years," *European Commission. Economic Papers,* 2005. Available at: http://ec.europa.eu
/economy_finance/publications/publication692_en.pdf

See also L. Jonung, "The Swedish Model for Resolving the Banking Crisis of 1991–93. Seven Reasons Why It Was Successful." Available at: http://ec.europa.eu/economy
_finance/publications/publication14098_en.pdf

20. OECD Social Expenditure Database 2008 edition.

21. Source for Figure 7.3: D. Stuckler S. Basu M. Suhrcke, A. Coutts, M. McKee. 2009. "The Public Health Impact of Economic Crises and Alternative Policy Responses in Europe," *The Lancet* v374:315–23.

22. Source for Figure 7.4: Stuckler, et al. "The Public Health Impact of Economic Crises and Alternative Policy Responses in Europe."

23. Jonung and Haberg, "How Costly Was the Crisis of the 1990s?

24. Our colleague, the medical doctor Sir Michael Marmot, had already warned UK policymakers in 2011 that the "scale of youth unemployment was a public health emergency." See Michael Marmot. 2011. "Scale of Youth Unemployment Is a Public Health

Emergency, Marmot Says," *British Medical Journal*. Available at: http://www.bmj.com/content/343/bmj.d7608?tab=related

25. For a version that is at the time of this writing available online, see "Recession and Unemployment Could Be Blamed for 1,000 More Suicides," *London Evening Standard*, 2012. Available at: http://www.standard.co.uk/news/health/recession-and-unemployment-could-be-blamed-for-1000-more-suicides-8049459.html

26. Cited in B. Barr, D. Taylor-Robinson, A. Scott-Samuel, M. McKee, D. Stuckler. 2012. "Suicides Associated With the 2008–10 Economic Recession in England: A Time-Trend Analysis," *British Medical Journal* v345:e5142. Available at: http://www.ncbi.nlm.nih.gov/pmc/articles/PMC3419273/

27. H. Stewart, "Osborne's Austerity Drive Cut 270,000 Public Sector Jobs Last Year," *The Guardian*, March 14, 2012. Available at: http://www.guardian.co.uk/business/2012/mar/14/osborne-austerity-270000-public-sector-jobs

In Europe, policy discussions took a similar denialist tone. Nine times during sessions of EU Parliament, members of that parliament raised concerns about rising suicides. John Dalli, the EU Health Commissioner, said, "The Commission is aware of the article by David Stuckler et al [but] it needs to be taken into account that there is a range of different economic, social and health factors and causes involved." In other words, the government was going to claim that the problem was so "multi-factorial" that there was nothing to do about it; the problem would just be buried in bureaucratic language. Another response by Mr. Andor, representing work initiatives, also noted that very little was being done. "The Commission is not aware of mental health support structures in Member States to address mental health problems arising specifically from unemployment. Public employment services can offer personalised support, which the Commission encourages."

28. There was one further test to assess whether the relationship between ALMPs and suicidality was causal: whether a correlation from the past can predict what happens in the future. While we found that UK, US, and Spain were experiencing significant rises in economic suicides, we saw the mental health of Sweden's population was protected from the Great Recession. During Sweden's recession, GDP in the country fell by as much as in the US, but thanks to the ALMPs, unemployment rose to a lesser degree during the recession, from 6.1 percent in 2007 to 9.1 percent at the peak in 2010. Meanwhile there was no obvious impact on suicides. In 2007, Sweden's suicide rates were 11.4 per 100,000 people under age sixty-five. In 2010, these rates had actually dropped, to 11.1 per 100,000 under age sixty-five.

29. D. Wasserman. *Mental Health and Suicidal Behaviour in Times of Economic Crisis: Impact and Prevention*. Mental Health and Suicidal Behaviour in Times of Economic Crisis: Impact and Prevention, Stockholm, Sweden, 2009.

Chapter 8: A Plague on All Your Houses

1. The bird deaths were "signaling the Apocalypse," one resident proclaimed after the Sunday sermon at the Valley Baptist Church. "Local Men Suffer State's First West

Nile Deaths," *Bakersfield Californian,* Oct 3, 2011. Available at: http://www.bakers fieldcalifornian.com/local/x651158822/Two-local-men-suffer-states-first-West-Nile -deaths

2. CDC. Symptoms of West Nile Virus. Available at: http://www.cdc.gov/ncidod /dvbid/westnile/qa/symptoms.htm

3. "Heat Death in Kern Country," *Bakersfield Californian,* June 21, 2007. Available at: http://www.bakersfieldcalifornian.com/local/x1756813242/Heat-death-in-Kern -County

4. M. Engel, "Virus Linked to Foreclosures," *Los Angeles Times,* Oct 31, 2008. Available at: http://articles.latimes.com/2008/oct/31/science/sci-westnile31

5. "Governor Declares State of Emergency for Kern County over West Nile," *Bakersfield Californian,* Aug 2, 2007. Available at: http://www.bakersfieldcalifornian.com /local/x1018063026/Governor-declares-state-of-emergency-for-Kern-County-over -West-Nile-virus

W. K. Reisen, R. M. Takahashi, B. D. Carroll, R. Quiring. 2008. "Delinquent Mortgages, Neglected Swimming Pools, and West Nile Virus, California," *Emerging Infectious Diseases* v14(11): 1747–49. Available at: http://www.ncbi.nlm.nih.gov/pmc /articles/PMC2630753/

6. "Fight the Bite! City Gets Sprayed for West Nile Virus." Available at: http:// fightthebite.blogspot.com/2007/08/bakersfield-prepare-to-be-sprayed.html

7. S. Russell, "West Nile Virus Upturn Traced to Dry Climate," *SFGate,* July 21, 2007. Available at: http://www.sfgate.com/health/article/CALIFORNIA-West-Nile-virus -upturn-traced-to-dry-2551675.php

8. RealtyTrac Staff foreclosure activity increases 81 percent in 2008. 2009. Available at: http://www.realtytrac.com/ContentManagement/pressrelease.aspx?ChannelID=9& ItemID=5681. Accessed May 5, 2009.

"Foreclosure Statistics for US, Mass., During Recession," *Boston Globe,* Dec 2, 2012. Available at: http://www.bostonglobe.com/business/2012/12/02/foreclosure-statistics -for-mass-during-recession/GUf8zjEWw0xM3DQjhuYarN/story.html

L. Christie, "California Cities Fill Top 10 Foreclosure List," *CNN Money,* July 14, 2007. Available at: http://money.cnn.com/2007/08/14/real_estate/California_cities_lead _foreclosure/index.htm; Reisen, Takashi, Carroll, Quiring, "Delinquent Mortgages, Neglected Swimming Pools, and West Nile Virus."

One of the victims was ninety-six-year-old Marguerite Wilson. She didn't have any standing water around her northeast Bakersfield home for mosquitoes to breed in, but must have been bitten around town. Her obituary described, "a college graduate in her 40s. A congressional intern in her 70s. A world traveller in her 90s." Senator Roy Ashburn, whose campaign she had supported, said "she defied age." "It is hard to believe that a woman can make it through 96 years and then die from a bite from a mosquito," her granddaughter said. Her traveling partner Diane Flynn reflected that "I really and truly wanted her death to spark an interest in mosquito abatement."

9. Mosquitoes weren't the only threat. In July 2008, Sheyenne Jenkins, a five-year-old girl, went out to play in the backyard of home in Avon, Indiana, while her grandparents were babysitting her. She wandered into the neighbors' yard—a foreclosed home that had been abandoned with a backyard pool full of water. The pool's cover, without anyone to tend to it, had begun to sag beneath the surface. Somehow, Sheyenne fell in. By the time that she was found, it was too late."I'm angry that nothing was done. I'm angry that my daughter was taken away because nothing was done," Sheyenne's mother said. Repossessed homes were left by banks to fall into disrepair. As NBC News reporter Kerry Sanders put it, "Sheyenne's tragedy is a worst-case example of the unintended consequences of foreclosure." M. Celizic, "Foreclosed Homes' Pools Can Be Death Traps," NBC News, 2009. Available at: http://today.msnbc.msn.com/id/31795988/ns/today-money/t/foreclosed-homes-pools-can-be-death-traps/

10. Not just having a home, but the quality of the house and neighborhood impacts health. Damp, mold, and cold in substandard housing create the toxic living conditions that exacerbate childhood asthma and winter deaths. When people live in poorly ventilated, close quarters, it's easier to spread airborne diseases such as tuberculosis. One RAND study in the 1990s compared neighborhoods that were equally deprived but found that those with substandard housing had a dramatic effect on increased risk of dying prematurely. Substandard housing and deprived neighborhoods have further been found to be linked to greater rates of child mortality, HIV and sexually transmitted diseases, diabetes, cardiovascular disease, violent deaths, among many other health threats. As one systematic review concluded, "Investment in housing can be more than an investment in bricks and mortar: It can also form a foundation for the future health and well-being of the population." For more details see p. 11, Department of Health, 2010. Available at: http://www.dh.gov.uk/prod_consum_dh/groups/dh_digitalassets/@dh/@en/@ps/documents/digitalasset/dh_114369.pdf

11. G. G. Bennett, M. Scharoun-Lee, R. Tucker-Seeley, "Will the Public's Health Fall Victim to the Home Foreclosure Epidemic?" *PLoS Medicine,* 2009. Available at: http://www.plosmedicine.org/article/info%3Adoi%2F10.1371%2Fjournal.pmed.1000087; D. Alley, et al. 2011. "Mortgage Delinquency and Changes in Access to Health Resources and Depressive Symptoms in a Nationally Representative Cohort of Americans Older Than 50 Years," *American Journal of Public Health* v101(12): 2293–98. Available at: http://ajph.aphapublications.org/doi/abs/10.2105/AJPH.2011.300245

The researchers also controlled for pre-existing symptoms and behaviors (implying that these effects were truly related to the mortgage payment difficulties themselves, rather than being a mere correlation).

12. C. E. Pollack, et al. 2011. "A Case-Control Study of Home Foreclosure, Health Conditions, and Health Care Utilization," *Journal of Urban Health* v88(3): 469–78. Available at: http://link.springer.com/article/10.1007%2Fs11524-011-9564-7?LI=true

13. J. Currie and E. Tekin, "Is There a Link Between Foreclosure and Health?" NBER Working Paper No. 17310, 2012. Available at: http://www.nber.org/papers

/w17310.pdf; S. M. Kalita, "Tying Health Problems to Rise in Home Foreclosures," *Wall Street Journal*, 2011. Available at: http://online.wsj.com/article/SB10001424053111 904199404576538293771870006.html

Similarly, in the UK, emergency room visits rose but to a lesser degree, from 12.3 million emergency room visits to 13.8 million: http://www.hesonline.nhs.uk/Ease /servlet/ContentServer?siteID=1937&categoryID=1834

14. J. Nye, "How Foreclosures Ate America," *Daily Mail*, Oct 2, 2012. Available at: http://www.dailymail.co.uk/news/article-2212071/How-foreclosures-ate-America -Incredible-interactive-map-shows-wave-property-repossession-past-years.html #axzz2KA5qnpGS. In January 2009, the month Obama came into office, there were 274,399 foreclosures nationwide, a figure which continued to its upward march to 341,180 in March 2010.

15. US Conference of Mayors, *A Hunger and Homelessness Survey, 2007*. Available at: http://usmayors.org/uscm/home.asp; see also http://www.nationalhomeless.org/fact sheets/How_Many.html; quoted in P. Markee, "The Unfathomable Cuts in Housing Aid," *The Nation*, Dec 4, 2011. Available at: http://www.thenation.com/article/165161 /unfathomable-cuts-housing-aid

16. Unemployment, poverty, and foreclosure are three main risk factors for homelessness associated with the recession. Other factors include alcohol and drug use, mental health problems, and domestic violence. See National Alliance to End Homelessness. Foreclosure and Homelessness, 2013. Available at: http://www.endhomelessness.org /pages/foreclosure. A 2009 survey of homeless support organizations found that between 5 percent (the estimate of those working at homeless shelters) and 20 percent (the figure given by service-only providers) of their clients were homeless due to foreclosure. Foreclosures and Homelessness: Understanding the Connection. Institute for Children, Poverty, and Homelessness, 2013. Available at: http://www.icphusa.org/filelibrary/ICPH _policybrief_ForeclosuresandHomelessness.pdf

"Hunger and Homelessness Survey: A Status Report on Hunger and Homelessness in America's Cities: A 25-City Survey," The United States Conference of Mayors, 2008, p. 22.

US Department of Housing and Urban Development. *The Third Annual Homeless Assessment Report to Congress* (Washington, DC: US Department of Housing and Urban Development, 2007). Between 2006 and 2007, homelessness had dropped by 11 percent but with rising foreclosures in subsequent years, homelessness rates increased, reaching a new peak in 2009. A survey of twenty-five city mayors asked if they had adopted a policy to prevent homelessness among families whose homes were foreclosed; thirteen cities replied that they had but ten cities had not and two did not know.

M. W. Sermons and P. Witte, "State of Homelessness in America," National Alliance to End Homelessness. Available at: http://b.3cdn.net/naeh/4813d7680e4580020f_ky 2m6ocx1.pdf. The homelessness numbers are estimated slightly differently in this report for unsheltered homeless persons to account for a change in the classification of homeless persons that took effect with the implementation of HPRP. Two main homelessness estimates exist: point-in-time and prevalence. Point-in-time tends to understate the "transitional homeless," persons who rapidly find shelter. To obtain a complete view of homelessness, it is also necessary to examine data on the number of persons who experience homelessness in a given year. Here we present both data sources. For prevalence estimates see HUD, The Annual Homeless Assessment Report to Congress. Available at: http://www.huduser.org/Publications/pdf/ahar.pdf

P. S. Goodman, "Foreclosures Force Ex-Homeowners to Turn to Shelters," *New York Times,* 2009. Available at: http://www.nytimes.com/2009/10/19/business/economy/19foreclosed.html?pagewanted=all&_r=0

17. "Homeless Children: The Hard Times Generation," CBS News, March 6, 2011. Available at: http://www.cbsnews.com/8301-18560_162-20038927.html

18. J. J. O'Connell, *Premature Mortality in Homeless Populations: A Review of the Literature* (Nashville, 2005). Similar risks were observed in the UK. One group studying single homeless people carefully sifted through the Coroner's Courts records to obtain data from the inner-city areas of London, Manchester, and Bristol from September 1995 to August 1996. From the courts' detailed records, it was possible to obtain age, gender, place of death, causes of death, and events that led to death among 365 homeless persons. They were also able to link that data to hospital records, which had allocated people who were NFA (not fixed abode) without a postcode to a special code: "ZZ99 3VZ."

A national UK audit of the homeless also found that four-fifths had a physical health problem, and about three-quarters had mental health issues, with similar patterns found in the US.

19. "Hunger and Homelessness Survey," p. 45; Institute for Children, Poverty and Homelessness, "Foreclosures and Homelessness: Understanding the Connection," 2013. Available at: http://www.icphusa.org/filelibrary/ICPH_policybrief_Foreclosuresand-Homelessness.pdf. We estimated that across the country there were about twenty-five homeless persons for each 1,000 foreclosures.

20. Homeless Assistance, US Department of Housing and Urban Development. Available at: http://portal.hud.gov/hudportal/HUD?src=/program_offices/comm_planning/homeless

A. Lowrey, "Homeless Rates in the U.S. Held Level Amid Recession, Study Says, but Big Gains Are Elusive," *New York Times,* Dec 10, 2012. Available at: http://www.nytimes.com/2012/12/10/us/homeless-rates-steady-despite-recession-hud-says.html?_r=0

21. However, for many such programs, to qualify, people had to be sober, which meant that the highest-risk groups—the heaviest drinkers, the crack and the heroin users—weren't eligible.

One "Housing First" program in Seattle launched in December 2005 sought to help an estimated 500 chronically publicly inebriated persons in downtown Seattle. The program came to be known as 1811 Eastlake, the street address where seventy-five units of residential housing were built. The researchers tried to assess what might happen if these high-risk groups were included, even allowing participants to drink in their rooms. Needless to say, 1811 Eastlake was overrun with homeless applicants wishing to take part.

The situation created a unique opportunity for researchers to conduct a natural experiment. The researchers were able to compare people who participated in Seattle's Housing First program for chronically homeless persons with severe alcohol problems against people who were on a wait-list for the program.

Participants in the program were estimated to cost society $4,066 per person per month in hospital, jail, and housing bills. Once provided with permanent housing, their total costs dropped to $1,492 after six months, and to $958 by the end of the year. The benefits had largely come from participants drinking less than those who remained homeless.

Finding housing helped avoid health hazards, but the ultimate health effect depended on the quality of the neighborhood. A 2011 study published in *The New England Journal of Medicine* randomly assigned 4,498 women with children living in public housing in high-poverty urban areas to one of three groups: 1,788 received housing vouchers, which could be redeemed only if they moved to a low-poverty area (where less than 10 percent of residents are poor); 1,312 received unrestricted, traditional vouchers; and 1,398 placed into a control group that was offered neither of these opportunities. From 2008 through 2010, as part of a long-term follow-up study, researchers measured data on their health outcomes. They found that simply moving from a neighborhood with a high level of poverty to a community with a lower level of poverty was associated with significant reductions in the obesity and diabetes. These remarkable benefits appeared to happen because wealthier neighborhoods offered their residents better access to healthier food, along with more green space that made it easier and more desirable to walk without the fear of crime and gang-related violence.

22. Fairmount Ventures Inc. *Evaluation of Pathways to Housing Philadelphia*, 2011. Available at: https://www.pathwaystohousing.org/uploads/PTHPA-ProgramEvaluation

Finding housing helped avoid health hazards, but the ultimate health effect depended on the quality of the neighborhood. A 2011 study published in *The New England Journal of Medicine* randomly assigned 4,498 women with children living in public housing in high-poverty urban areas to one of three groups: 1,788 received housing vouchers, which could be redeemed only if they moved to a low-poverty area (where less than 10 percent of residents are poor); 1,312 received unrestricted, traditional vouchers; and 1,398 placed into a control group that was offered neither of these opportunities. From 2008 through 2010, as part of a long-term follow-up study, researchers measured data on their health outcomes. They found that simply moving from a neighborhood with a high level of poverty to a community with a lower level of poverty was associated with significant reductions in the obesity and diabetes. These remarkable benefits appeared to happen because wealthier neighborhoods offered their residents better access to healthier food, along with more green space that made it easier and more desirable to walk without the fear of crime and gang-related violence.

23. J. Eng, "Homeless Numbers Down, but Risks Rise," NBC News, Jan 18, 2012. Available at: http://usnews.nbcnews.com/_news/2012/01/18/10177017-homeless-numbers-down-but-risks-rise?lite

The number of beds of permanent supportive housing rose from 195,724 in 2008 to 274,786 in 2012, with significant financing from the HPRP program. Available at: https://www.onecpd.info/resources/documents/2012AHAR_PITestimates.pdf

24. V. Busch-Geertsema and S. Fitzpatrick. 2009. "Effective Homelessness Prevention? Explaining Reductions in Homelessness in Germany and England," *European Journal of Homelessness* v2:69–96. UK Housing benefit fact sheet. Available at: https://www.gov.uk/housing-benefit/what-youll-get; where this was not enough to meet rent payments, it was also possible to apply for "discretionary housing payments" to help make up the difference.

Housing has long been a key target of public health intervention. The founder of the Yale School of Public Health, C. E. A. Winslow, gave a famous speech to the American Public Health Association in 1937. "Housing as a public health problem," he argued, was a fundamental goal in public health. "We call you today to a new contest even harder than the old ones—the fight for decent hygienic housing for the American peoples." He pointed to the example of Britain, noting, "No British health officer publishes an annual report without a section on housing in the positive sense, and the same inevitable laws of social progress are pressing on us in this country that have operated there."

25. R. Ramesh, "Warning on Benefit Cuts amid Rise in Homelessness," *The Guardian*, Dec 4, 2012. Available at: http://www.guardian.co.uk/society/2012/dec/04/benefit-cuts-rise-homelessness

The total austerity figure was later slightly revised down to reach total spending cut of £81 billion by 2014–15 as set out in the June budget. This included 11 billion in welfare reform savings and 3.3 billion from a two year freeze in public-sector pay. HM Treasury Spending Review 2010. Cm 7942. UK Treasury, Oct 2010.

R. Bury, "Social Housing to Be Hit With £8bn Cuts," *Inside Housing*, 2010. Available at: http://www.insidehousing.co.uk/social-housing-%E2%80%98to-be-hit-with-%C2%A38bn-cuts%E2%80%99/6512119.article

"Housing Benefit Cuts," *Crisis UK*, 2012. Available at: http://www.crisis.org.uk/data/files/publications/Crisis%20Briefing%20-%20Housing%20Benefit%20cuts.pdf. The Scottish government followed suit, cutting its own affordable housing budget by 31 percent.

"Social Housing Budget 'To Be Cut In Half'," BBC, Oct 19, 2010. Available at: http://www.bbc.co.uk/news/uk-politics-11570923

26. US Department of Housing and Urban Development, *Point-in-Time Estimates of Homelessness: Volume I of the 2012 Annual Homeless Assessment Report* (AHAR), 2012. Available at: https://www.onecpd.info/resource/2753/2012-pit-estimates-of

-homelessness-volume-1-2012-ahar/; UK Government, "Live Tables on Homelessness." Available at: https://www.gov.uk/government/statistical-data-sets/live-tables-on-home lessness. Homelessness rose in London from 9,700 households to 11,680 households between 2010 and 2011 (Department for Communities data). In the city of London, the number of people sleeping on the streets rose by 8 percent; youth were particularly negatively affect, as among those aged under twenty-five, homelessness rates rose by a third.

27. SSAC (November 2010) Report on S.I. No 2010/2835 and S.I. No. 2010/2836. Cited on p. 19 in http://www.crisis.org.uk/data/files/publications/Crisis%20Briefing %20-%20Housing%20Benefit%20cuts.pdf

28. "Homelessness: A Silent Killer," *Crisis UK,* 2011. Available at: http://www.crisis .org.uk/data/files/publications/Homelessness%20-%20a%20silent%20killer.pdf

The epidemiological study tried to disentangle homelessness from pre-existing health problems by evaluating people's health over time. These researchers identified and followed 6,323 homeless adults over five years and compared them with 12,451 people of the same age and gender in the general population. The homeless people, they discovered, were 4.4 times more likely to die than those with homes. But more interestingly, even when the researchers adjusted for the risks linked to past hospitalizations and current disabilities, it was found that not having a house posed a significantly greater risk of dying prematurely. In other words, the homeless who started out being healthy ultimately ended up being sicker.

A Department of Health report in 2010 estimated the healthcare costs alone of UK homelessness at about £2,115 per person per year. Department of Health. March 2010. Healthcare for single homeless people. March 2010. Based on 10,000 persons made homeless, this would result in a cost of an additional £20 million per annum. Unison Briefing on the Coalition Government's Housing Policies, Unison, London. Available at: http://www.unison.org.uk/acrobat/B5199.pdf

S. Salman, "How Have the Cuts Affected Housing?" *The Guardian,* Mar 30, 2011. Available at: http://www.guardian.co.uk/society/2011/mar/30/cuts-housing

29. "Tuberculosis Rises 8% in London—HPA Figures," BBC News, 2012. Available at: http://www.bbc.co.uk/news/uk-england-london-17485728

A. Gerlin, "Ancient Killer Bug Thrives in Shadow of London's Canary Wharf," Bloomberg, Feb 23, 2012. Available at: http://www.bloomberg.com/news/2012-02-23 /ancient-killer-bug-thrives-in-shadow-of-london-s-canary-wharf-skyscrapers.html

30. "Homeless Crisis as 400 Youths a Day Face Life on the Streets of Britain," *Mirror,* 2011. Available at: http://www.mirror.co.uk/news/uk-news/homeless-crisis-as-400 -youths-a-day-95173

L. Moran, "Is Greece Becoming a Third World Country? HIV, Malaria, and TB Rates Soar as Health Services Are Slashed by Savage Cuts," *The Mail,* 2012. Available at: http://www.dailymail.co.uk/news/article-2115992/Is-Greece-world-country-HIV -Malaria-TB-rates-soar-health-services-slashed-savage-cuts.html

31. ECDC, "West Nile Virus Infection Outbreak in Humans in Central Macedonia, Greece," ECDC Mission Report, July–August 2010. Available at: http://www.ecdc .europa.eu/en/publications/publications/1001_mir_west_nile_virus_infection_out break_humans_central_macedonia_greece.pdf

32. Greece estimates that the homeless population rose to 20,000 in 2011, a rise of 25 percent between 2009 and 2011. Ireland's number of households increased from 1,394 in 2008 to 2,348 in 2011. See "Major Increase in Homelessness," *Irish Times,* Dec 19, 2012. Available at: http://www.irishtimes.com/newspaper/breaking/2012/1219/breaking53.html. See also "On the Way Home?" FEANTA Monitoring report on homelessness and homeless policies in Europe. The European Federation of National Organisations Working with the Homeless, 2012. Available at: http://www.feantsa.org/IMG/pdf/on_the_way_home.pdf

33. See "On the Way Home?"

34. Markee, "Unfathomable Cuts in Housing Aid."

35. "Stampede Chaos as Thousands of Dallas Residents Apply for Housing Vouchers," *Above Top Secret,* July 16, 2011. Available at: http://www.abovetopsecret.com/forum /thread729362/pg1

"Oakland Opens Waiting List for Section 8 Vouchers," *SFGate,* Jan 26, 2011. Available at: http://www.sfgate.com/bayarea/article/Oakland-opens-waiting-list-for-Section -8-vouchers-2478260.php

"City's Homeless Count Tops 40,000," *Wall Street Journal,* Nov 9, 2011. Available at: http://online.wsj.com/article/SB10001424052970204190704577026511791881118. html?mod=googlenews_wsj

36. RealtyTrac, January 2013 Foreclosure Rate Heat Map, 2013. Available at: http:// www.realtytrac.com/trendcenter/default.aspx?address=Duval%20county%2C%20FL &parsed=1&cn=duval%20county&stc=fl

Council on Homelessness. 2011 Report. Submitted June 2011 to Governor Rick Scott, p. E-2. Available at: https://docs.google.com/viewer?a=v&q=cache:lQVq Dby8TywJ:www.dcf.state.fl.us/programs/homelessness/docs/2011CouncilReport.pdf+& hl=en&gl=uk&pid=bl&srcid=ADGEESjrwRb_ph_xCzTBGQ4vRvnrVQvXIAnreS Vi3MrT6xlXE6f_5aJ9k_iJW1ZegjE0Wt3IxIbP2ENvqMUzgI-HD0CdbLwc ge14wysl9dDI6FAp_lHqqjTxoSGwOyc3jkZf9dsuR6b5&sig=AHIEtbTSHKoz wOFJZyewSqHKbsh-xJFoIA

37. As the CDC reported, "This outbreak represents one of the most extensive TB outbreaks that the CDC has been invited to assist with since the early 1990s, both in terms of its size and rapid growth."

While some commentators in Florida were quick to blame the immigrant population for importing the disease, the CDC found that all but three of the ninety-nine cases were among US citizens.

38. K. Q. Seelye, "Public Health Departments Shrinking, Survey Finds," *New York Times,* March 1, 2010. Available at: http://prescriptions.blogs.nytimes.com/2010/03/01 /public-health-departments-shrinking-survey-finds/

Conclusion

1. *Merriam Webster Collegiate Dictionary.*

2. Naomi Klein, *The Shock Doctrine* (New York, 2007).

3. Source for Figure C.1: EuroStat 2013 Statistics. Gross domestic product is per capita, purchasing-power-parity adjusted and constant 2005 dollars. Estonia, Latvia, Lithuania, and Hungary are calculated as peak-to-trough austerity in 2008–10 to reflect earlier initiation of austerity. The association of budgetary changes with changes in gross domestic product is consistent and statistically significant even after adjusting for the depth of prior recession.

4. Laura Tiehan, Dean Jolliffe, Craig Gundersen, "Alleviating Poverty in the United States: The Critical Role of SNAP Benefits," US Department of Agriculture, ERR-132, April 2012. Available at: http://www.ers.usda.gov/publications/err-economic-research -report/err132.aspx; Parke E. Wilde, "Measuring the Effect of Food Stamps on Food Insecurity and Hunger: Research and Policy Considerations," *Journal of Nutrition*, Feb 2007. Available at: http://jn.nutrition.org/content/137/2/307.full

5. Health Impact Assessments were used for selected policies by the UK's Labour government before the Tories came into power in 2010. We are grateful to Klim McPherson for the suggestion to institute an Office of Health Responsibility.

6. A. Reeves, S. Basu, M. Mckee, C. Meissner, D. Stuckler. "Does Investment in the Health Sector Promote or Inhibit Economic Growth?" *Health Policy*, forthcoming.

RESEARCH PUBLICATIONS

B. Barr, D. Taylor-Robinson, A. Scott-Samuel, M. McKee, D. Stuckler. "Suicides associated with the 2008–2010 recession in the UK: a time-trend analysis." *British Medical Journal*. August 2012, v345: e5142.

A. Bessudnov, M. McKee, and D. Stuckler. "Inequalities in male mortality by occupational class, perceived social status, and education in Russia, 1994–2006." *European Journal of Public Health*. June 2012, v22(3): 332–37.

J. Bor, S. Basu, A. Coutts, M. McKee, D. Stuckler. "Alcohol use during the Great Recession of 2008–2009." *Alcohol and Alcoholism*. January 2013. In press.

M. Bordo, C. Meissner, and D. Stuckler. "Foreign currency debt, financial crises and economic growth: A long run view." *Journal of International Money and Finance*. May 2010, v29: 642–65.

R. De Vogli, M. Marmot, and D. Stuckler. "Excess suicides and attempted suicides in Italy attributable to the Great Recession." *Journal of Epidemiology and Community Health*. August 2012. In press.

R. De Vogli, M. Marmot, and D. Stuckler. "Strong evidence that the economic crisis caused a rise in suicides in Europe: the need for social protection." *Journal of Epidemiology and Community Health*. January 2013. In press.

M. Gili, M. Roca, S. Basu, M. McKee, D. Stuckler. "The mental health risks of unemployment, housing payment difficulties, and evictions in Spain: evidence from primary care centres, 2006 and 2010." *European Journal of Public Health*. February 2013, v23(1): 103–8.

P. Hamm, L. King, and D. Stuckler. "Mass privatization, state capacity, and economic growth in post-communist countries: firm- and country-level evidence." *American Sociological Review*. April 2012, v77(2): 295–324.

M. Karanikolos, P. Mladovsky, J. Cylus, S. Thomson, S. Basu, D. Stuckler, J. P. Mackenbach, M. McKee. "Financial crisis, austerity, and health in Europe." *The Lancet*. In press.

A. Kentikelenis, M. Karanikolos, I. Papanicolas, S. Basu, M. McKee, D. Stuckler. "Effects of Greek economic crisis on health are real." *British Medical Journal*. December 2012, v345: e8602.

A. Kentikelenis, M. Karanikolos, I. Papanicolas, S. Basu, M. McKee, D. Stuckler. "Health effects of financial crisis: omens of a Greek tragedy." *The Lancet.* October 2011, v378(9801): 1457–58.

A. Kentikelenis, M. Karanikolos, I. Papanicolas, S. Basu, M. McKee, D. Stuckler. "Reply to Polyzos." *The Lancet.* March 2012, v379: 1002.

L. King, P. Hamm, and D. Stuckler. "Rapid large-scale privatization and death rates in ex-communist countries: an analysis of stress-related and health system mechanisms." *International Journal of Health Services.* July 2009, 39(3): 461–89.

M. McKee and D. Stuckler. "The assault on universalism: How to destroy the welfare state." *British Medical Journal.* December 2011, v343: d7973.

M. McKee and D. Stuckler. "The consequences for health and health care of the financial crisis: a new Dark Age?" In Finnish. *Sosiaalilääketieteellinen Aikakauslehti.* March 2012, v49: 69–74.

M. McKee and D. Stuckler. "Older people in the United Kingdom: under attack from all directions." *Age and Ageing.* January 2013, v42(1): 11–13.

M. McKee, S. Basu, and D. Stuckler. "Health systems, health and wealth: the argument for investment applies now more than ever." *Social Science & Medicine.* March 2012, v74(5): 684–87.

M. McKee, M. Karanikolos, P. Belcher, D. Stuckler. "Austerity: a failed experiment on the people of Europe." *Clinical Medicine.* August 2012, v12(4): 346–50.

M. McKee, D. Stuckler, J. M. Martin-Moreno. "Protecting health in hard times." *British Medical Journal.* September 2010. v341: c5308.

C. Quercioli, G. Messina, S. Basu, M. McKee, N. Nante, D. Stuckler. "The effect of health care delivery privatization on avoidable mortality: longitudinal cross-regional results from Italy, 1993–2003." *Journal of Epidemiology & Community Health.* 2013, v67(2): 132–38.

B. Rechel, M. Suhrcke, S. Tsolova, J. Suk, M. Desai, M. McKee, D. Stuckler, I. Abubakar, P. Hunter, M. Senek, J. Semenza. "Economic crisis and communicable disease control in Europe: A scoping study among national experts." *Health Policy.* December 2011, v103(2–3): 168–75.

A. Reeves, D. Stuckler, M. McKee, D. Gunnell, S. Chang, S. Basu. "Increase in state suicide rates in the USA during economic recession." *The Lancet.* November 2012, v380(9856): 1813–14.

D. Stuckler and S. Basu. "International Monetary Fund's effects on global health: before and after the 2008 financial crisis." *International Journal of Health Services.* September 2009, 39(4): 771–81.

D. Stuckler, S. Basu, P. Fishback, C. Meissner, M. McKee. "Banking crises and mortality during the Great Depression: Evidence from U.S. urban populations, 1929–1937." *Journal of Epidemiology and Community Health.* June 2012, 66(5): 410–19.

D. Stuckler, S. Basu, P. Fishback, C. Meissner, M. McKee. "Was the Great Depression a cause or correlate of falling mortality?" *Journal of Epidemiology and Community Health.* November 2012. In press.

D. Stuckler, S. Basu, and M. McKee. "Budget crises, health, and social welfare." *British Medical Journal.* July 2010, 340: c3311.

D. Stuckler, S. Basu, and M. McKee. "Effects of the 2008 financial crisis on health: A first look at European data." *The Lancet.* July 2011, v378(9876): 124–25.

D. Stuckler, S. Basu, and M. McKee. "How government spending cuts put lives at risk." *Nature.* May 2010, v465: 289.

D. Stuckler, S. Basu, and M. McKee. "Public health in Europe: Power, politics, and where next?" *Public Health Reviews.* July 2010, v1: 214–42.

D. Stuckler, S. Basu, M. McKee, M. Suhrcke. "Responding to the economic crisis: A primer for public health professionals." *Journal of Public Health.* August 2010, v32(3): 298–306.

D. Stuckler, S. Basu, M. McKee, et al. "An evaluation of the International Monetary Fund's claims about public health." *International Journal of Health Services.* March 2010, v40(2): 327–32.

D. Stuckler, S. Basu, M. Suhrcke, A. Coutts, M. McKee. "Financial crisis and health policy." *Medicine & Health.* September 2009, pp. 194–95.

D. Stuckler, S. Basu, M. Suhrcke, A. Coutts, M. McKee. "The public health effect of economic crises and alternative policy responses in Europe: an empirical analysis." *The Lancet.* July 2009, 374(9686): 315–32.

D. Stuckler, S. Basu, M. Suhrcke, M. McKee. "The health implications of financial crisis: A review of the evidence" *Ulster Medical Journal.* September 2009, 78(3): 142–45.

D. Stuckler, S. Basu, S. Wang, M. McKee. "Does recession reduce global health aid? Evidence from 15 countries, 1975–2007." *Bulletin of the World Health Organization.* April 2011, v89: 252–57.

D. Stuckler, L. King and S. Basu. "International Monetary Fund programs and tuberculosis outcomes in post-communist countries." *PLoS Medicine.* July 2008, 5(7): e143.

D. Stuckler, L. King, and S. Basu. "Reply to Murray and King." *PLoS Medicine.* July 2008, 5(7): e143.

D. Stuckler, L. King, and A. Coutts. "Understanding privatisation's impacts on health: Lessons from the Soviet Experience." *Journal of Epidemiology and Community Health.* July 2008, 62(7): 664.

D. Stuckler, L. King, and M. McKee. "The disappearing health effects of rapid privatization: a case of statistical obscurantism?" *Social Science & Medicine,* March 2012, 75: 23–31.

D. Stuckler, L. King, and M. McKee. "Mass privatisation and mortality." *The Lancet.* April 2009, 373(9671): 1247–48.

D. Stuckler, L. King, and M. McKee. "Mass privatisation and the post-communist mortality crisis: a cross-national analysis." *The Lancet*. January 2009, 373(9661): 399–407.

D. Stuckler, L. King, and M. McKee. "Reply to Earle and Gerry." *The Lancet*. January 2010, v375(9712): 372–74.

D. Stuckler, L. King, and M. McKee. "Response to Gentile: Mass privatization, unemployment, and mortality." *Europe-Asia Studies*. June 2012, v64(5): 949–53.

D. Stuckler and M. McKee. "There is an alternative: public health professionals must not remain silent at a time of financial crisis." *European Journal of Public Health*. February 2012, v22(1): 2–3.

D. Stuckler, C. Meissner, and L. King. "Can a bank crisis break your heart?" *Globalization and Health*, January 2008, 4(1): 1–12.

M. Suhrcke, M. McKee, D. Stuckler, et al. "Contribution of health to the economy of the European Union." *Public Health*. October 2006, 120: 994–1001.

M. Suhrcke, M. McKee, D. Stuckler, et al. "The economic crisis and infectious disease control." *Euro Surveillance*. November 2009, v14(45).

M. Suhrcke and D. Stuckler. "Will the recession be bad for our health? It depends." *Social Science & Medicine*. March 2012, v74(5): 647–53.

M. Suhrcke, D. Stuckler, J. Suk, et al. "The impact of economic crises on communicable disease transmission and control: a systematic review of the evidence." *PLoS One*. June 2011, v6(6): e20724.

ACKNOWLEDGMENTS

We are deeply indebted to our many colleagues who have worked with us over the years and provided unparalleled support and guidance, offering their critical eyes and vast repositories of wisdom to review this book as it came together. First of these, we are indebted to Martin McKee, our dear friend and close colleague who worked with us tirelessly in this research and continues to prove himself a paragon of integrity and virtue in public health. We also appreciate our many collaborators, without whose support the research that went into this book would not be as well-developed: Adam Coutts, Christopher Meissner, Marc Suhrcke, Price Fishback, David Taylor-Robinson, Benjamin Barr, Alexander Kentikelenis, Irene Papanicolas, Michael Marmot, Roberto De Vogli, Marina Karanikolos, Alexey Bessudnov, Johan Mackenbach, Lawrence King, Jose Martin-Moreno, Vicente Navarro, Michael Harhay, Jacob Bor, Karen Siegel, Chris McClure, Margalida Gili, Miquel Roca, David McDaid, David Gunnell, Shu-Sen Chang, Jan Semenza, Gauden Galea, Aaron Reeves, Patrick Hamm, and Ben Cave. Additionally we appreciate the time and energy of those who provided constructive comments, criticisms, and advice at various stages of the book's development, including Vladimir Shkolnikov, Sigur Sigurgeirsdottir, Shah Ebrahim, Ron Labonte, John Thompson, Margaret Whitehead, and Bo Burgstrom. Inevitably, we are unable to thank by name all the peer-reviewers who have contributed anonymous feedback that helped strengthen our analysis. Peer-review is a thankless task, and for those who contributed, we are ever grateful.

A special thanks goes to Molly Crockett for her extraordinary assistance in editing and revising the manuscript. We are also grateful to Michelle Spring for introducing us to the world of trade publishing and helping us to craft the initial book proposal. We are particularly thankful to Shah Ebrahim and Fiona Taylor for giving us refuge in Delhi during the final stages of this writing.

David would additionally like to thank his parents, Danny and Margit, and his sister, Michelle, for their unwavering support. His research has benefited from the insights and direction of Mary Ridgway, Lowell Levin, Mark Schlesinger, Larry King, Paul Schultz, Christopher Meissner, and especially Martin McKee. Thanks to the continued support and friendship of Chris Lockamy, Elizabeth Rush, and Louis Caron.

Sanjay would also like to thank his parents for always encouraging him to "read, read, read, read everything" (as per Faulkner), and his mentors Christine Balone for teaching him to write, Lee Marek for the gift of science, Rudolph Tanzi for the experimental spirit, and Noam Chomsky for being the quintessence of the public intellectual. Special thanks to Paul Farmer for always humbly bestowing on him the lessons of social justice; Jim Yong Kim for teaching him how to pick the right battles; Joseph Dumit for insights on academia; and Anita Desai, Alan Lightman, and Jean Jackson for the gift of the pen. For their mentorship in medicine and epidemiology, thanks to Rick Altice, R. Douglas Bruce, Gerald Friedland, Edward Kaplan, Sharad Jain, Stanton Glantz, Robert Lustig and Jack Farquhar. Thanks to John Ioannidis for role-modeling the ideal of a critical scientist, and for everyone at the Stanford Prevention Research Center for their family spirit and passion in the pursuit of public health. Thanks to the continued support and friendship of Jason Andrews, C. Brandon Ogbunagafor, Jay Varellas, Russell Bither-Terry, Sandeep Kishore, Amy Kapczynski, Gregg Gonsalves, Duncan Smith-Rohrberg Maru and the Nyaya Health team. For their encouragement and constructive criticism in writing, thanks as well to Sandy Close, Viji Sundaram, Richard Rodriguez and the folks at New America Media. And thanks most of all to Palav Babaria, the love of my life, who forgave many sleepless nights, and who always provides a critical lifeline of grounded insight, encouragement and partnership.

This book would not have been possible without the dedication of an incredible editorial team. Thanks to Lara Heimert at Basic Books for her "fierce but loving" edits to strengthen our manuscript, to Norman MacAfee for his indelible camaraderie and eleventh-hour marathon editing sessions, and to Thomas Penn at Penguin for his intellectual spirit, vast historical knowledge, and keen eye for detail. We are very grateful for support from Katy O'Donnell and the team at Basic at every step of the book's development; Karen Browning and the team at Penguin for their support to produce the book; and Iris Tupholme and the HarperCollins crew for their coordination and wisdom. Thanks finally to Patrick Walsh and his team at Conville and Walsh for being the most supportive agency a new pair of authors could hope for.

INDEX